INSIGHT
GUIDES

MOROCCO

Edited by Dorothy Stannard
Editorial Director: Brian Bell

A P A
PUBLICATIONS

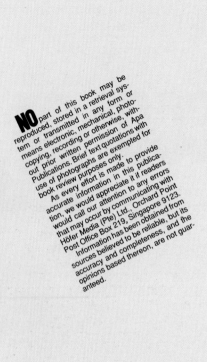
MOROCCO

First Edition
© 1989 APA PUBLICATIONS (HK) LTD
All Rights Reserved
Printed in Singapore by Höfer Press Pte Ltd

ABOUT THIS BOOK

Dorothy Stannard, project editor of *Insight Guide: Morocco*, first visited the country in her early twenties. Relying on local transport, she and a girlfriend trekked through valleys and crossed deserts. Colleagues and friends attempted to dissuade them from the trip with tales of strange sects and scimitar-wielding Berbers. To these alarmists' surprise, they returned committed fans of Morocco and Moroccans. They'd had their adventures—and they were already planning to go back.

In between travelling, Dorothy Stannard worked in London as an assistant editor on *Punch* magazine.

It was in Tangier that she met (and was fed by) **Anne Lambton**, who here writes about Moroccan cooking—reckoned one of the most underrated cuisines of the world. Mrs Lambton lives in a quarter of Tangier known as The Mountain, a leafy suburb long associated with English expatriates. She is full of enthusiasm for present-day Tangier, not in the least sorry to have missed the legendary international era. Her friend, however, the Honourable **David Herbert**, second son of the Earl of Pembroke and author of several novels, experienced Tangier in full swing. He has been described as its "unofficial social arbiter". For this book, he recalls the famous parties given by his friend Barbara Hutton, the Woolworth heiress, who for many years owned a house in Tangier's medina.

Like the literary captain of Morocco, novelist Paul Bowles, **Stanley Reynolds** grew up in New England. Walking into a bar in 1957, he met, and a little later married, a young Englishwoman, and in 1958 he left the USA to settle in her hometown of Liverpool. As a young journalist, he graduated from the *Liverpool Echo* to *The Guardian* to *Punch* magazine, where in the wake of such predecessors as Anthony Powell, he became a literary editor. Here he writes about the draw of Morocco to the novelists of the 1950s—Paul Bowles and beat writers William S. Burroughs, Jack Kerouac and Brion Gysin. Reynolds, now a freelance journalist, is contemplating abandoning the inconsequential world of journalism to resume more serious writing. Tangier, he says, would be an excellent place to complete his epic poem.

Another contributing literary man is **Nicholas Shakespeare**, books editor of London's *Daily Telegraph*, novelist and son of the British Ambassador to Morocco. In 1988 he travelled to the Spanish enclave of Ceuta to glean information for his second novel. He said of the trip: "I had gone there in high hopes that I might find it a suitable place to set a novel. I was not disappointed. But while prepared to make Ceuta home to a number of paper characters, I would not willingly despatch any flesh and blood creature to the Cafeteria Nizi in the Plaza de los Reys."

Stephen Ormsby Hughes, author of the history section, has witnessed the whole compass of Moroccan affairs since Independence. Formally an RAF Coastal Command pilot, he first went to Morocco in 1953 to edit an English-language daily newspaper in Casablanca. Two years later the paper closed down but he stayed on as correspondent of the Associated Press. He also worked for the *New York Times*, *Time* magazine and the BBC until joining Reuters in 1961. In addition to the history section, he has contributed a feature on the subtle definition of the Moroccan refrain *"In sha' Allah"*.

Also living in Rabat, **Reg Veale** is the Director of Studies at the British Council

Stannard   *Ormsby Hughes*   *Veale*

Language Centre there. He has spent all his working life overseas—in Fiji, Malaysia and Morocco—teaching English as a foreign language and managing language schools. In conjunction with his friend **Tiina Britten**, born in the Ivory Coast and educated in French Lycees in West Africa and Morocco, he wrote the chapters on Rabat, Casablanca and the southern coastline.

Tackling the Imperial cities of Morocco, **Polly Phillimore** (Fez, Méknès and Moulay Idriss) and Robert Hartford (Marrakesh) are longstanding visitors to Morocco. Polly has travelled all over the world: South and North America, Asia, Africa, as well as east and west Europe. She joined the British Consumers' Association in 1986 to work on its travel publication *Holiday Which?* but found combining work with her favourite hobby far too pleasurable. In 1988 she left the magazine to teach autistic children in Inner London but returned to her former job and the travelling life after six months. Morocco, she says, is a country that can get under your skin.

Robert Hartford is primarily a music critic and author of music biographies. His second love, however, acquired during a youth spent hacking round the globe, is foreign travel. He writes travel features for British newspapers and magazines, including *The Independent* and *Punch*, and recently has added lecturing, on cultural tours and cruises, to his work activities.

Robin Collomb is an established expert on the Atlas Mountains, knowing not only the roads through the region but every gorge and col. He says that from the age of 11 he misspent his youth potting mountain peaks all round the world. He arrived in Morocco in the 1970s, some 1,700 summits and 35 years later, and duly wrote and published a guide-book to the Atlas for mountaineers and trekkers. That's just one of nearly 40 titles he has chalked up.

Short features have been contributed by other enthusiasts of their subject. **John Offen**, writing about architecture, is an interior designer living in Paris and currently completing a book on Moroccan style. **Dave Muddyman**, covering music (the beauty of which Brion Gysin thought might be reason enough to become a Muslim), is a musician. He regularly travels to Morocco to record and accompany musicians performing in the cafés of the medinas. Asilah, on the northwest coast, is his favourite haunt. **Mark Griffiths**, writing about the film location business in Morocco, is a young filmmaker who between assignments dabbles in freelance journalism, turning experiences of exotic locations into travel features.

The Travel Tips section was compiled by **David Dickinson**, who served a tough travel research and writing apprenticeship on *Holiday Which?* magazine before becoming an assistant editor on the Consumers' Association health magazine. He escaped the fact-checking and information hauling involved in compiling the Travel Tips to fly to Agadir and cover the long coastal stretch down to Layounne. Dickinson enjoys adventurous comfort—which, a plague of locusts apart, was what he found in Morocco's deep south.

Apart from the writers and photographers who contributed to the book, the project editor would like to thank her brother **David Stannard**, who accompanied her on her latest trips to Morocco and, uncomplainingly, undertook most of the driving throughout. Credit for the maps goes to **Kaj Berndtson Associates**. Proof-reading and indexing was completed by **Rosemary Jackson Hunter**.

Reynolds

Phillimore

Collomb

Dickinson

HISTORY AND FEATURES

23 The Moroccans
—by Dorothy Stannard

31 History: Before Islam
—by Stephen Ormsby Hughes

35 History: The Arrival of Islam
—by Stephen Ormsby Hughes

41 History: The Dynasties
—by Stephen Ormsby Hughes

49 History: European Encroachment
—by Stephen Ormsby Hughes

57 History: Since Independence
—by Stephen Ormsby Hughes

62 In Sha'Allah: Yes, No or Maybe
—by Stephen Ormsby Hughes

66 The Spanish Enclaves
—by Nicholas Shakespeare

71 Les Femmes
—by Dorothy Stannard

75 The Novelist as Tourist
—by Stanley Reynolds

79 A Wild Time Was Had By All
—by David Herbert

85 Food and Drink
—by Anne Lambton

91 The Essence of Architecture
—by John Offen

99 Making Music
—by David Muddyman

103 Skiing
—by Robin Collomb

PLACES

113 Introduction

117 Tangier
—by Dorothy Stannard

131 The Rif
—by Dorothy Stannard

134 Kif Growing in the Rif
—by Dorothy Stannard

145 The Northwest Coast
—by Dorothy Stannard

151 Rabat
—by Reg Veale and Tiina Britten

167 Casablanca
—by Reg Veale and Tiina Britten

173 South of Casablanca
—by Reg Veale and Tiina Britten

181 The Imperial Cities: Introduction

183 Fez
—by Polly Phillimore

188 The Future of the Medina
—by Polly Phillimore

201 Méknès
—by Polly Phillimore

207 Moulay Idriss
—by Polly Phillimore

211 Volubilis
—by Polly Phillimore

219 Marrakesh
—by Robert Hartford

230 **The Hard Sell**
—by Dorothy Stannard

237 **The Southwest Coast**
—by Dorothy Stannard

243 **The Atlas Mountains**
—by Robin Collomb

261 **The South**
—by Dorothy Stannard

269 **On Location: Film-making**
—by Mark Griffiths

275 **Agadir**
—by David Dickinson

281 **The Deep South**
—by David Dickinson

287 **Real Blue Men and Fake Blue Men**
—by Dorothy Stannard

MAPS

114 Morocco
118 Tangier
152 Rabat
168 Casablanca
184 Fez
202 Méknès
220 Marrakesh
244 The Atlas Mountains
248 The High Atlas
262 The South: the Draa and Ziz Valleys
276 Agadir
283 The Deep South

TRAVEL TIPS

GETTING THERE
290 By Air
290 By Sea
290 By Rail
290 By Road

TRAVEL ESSENTIALS
291 Visas & Passports
291 Money Matters
291 Health
292 What to Wear
292 What to Bring
292 On Arrival
292 Customs Formalities
293 Reservations
293 Extension of Stay
293 On Departure

GETTING ACQUAINTED
293 Government
294 Geography
295 Language
295 Time Zone & Climate
296 Weights & Measures
296 Business Hours
297 Holidays
297 Festivals
297 Islam & Ramadan

COMMUNICATIONS
299 Newspapers
299 Post &
     Telecommunications

EMERGENCIES
300 Security & Crime
300 Loss
300 Medical Services

GETTING AROUND
301 Orientation
301 Maps
301 Airport/City Links
302 City Transport
302 Local Transport
302 Private Transport
303 Internal Flights
303 On Foot &
     By Thumb
304 Complaints

WHERE TO STAY
304 Hotels

FOOD DIGEST
306 What to Eat
306 Where to Eat
308 Drinking Notes

THINGS TO DO
309 City
310 Country

NIGHTLIFE
312 Folklore/Fantasias

SHOPPING
314 What to Buy
314 Export Procedures
314 Complaints

SPORTS
315 Participant

SPECIAL INFORMATION
316 Doing Business
316 Gays
317 Disabled
317 Students

LANGUAGE
317 Useful Words

FURTHER READING
319 Films

USEFUL ADDRESSES
319 Tourist Ofices
319 Embassies & Consulates

THE MOROCCANS

For centuries Europeans have enjoyed explaining the character of the Moor. Early visitors to Morocco, arrogantly convinced of their own superior, civilised values, considered it their right, even their duty, to warn of the dark, lazy, deceitful, polygamous—and therefore lascivious—infidels on Europe's doorstep. Sir John Drummond Hay, Britain's consul in Tangier for the last half of the 19th century, wrote: "They combine all possible vices."

The problem, of course, was that Moroccans did not conform to the familiar (if often hypocritical) morals of Paris or London. More outrageous was that they displayed no interest in developing a deferential regard for them. They remained unshaken in their religious beliefs and scorned Christians. A more reverent attitude had to be taught.

Even these days, some of these Western prejudices and clichés remain, albeit tempered by faint praise of Moroccan hospitality or family values. In the popular imagination—and that includes that of the media—Moroccans, like any other oriental people (though in this case well west of London), are described as "chauvinists", "fatalists", and "hedonists"—simple stereotypes, even for the press, when one considers Morocco's eclectic racial origins.

Broadly, the people may be divided into the urban and rural populations. The Berbers, the indigenous race, are still more likely to live in the mountainous *bled*, or countryside, where they migrated in the face of the first Arab invaders; and the Arabs, in the towns and cities of the plains. The Berbers are of three main types (sub-divided into countless tribes): the Riffians of the north; the Chleuhs from the Middle and High Atlas; and the Soussi, found in the southwest. Their origins are uncertain; theories include the possibility of European derivations, probably based on the not

unusual occurrence of fair colouring and blue or green coloured eyes.

Nowadays many Moroccans are, of course, of mixed race and it is splitting hairs to say whether one is pure Berber/Arab or whether or not there is any black African ancestry in the blood (originating from the black slaves imported from Mali during the Saadi dynasty). But there are villages in Southern Morocco, particularly in the Dades, Tafilalt and Draa valleys, where pockets of unadulterated Arabs exist in re-

gions that are otherwise Berber: for example, Erfoud in the Tafilalt and Tamagroute in the Draa. Here the women, in contrast to their Berber counterparts, are shrouded in heavy black *haik*, to the extent of covering all their charms apart from one eye.

The so-called Arab/Berber divide is now dismissed as a myth propagated by the French during the French and Spanish protectorates to help justify their policies in Morocco and to undermine the solidarity of resistance. Nonetheless, Berber—either Shilha, Soussia or Riffia—are totally different languages to Arabic, with many dialects. Whereas a Berber usually

Preceding pages: crossing the courtyard of the Kairouyine Mosque, Fez; a young population; desert places; discussing the date harvest. **Left**, Berber girl from the Dades Valley. **Above**, a water seller poses.

understands Arabic (and in order to write, must use it), Berber remains incomprehensible to most Arabs.

The two races have, though, developed much in common. Although the Berbers needed little coercion to embrace Islam, they adapted it to include favourite pagan customs. Islam is not supposed to accept any intermediary between an individual and God, but, contradictorily, Morocco is littered with the square, white-domed buildings housing the tombs of holy men, *marabout*, to which the troubled and the sick, especially women, like to make pilgrimages.

In fact, a woman is more likely to visit the

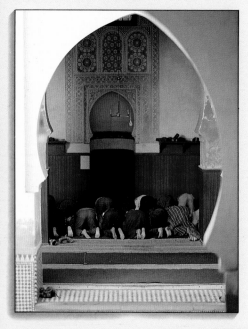

tomb of her favourite holy man (or even a supposedly sacred stream or tree) to seek assistance than go to the mosque. She may camp for weeks at a *koubba*, where she will pray or grieve.

Magic, too, is a fecund and potent force. As Paul Bowles, the American novelist and composer living in Tangier, wrote in his autobiography *Without Stopping*: "Sorcery is burrowing invisible tunnels in every direction, from thousands of senders to thousands of unsuspecting recipients."

Every medina contains a *shouaf* to which not only the gullible and uneducated go to purchase weird concoctions or find advice;

the apothecaries in the markets trade in dried bits of animal skin and pickled reptiles; benevolent and evil *djin* (spirits) are thought populous; and the power of the so-called "Evil Eye", meaning the spells cast over one by an ill-wisher, isn't taken lightly. The newspapers are full of lurid tales of revenge through witchcraft.

Again, Islam doesn't exactly endorse the use of magic, but that it can tolerate it is another indication of its flexibility as a religion. In theory, Islam recognises both the other "written" religions, i.e. Judaism and Christianity, and in spite of the colourful accounts of Christian slavery in the 17th century and the departure of most Jews at Independence, Morocco claims historical respect for both. Many Jews emigrated there from Spain to escape the Inquisition.

King Hassan II, in his autobiography *The Challenge*, is proud of Morocco's history of religious tolerance. He claims the Jewish quarter, the *mellah*, was always built close to the palace in a city so that it should benefit from royal protection. This may be true, but the Jews had also to pay a special tax for the privilege.

Certainly, Islam is forgiving towards Muslims themselves. There are five "pillars" to the faith (the testament that there is no god but God; the observance of prayers; the giving of alms to the poor; fasting at Ramadan; and the pilgrimage to Mecca at least once in a lifetime), but the Koran (the word of God given to the Prophet) and the Hadith (the sayings of the Prophet on Islamic conduct in everyday life) allow for the frailty of the flesh time and time again.

If you can't do so and so, the Prophet is usually reported to have said, do such and such, the next best thing, instead. Sexual intercourse, providing it is within marriage, is considered beneficial to the holiest of men.

Equally, in the strand of Islam known as Sufism is found a way of including other, more mystical drives—towards asceticism and meditation and the forming of exclusive sects—that have more in common with Roman Catholicism than orthodox Islam. At one time, those claiming *baraka*, a blessing supposedly bestowed by Allah on any direct descendants of the Prophet (quite a marketable asset), acquired the status of saints, deemed capable of miracles and liable to inspire trances and self-mutilations—not behaviour recommended in any obvious way by the Koran.

Such practices have tended to die out, or go underground, but some remnant of their spirit is still alive in the music of the *gnaoua*.

Traditionally, *baraka* also endowed its possessor with more civil authority than anyone else—which, in a country of constant tribal feuding, provided at least some kind of independent jurisdiction. Thus it has also helped determine and preserve the succession to the sultancy. Mohammed V's claim to the throne in 1956 was helped by the fact that his lineage can be traced back to the Prophet via Ali (the Alaouite dynasty), even though, according to the Koran, all men are

It is interesting that, in the 1980s, when there are a million and one social improvements Moroccans need, King Hassan chose to underline his piety by having a new mosque built in Casablanca costing countless millions (estimates differ unbelievably). Generally, the project was supported by the Moroccan people, who were each asked by special house-visiting officials to contribute to the expense of building it—their 60th-birthday present to their King.

International consensus is that Morocco has done well since independence—all things considered, including problems of earthquake and droughts. Certainly, arriving

equal and there should be no religious hierarchy in Islam.

Naturally, following independence there were deep social and economic problems and Mohammed V and his son Hassan were bolstered by what had effectively become a "Divine Right". A revolution would need to challenge a God-given mandate to rule. Again in his autobiography, King Hassan stresses his descent from the Prophet and his dramatic accounts of his escapes from would-be assassins do rather suggest a charmed life.

Left, the sacred. **Right**, the profane.

in Rabat for the first time or driving into Casablanca along the salubriously residential Anfa road, one is struck by the sense of established prosperity. The French civic architecture and the chi-chi patisseries along Boulevard Mohammed V in Rabat give the impression of a town bourgeois enough for Madame Bovary to kick against.

France has left its legacy in the country's administration: in common with Europe rather than other parts of the Muslim world, Friday is a normal working day and Saturday and Sunday a weekend holiday; administratively the country is divided into provinces (or *préfectures* in the cases of

Rabat and Casablanca) and sub-divided into communes; when conducting business the educated frequently talk to one another in French rather than Arabic; and bright students are assisted by the Moroccan government to attend foreign, usually French, universities. Often such students return with outlooks that have altered.

Superficially, therefore, Morocco can seem European rather than North African. But, in fact—unlike other Arab countries, whose cultures bear the heavy-handed stamp of their colonisers, the Ottomans—it retains much of its pre-Protectorate variety of character. Its Europeanisation is only the façade, even in the cities.

lyrics. It degenerated into popular commercial music before it had much political impact, but not before it had been noticed. King Hassan, conscious of skating on thin ice (and aware of the demise of the Shah of Iran) has been careful to encourage national pride, foster useful relations with Europe and America, and watch his own back, all at the same time.

By Arab and African standards he has produced a liberal kingdom. It is a country, though, where royal contacts are tantamount to success (though it should be remembered that what seems like nepotism, preferment, has a long tradition in the Muslim East), and it is a monarchy in its full sense; constit-

The *bidonvilles* of Casablanca, shanty-towns built by those who, following World War II and the rapid industrialisation of Morocco, migrated from the country to towns, exist in conditions that have never improved—theirs is not the kind of picturesque poverty captured on postcards or promoted by the Tourist Office.

In the 1970s a delayed reaction to the colonialism of the first half of the century heralded a mood of Moroccan nationalism. Groups of musicians, notably Nass el Ghiwane and Jilala, revived a popular ancient folk music known as El Malhoune, incorporating anti-establishment, leftist

utionally, the monarch can overrule any decision made by the elected parliament.

The King's authority is underlined at all levels. In every public building, be it an ever-so-humble sandwich shop, a framed portrait of King Hassan hangs. Even such places as Scott's, a gay discothèque in Tangier, are graced by a royal photograph.

Delicate situation: Since the attempted *coups d'états* in the 1970s particularly, press and broadcasting are carefully controlled. The riots which erupted in Algiers in the autumn of 1988 made headline news in Britain and Europe. In Morocco they were not reported at all, partly because Morocco was then engaged in delicate negotiations with Algeria over their support of Polisario, and presumably because it was a situation which could equally happen there, and has—as recently as 1984.

The danger is one of an educated proletariat who have little or no work. Official employment is extremely low; a high percentage of people are engaged in casual, seasonal or itinerant work (as in any country in the Third World, there are an amazing number of street vendors and pedlars engaged in the business of the first world at its most primitive level).

A population of 24 million and an accelerating birthrate exacerbate such

difficulties and have at last prompted timid attempts at birth control. King Hassan has referred to the need for contraception in his speeches—a move which at one time would have been condemned as anti-religious.

Chronic unemployment must also account in part for the vast numbers of male and female brothels, particularly in Marrakesh and Casablanca. Although its claim to be the oldest profession in the world is as true here as anywhere, prostitution proliferated in Morocco under the French and Spanish

Left, intimate dialogue between females. **Above**, a participant in a *moussem*.

protectorates. Military brothels were set up to cater for the French armies. At independence the number of registered prostitutes in Marrakesh was calculated to be 16,000.

Western homosexuals still find a ready supply of catamites in Tangier and Marrakesh, while rich Gulf Arabs, escaping the strict regimes of home, take advantage of Morocco's more liberal attitudes to establish private female brothels. These are not apparent to the average tourist, whose impression is of veiled women and sexual suppression.

On a more domestic note, social and family traditions, national and regional, are fervently followed. As well as the annual (according to the Muslim calendar) religious festivals—the birthday of the Prophet; Ramadan; the feast of the lamb (Aid el Kebir) commemorating the Prophet Abraham's sacrifice of a sheep in place of his son, and held 50 days after Ramadan—family events are loaded in ritual.

After the birth of a child a lamb is always slaughtered—two lambs if the baby is given two names. If the family is very poor, it may be just a chicken that is killed, or if they are impoverished, a rabbit. For the circumcision of boys at the age of four—these days aided by a local anaesthetic—another feast is held and the boy is plied with money.

Arranged marriages, when a man's mother selects his bride (the woman must always wait to be chosen) still happen, especially in the low and high class families. Weddings are usually elaborate 15-day affairs (not even counting the preliminary official ceremony which happens a year or two before). But young Moroccans now often choose their own partners, and a few opt for a simple ceremony. Probably more than in any other Arab nation, traditionalists and modernists comfortably coexist.

If the Moroccan virtue is tolerance, how many of the vices Sir John Drummond Hay claimed for the Moroccan people are true? Well, even their ardent admirers would cite one: their special, developed sense of non-urgency (dare it be said, languor). In October 1980 King Hassan himself kept the Queen of England waiting—an incident which merited the description "snub" in a feature entitled "The King who kept the Queen Waiting" published in London's outraged *Sunday Times*.

Over 50,000 years ago Neanderthal man lived in Morocco. A specimen of his remains was found in caves at Tamara beach near Rabat in 1933. The so-called "Rabat man" seems to have been a boy about 16 years old. He lived at a time when the country was physically very different from what it is today, covered with dense forests full of wild animals.

Part of the history of these people and their descendants is written on rocks. Engravings on flat slabs of rock—some can be seen near Tafraout southeast of Agadir—show that besides prehistoric man the area was populated by lions, panthers, giraffes, ostriches, elephants and antelopes.

There is evidence that there may have been some sort of civilisation about 5,000 years ago, as indicated by the discovery of rock carvings representing a ram with a solar disc between its horns similar to the god Ammon Ra of Thebes.

The Greeks have left legends. Fabulous Atlantis is said to have sunk into the sea somewhere west of Spain and Morocco. Then there is the myth of Hercules forcing apart Europe and Africa to create the Straits of Gibraltar, a feat remembered in the Caves of Hercules near Tangier, and in the "Pillars of Hercules"—the rocks of Gibraltar and Ceuta. Some say the Garden of the Hesperides was also in Morocco and that the golden apples Hercules found were in fact oranges—an unlikely tale because oranges originated in Asia and were introduced into Morocco long after his time.

The Phoenicians: We know slightly more (but not much) about Morocco from the 12th century B.C. onwards, thanks to the Phoenicians who set up trading posts along the coast. Punic remains have been found at Russadir (Melilla), Tamuda (Tetouan), Ceuta, Tingis (Tangier), Lixus (Larache), Thymiaterion (Mehdia near Kenitra), Sala (Rabat) and Karikon Telichos (Essaouira).

They were probably trading posts rather than settlements, although a number of

Punic tombs have been found near Tangier and Rabat. There is a record of how the Phoenician navigator Hanno sailed between the Pillars of Hercules in 460 B.C. and down the African coast, perhaps as far as the Equator, founding on the way another trading post at Cerne, which may be Dakhla in the Western Sahara.

We know practically nothing of the people who lived in Morocco in Phoenician times up to the fall of Carthage in 140 B.C.. There is no evidence that the sailors or merchants of

Carthage ever penetrated inland, perhaps simply because they were not interested in colonisation, or because the Berbers were a fierce warrior race and the traders were unable to conquer them.

At all events, the Romans, who dominated the area for over four centuries until A.D. 429, found the Berbers, or the Barbarians as they called them, an intractable race who gave the Legions constant trouble when they were founding permanent Roman settlements. Among these outposts of the Roman Empire were Tingi (Tangier), Zilis (Asilah), Lixus, Valentia Banasa on the Sebou River near Kenitra, Sala Colonia and Volubilis.

Preceding pages: *Fantasia in front of Méknès* by **Eugène Delacroix.** <u>Left</u>, **Volubilis.** <u>Above</u>, **bronze head of Juba II.**

Ruins can be seen today in Rabat at Chella, the Roman Sala Colonia. The name survives in Salé, Rabat's sister town on the other side of the river, still called Sala in Arabic. The most impressive remains are at Volubilis, 19 miles (30 km) north of Méknès, which was probably the capital of the Roman province of Mauritania Tingitana encompassing northern Morocco.

The most remarkable local figure of the Roman period was undoubtedly King Juba II who ruled Mauritania Tingitana for perhaps half a century. He died in A.D. 23, in his seventies. He had three claims to fame: he married Cleopatra Selene (The Moon), daughter of Anthony and Cleopatra; he was

one of the most prolific writers of his time in Latin, Greek and Punic, and he founded a purple dye works at Essaouira.

The highly-prized purple dye was extracted from shellfish, each of which, it was said, had a drop "no bigger than a single tear". It was used to make the imperial purple robes of the Caesars. On the wind-swept islets near the coast of Essaouira deep deposits of seashells are thought to be evidence of this industry.

Juba's successor, King Ptolomy, came to grief because of the dye. He is depicted as a vain man who spent his 17-year reign in extravagance. On a visit to Rome he wore a robe of imperial purple of such magnificence that it aroused the jealousy of the malevolent Emperor Caligula. Incensed that a "Barbarian kinglet" should dare to wear imperial purple, Caligula decided to have the provincial upstart assassinated.

The Romans also exploited fish factories in Morocco to make *garum*, a sauce used in cooking. The remains of two of the factories can be seen at Lixus near Larache and at Tangier close to the Caves of Hercules, where the Romans, and probably the Phoenicians before them, used to quarry mill stones.

In the third century, Christian evangelisation of Rome's African provinces began. It seems that many Berbers embraced the new religion since there were numerous bishoprics including four in Morocco. In some cities the Latin and Christian ways of life survived the fall of the Western Empire of Byzantium. Latin inscriptions in Volubilis are dated as late as the seventh century.

In this period there were also Jewish communities, founded after the Exodus from Egypt. These form the oldest religious denomination to survive without interruption in the country down to the present day.

A dark age: The Vandal invasion of 429 wiped out what was left of Roman Catholic civilisation. King Genseric of "Vandalusia" in southern Spain set out from Tarifa with 80,000 people, including 15,000 troops, who swept through Morocco and along the North African coast, destroying everything in their path in an orgy of looting and burning that culminated in the sack of Rome in 455.

It is thought that Vandal depredations were such that the North African Berbers were forced to become nomads, helped by the camel, which had been introduced in about the third century.

Although Emperor Justinian restored Catholicism to North Africa after the Vandals (considered to be Christian heretics) were defeated by Belisarius in 533, Morocco and indeed most of North Africa entered a period of obscurity in the next century. And then, 3,000 miles away in the east, a new fire of religious fervour burst into flame which was to sweep along the Mediterranean coast and bring Islam to Morocco.

Above, mosaic from Lixus, now in the archaeological museum in Tetouan. **Right**, invasion of the Vandals.

THE ARRIVAL OF ISLAM

El Maghreb El Aksa, or the "Farthest West" as Morocco is known in Arabic, was seen in Arabia, the birthplace of Islam, as a reservoir of misguided infidels who needed to be converted to the new faith *besiff* (by the sword). The first of these military missionaries was one of the greatest of North African heroes, Sidi Okba ibn Nafi.

Inspired by fervent dedication to the teachings of the Koran, Okba left Arabia in A.D. 666, 34 years after the death of the Prophet Mohammed, at the head of an Arab cavalry force. By all accounts, admittedly written by Arab historians centuries after the event, the expedition was a splendid sight as it drove westwards, the curvetting steeds and their scimitar-wielding warriors sweeping through deserts and mountains to spread the divine revelation.

Converting pagans: In fact, Okba made three expeditions, apparently covering over 5,000 miles on horseback to convert pagans, Christians and Jews. He paused for a time to found the city of Kairouan in Tunisia and finally arrived in Morocco on his third thrust westwards in the year 684.

In Tangier he met the Count Julian, a shadowy figure who was the Christian Visigoth governor of territory on both sides of the Straits of Gibraltar. Okba considered the possibility of invading Spain, but Julian told him it was well-defended and advised him to go instead into the pagan regions of southern Morocco.

Arab chroniclers say that in the Souss valley near Taroudant he defeated a Berber army so big that "Allah alone could count them", an oriental hyperbole frequently used to describe the exploits of the Arab invaders.

Somewhere later, perhaps on the beach of Agadir bay, he rode his charger into the waves and cried: "Allah! If this sea did not stop me, I would go into distant lands to Doul Karnein (where the sun sets), forever fighting for your religion and slaying all who did not believe in you or adored other gods than you!"

Left, removing shoes—a mark of respect. **Above**, *Religious Fanatics in Tangier* by Eugène Delacroix.

Okba made no attempt to rule Morocco, evidently happier on a horse than on a throne. He quickly withdrew to be slain in a battle with Berbers in Algeria, where his tomb is still revered. Thirty years later another Arab conqueror, Musa ibn Noseir, arrived to subjugate Moroccan tribes between Tangier and the Tafilalt oases in the name of the Umayyad Caliph of Damascus.

Zealous Berbers: The commander of Musa's forces was a Berber chieftain, Tarik ibn Ziad, a glorious hero enshrined in history

and literature as the man who led the Muslim invasion of Spain. With an army of Berber warriors he routed the Visigoths in 711 to begin seven centuries of brilliant civilisation at a time when the rest of Europe lived in the Dark Ages.

Tarik's army landed on the bay of Algeciras near the limestone pinnacle which was named after him, Jebel Tarik or Tarik's mountain, today known as Gibraltar. From this foothold the Muslim armies were to spread with spectacular speed across Spain and into France, where they were finally halted by Charles Martel at the battle of Poitiers in 732.

It seems certain that these armies were composed almost entirely of Berbers rather than Arabs. They had voluntarily embraced Islam and, like many recent converts, were the most fervent if not fanatical supporters of the faith, whose simplicity and conquering spirit suited their temperament. In Morocco they also revolted against attempts at Arab domination and the greedy exactions of the eastern caliph's tax collectors.

In Morocco they founded several independent Muslim kingdoms of the Kharijite sect, which emerged following one of numerous schisms caused by bloody quarrels in the east over succession to the caliphate after the Prophet's death. The heretical king-

Arabian rebels: These three groups of Arabs were expelled from Arabia by the caliphs because they were too troublesome. The historian Ibn Khaldoun likened the Hilalis to "an army of locusts destroying everything in their path". Desert bedouins with an insatiable appetite for plunder, they streamed into North Africa but were halted by the Almohad dynasty.

The powerful Almohad monarch Yacoub el Mansour, who had created an empire comprising Muslim Spain and most of North Africa, deported the more turbulent Hilali tribesmen and settled others in the Gharb, Haouz and Temesna areas on the coastal plains of Morocco where they would form

doms already existed when another Arab hero arrived in 788, accompanied only by an ex-slave to establish what was to be the first orthodox Muslim dynasty in Morocco.

Idriss, a descendant of the Prophet, was fleeing from the Abbasid caliphate and he took refuge in Walili (Volubilis), where the local Berber tribesmen proclaimed him sultan. His reign was short-lived and the dynasty expired in 974.

The next three Moroccan dynasties were all Berber. There were still very few Arabs around until the invasions of the Beni Hilal and Beni Solaim in the 11th century and the Maaqil in the 13th century.

only tiny Arab islands in a Berber sea.

In the 13th century the Maaqil bedouins from southern Arabia migrated rather more peacefully along the northern edge of the Sahara. As the Merinid dynasty declined, they crossed the Atlas mountain passes to settle in the Souss and Draa valleys and one group, the Zaers, pitched their tents at the gates of Rabat.

These movements of Arab invaders were slow but irresistible in times when Morocco was in turmoil between the fall and rise of dynasties. They left a lasting imprint. Firstly, they Arabised the countryside and, secondly, as pastoral nomads they tended to upset the Berbers' sedentary agricultural ways.

The last two Moroccan dynasties, the Saadians and the Alaouites, described themselves as *shorfas* , or pure Arabs descendant from the Prophet. The Saadians and Alaouites both originated as Arab families from the East who settled in the 12th century in the Zagora and Tafilalt oases, where they had lived modestly for centuries before seizing power.

In reality the two "Arab" dynasties ruled over a predominantly Berber nation and it remains highly questionable whether Morocco can be truly described as an Arab country if the term is taken to mean its racial origin. As Galbraith Welch Dwyer wrote in

Still, many Moroccans say they are Arabs, proud to belong to the conquering race of the Prophet, and some speak with a certain disdain of the Berbers as if they were an inferior race. This has led to the misconception that Morocco is divided between Arabs and Berbers, an idea that was espoused in colonial times by the French, when in fact if there is any division it is simply the same as anywhere in the world: between the urban and rural populations.

Nevertheless the Arabic-speaking Muslims of Morocco feel quite at home as members of the Arab League and of the Islamic Conference Organisation founded by King Hassan II. They have no identity

an excellent book for the general reader, *North African Prelude*, "The heroic blood of the original conquerors is today diluted almost out of existence."

Arab/Berber divide?: The Arab conquerors came in relatively small numbers a long time ago and most of them were males. The Hilali and other invasions had almost petered out by the time they reached Morocco, where through inter-marriage they melted into the Moorish family.

Left, wearing your beliefs on your heart—
badges inscribed with words from the Koran.
Above, Arab or Berber? It's difficult to tell.

problem, and their nationalism is a natural heritage handed down through a dozen centuries of independent Muslim rule.

Just as Europeans went west across the ocean to found Christian nations composed of many races in the Americas, so too the Arabs several centuries before went west over the sand seas of the Sahara to El-Maghreb El Aksa to bring Muslim civilisation to Morocco.

If the people of the New World are Americans, then there can be no doubt that "Moroccans" is the proper word to describe the patriotic people of Africa's equivalent to the Far West.

Harun el Rashid, the magnificent Caliph of Baghdad, hero of *The Thousand and One Nights*, was unwittingly responsible for the creation of the first Muslim dynasty in Morocco, the Idrissids, who ruled in the time of England's King Alfred and the Knights of the Round Table.

Idriss ibn Abdullah, a descendant of the Prophet Mohammed through his daughter Fatima and son-in-law Ali, was among rebels who disputed the legitimacy of the Abbasid caliphs of whom Harun el Rashid was the fifth.

The revolt was one of many due to the fact that the Prophet did not designate a successor and had no surviving son. Consequently Islam was plagued for centuries by discord over the legitimacy of its rulers. As we shall see, the lack of a clear-cut tradition, such as primogeniture, to establish succession, and the fact that polygamous rulers often had numerous sons, were to be the cause of anarchy many times in Morocco as rival pretenders fought for the throne.

Harun er Rashid sent his army to crush the rebels, and they were massacred near Mecca in 786, but Idriss escaped. After a two-year journey accompanied by only a faithful ex-slave, Rashid, he arrived in Morocco to take refuge in Walili, the former Roman town of Volubilis. Impressed by his erudition and piety, the superficially Islamicised Berbers made him their leader.

Hearing that the rebel had set up a kingdom, Harun el Rashid sent a Judas-like envoy, who killed Idriss with a poisonous potion in 791. But two months later Idriss's Berber concubine Kenza gave birth to a son. Nurtured by Kenza and the faithful Rashid, the boy became Sultan Idriss II and the dynasty was established.

The Idrissids founded the city of Fez where they were joined by hundreds of rebel families from Cordoba and Kairouan, bringing with them a sophisticated Arab civilisation which led to the creation of the Kairouyine University, today the oldest in the world.

On the death of Idriss II in 828 (probably also assassinated on orders from Baghdad) Kenza divided the small state between their 10 sons. This led inevitably to the decline of the dynasty and it expired in 974.

Moulay Idriss near Volubilis, the holiest city in Morocco, shelters the tomb of Idriss I, who is considered a saintly man. His son's shrine in Fez is also the object of pious devotion. Each year a *moussem* (pilgrimage) is made to their tombs to honour the founders

of Muslim Morocco and of the only dynasty which did not have to impose itself by force of arms.

Veiled Sultans: Youssef ibn Tashfin, a Berber from Adrar in what is now Mauritania where the men wore veils, was a religious zealot. He set up a *ribat* or hermitage in the desert from which to propogate the true faith. His movement was known as El Murabetun (people of the *ribat*), deformed by Europeans into Almoravids, the first of three Berber dynasties.

In an incredibly short time, the veiled Almoravid sultans created a Berber empire which covered northwest Africa as far as

Algiers and southern Spain. While the murderous Macbeth was king of Scotland, the Normans invaded England, and the first Crusade took Jerusalem, the Almoravids led by Tashfin swept up from the desert, founded Marrakesh in 1060, captured Fez in 1069, and then pushed on into Spain.

Muslim Spain, in the time of the romantic *Cid Campeador* Rodrigo Diaz de Vivar, was divided into 23 *Taifas*, or petty principalities. The Almoravids had little difficulty in dominating them on the pretext of helping to defeat Christian armies as they did at Zallaqa near Badajoz in 1086. They took Granada, Cordoba and Seville in the south, Badajoz, Valencia and Saragossa in the north, although they were unable to hold them for long. Tashfin's son Ali ruled the empire from 1120 to 1143 and with him the fierce and austere Almoravids abandoned the veil to become luxury-loving potentates in Andalusia.

The Almoravid dynasty disappeared almost as quickly as it had arisen out of the desert void, but not before spreading Andalusian culture throughout the Maghreb. Among their few remaining monuments are the mosque at Tlemcen in Algeria and ramparts, which they were the first to build, around Fez.

The greatest Berber: Ibn Toumert, known as The Torch, was another radical religious reformer who emerged at the beginning of the 11th century to preach a unitarian (*tawhid*) doctrine whose followers became known as *El Mowahhadidoun* or the Almohads. By the time the fiery Toumert died in 1130 he had gathered numerous Berber tribes around his banner.

The torch was passed to Abd el Moumin, an able warrior chieftain who proclaimed himself Caliph and Amir el Mumineen (Commander of the Faithful). Oriental historians called him The Greatest of all the Berbers. Moumin seized Marrakesh and Fez, controlled all Morocco by 1148, moved into Spain when called in by anti-Almoravid rebels, and raced across North Africa, defeating the Hilali Arab hordes at Sétif.

By the time he died Moumin had forged an empire even larger than that of the Almoravids', since it extended as far as Tripoli and most of Muslim Spain was reduced to vassaldom under his son Yacoub Youssef. His grandson, Youssef Yacoub, consolidated

Almohad power and won the title El Mansour (the victorious) when he crushed the Christians under King Alfonso VIII of Castille at the battle of Alarcos on 18 July 1195.

Yacoub el Mansour's reign was the zenith of the Almohad dynasty, a golden age of Andalusian brilliance. He surrounded himself with poets and philosophers, such as the Jewish thinker Maimonides, the court physician Ibn Tofail, and Ibn Rashid (Averroes, after whom the Casablanca hospital is named), who commented on the works of Aristotle and introduced him to Christian monks.

In Morocco he founded Rabat or *Ribat el Fath* (the camp of conquest), a vast enclo-

sure inside ramparts, that still stand with the Oudayas kasbah on a bluff overlooking the sea, and the monumental Bab er Rouah (gateway of souls). The camp was used to assemble troops for military expeditions to Spain.

In the period of their glory between 1160 and 1210, the Almohads built other landmarks such as the Giralda in Seville, the unfinished Tour of Hassan in Rabat, and the Koutoubia mosque in Marrakesh. But, like their predecessors, the reforming zealots inevitably sank into silken civilised ways. In their time, Alicante boasted 800 looms making silk cloth, the minting of fine gold coinage, and paper mills in Ceuta and Fez.

Towards the end of the dynasty, Sultan El Mamoun in 1230 was reduced to accepting 12,000 Christian cavalrymen from King Ferdinand of Castile and Leon in order to be able to retake Marrakesh from local dissidents. As part of the bargain he allowed the construction of a Catholic church in the city. A Marrakesh bishopric subsisted until the 14th century to serve foreign mercenaries.

The Black Sultan: The Beni Merin were a nomadic Berber tribe from the Sahara pushed westwards by the Hilali invaders. They settled northeast Morocco in the period when King John was forced by the English barons to sign Magna Carta in 1215, and the

reconquer lost territory, notably after one memorable battle on 8 September 1275 in which the army led by the Christian hero Don Nuno Gonzales de Lara was routed, a black day for the Cross.

Abou el Hassan, son of an Abyssinian mother and known as the Black Sultan, who ruled the Merinid empire from 1331 to 1351 (during the Hundred Years' War in Europe), was a prodigiously powerful and active man. He reorganised the empire between the Atlantic and the Gulf of Gabes in Tunisia and held it with an iron hand. He was less successful in Spain, where his army was beaten at the battle of Rio Salado near Tarifa in October 1340.

infamous Spanish Inquisition began in 1238 to persecute Muslims and Jews.

The Beni Merin took part in the battle of Alarcos and were aware of the rewards of the *jihad* (holy war) which they began waging—with the help of Christian mercenaries however—against the Almohads. By taking Fez on 20 August 1248, their leader Abou Yahya established the Merinid dynasty.

His son Abou Youssef crossed the Straits of Gibraltar four times to help the Muslims

Left, the Koutoubia Mosque, built by the Almohads in Marrakesh. **Above**, Chella, near Rabat, fortified by the Merenids.

Hassan died a disgusted man and was buried in Chella near Rabat. His own son Abou Inan had rebelled against him to rule until 1358 when he was strangled by a vizir in favour of a five-year-old pretender. Inan had lost control of what is now Algeria and Tunisia, the Maaqil Arab invaders started to move in, the Spanish connection was finished, and the Christians began their encroachments. The gangrene of anarchy set in under various infant sultans.

Although their political achievements could not be compared with those of the Almohads, the Merinids left a substantial cultural legacy in the shape of *medersa*, or colleges, in delicate Hispano-Moorish style, which can be seen in Fez, Méknès and Salé. The Bou Inania *medrassa* in Fez, finished in 1357 is one of the most remarkable, with a clepysdra water clock in the narrow street outside that at one time told the time with 13 brass gongs.

Christian encroachments: At the beginning of the 15th century, piracy became a way of attacking Christians and an excuse for the latter to intervene in Morocco. The Spanish kings were undoubtedly motivated also by a spirit of revenge after seven centuries of Muslim domination which was to end with the fall of Granada in 1492.

While Muslim and Jewish refugees began flooding into Morocco to escape the Inquisition, Spanish and Portuguese kings sent armies and navies after them. Henry III of Castile took Tetouan and massacred the population in 1399, Portugal grabbed Ceuta in 1415 and, after three attempts, finally took Asilah and Tangier with a fleet of 477 ships and 30,000 men in 1471.

After *Los Reyes Catolicos* Ferdinand and Isabella ousted the Muslims from Grenada, Spain occupied Melilla in 1497 with a fleet originally intended to take Columbus on his second voyage of discovery, while the Portuguese established fortresses on the Atlantic coast at Agadir, Azemmour and Safi, and the Ottoman Turks arrived on Morocco's doorstep at Tlemcen.

They were dark days for Morocco, enfeebled for a century by anarchy under the Wattasid dynasty (1465-1549), but they were a prelude to another glorious era. The renaissance came as a reaction to Christian intolerance: the bloody excesses of the Inquisition were matched by Moroccan xenophobia and fanaticism caused by the presence of infidels on the soil of *Dar el Islam*, the sacred House of Islam, that called for a holy war.

The spirit of the *jihad* coalesced around the Saadians, who overthrew the last of the Wattasids in 1557 and astounded Europe when they annihilated a Portuguese army of 20,000 at the Battle of the Three Kings on 4 August 1578.

Members of the Arab tribe of Beni Saad arrived in the 12th century to settle in the Draa valley near Zagora and later in the Souss near Taroudant. Claiming descent from the Prophet, they founded the Arab

dynasty by taking Marrakesh in 1525. After being driven out of Agadir in 1541, the Portuguese also abandoned the ports of Safi and Azemmour.

These reverses inspired 24-year-old King Sebastian of Portugal to seek revenge by launching a crusade against the "barbarians", albeit against the advice of his Jesuit mentors. But historians tell us Sebastian was a mystical fanatic who thought apparent anarchy in Morocco presented a golden opportunity for personal glory in the name of God.

Sebastian was joined by one of the Saadians, Mohammed el Mutawakkil, who was sultan for a brief period until he fled to Spain

after being overthrown by his brother Abd el Malik. Mohammed hoped to regain his throne. The cream of Portuguese nobility was assembled and embarked with a large fleet to land at Tangier and Asilah. The men marched southwards slowly and ponderously, lugging 36 bronze cannon.

Their progress was so slow that Abd el Malik was able to muster a force of 50,000 cavalry. The two armies met near Ksar el Kebir where the Portuguese suddenly found themselves trapped in a fork between the Loukos river and its tributary the Oued el Makhazin.

The tide rose to make it impossible to ford

the streams, while wave after wave of charging Moroccan cavalry cut them to pieces. Sebastian and Mohammed were drowned and Sultan Abd el Malik died of sickness before the battle was over. The disaster was complete for Portugal who later lost to Spain both its crown and its African possession, Ceuta.

The victory had a tremendous impact in Morocco after the death of the three kings, giving enormous prestige to Abd el Malik's brother Ahmed, proclaimed sultan on the battlefield. He became known as Ahmed el Mansour el Dehbi (the victorious and golden) after extracting huge ransoms for the Portuguese nobles captured in the battle.

haustion on the way. The rest arrived at Timbuctoo after marching for 135 days in probably one of the most gruelling gold rushes of all time. An offer made by local emperor Ishaq Askia to buy them off with 100,000 pieces of gold and 1,000 slaves was spurned by Ahmed as "insulting".

The Songai empire was destroyed and Ahmed named pashas to rule it. Goaded by greed, the pashas were unscrupulous (there were 149 of them between 1612 and 1750). Their unruly troops massacred the population or sent them into slavery in caravans carrying gold back to Marrakesh.

Laurence Maddock, an English trader in Marrakesh, counted 30 mule loads of gold

Since Spain was too powerful for him to attempt any exploits on the Iberian peninsular, Ahmed instead set out to conquer the salt and gold mines of the Songai empire on the banks of the Niger river. A ragtag army of 3,000 Christians, Kabyles, Ottomans and negroes, led by the Spanish renegade Jouder and trained by Turks, trekked across the Sahara. To paraphrase Wellington, it was the scum of the earth enlisted for lucre.

Half of the troops died of thirst and ex-

Left, piracy off the Atlantic coast. **Above**, cannons in Essaouira are a reminder today of a defensive past.

dust arriving in the city in a single day. The historian El Ifrani said court officials were paid in gold and there were 1,400 hammers at the palace to strike gold ducats.

To match his great wealth, Ahmed built himself a sumptuous palace, the Badi, with Italian marble bought kilo for kilo in exchange for sugar produced by Christian and Jewish renegades in the Souss valley. Foreign visitors marvelled at the magnificence of court ceremonial à la Turk, for Ahmed had spent his youth in Constantinople.

His notoriety spread throughout Europe. He corresponded several times with England's Queen Elizabeth I, proposing an

Anglo-Moroccan alliance against Spain after the defeat of the Spanish Armada by Sir Francis Drake in 1588.

He organised the Makhzen government, which survived with little change into the 20th century. Of the rest little remains. His palace was razed by the next dynasty. Among the few notable relics are the Saadian tombs built by Ahmed's son Moulay Zidan, which were walled up by his successors until the French came to Morocco.

One consequence of the Saadian era was that the influx of thousands of black slaves, white renegades and mercenaries changed the racial composition of the country. The result can be seen in the faces of Moroccans

was Moulay Ismail, whose 55-year reign was one of the longest and most brutal in Moroccan history. He was a cruel and profligate megalomaniac reputed to have had a harem of 500 women, over 700 sons and uncounted daughters.

Ismail was the brother of Moulay Rashid, the founder of the Alaouite dynasty and the scion of an Arab family which had emigrated from Arabia to the Tafilalt oasis in the 13th century. The family descended from El Hassan, son of Ali and the Prophet's daughter Fatima.

Ismail's reign is well-documented by Arab historians and also by European diplomats, monks and the slaves they came to

today, ranging from ivory white to brown and ebony black.

Ahmed died in August 1603, at a time when Shakespeare was writing his plays. He was undoubtedly the greatest of the 11 Saadian sultans, eight of whom were assassinated. Three of his sons fought over the succession for seven years, and for a time Morocco was divided into two states ruled from Fez and Marrakesh. A third proclaimed in Rabat-Salé was an independent corsair republic led by *Moriscos* expelled from Spain, the "Sallee Rovers" mentioned in Daniel Defoe's *Robinson Crusoe*.

Moulay Ismail: The next remarkable sultan

redeem from captivity at the hands of the corsairs. Some 2,000 Christian slaves and 30,000 other prisoners were employed for half a century in an orgy of building in Méknès, which he made his capital.

A hotchpotch of gigantic structures was built, mostly of adobe but also with some marble looted from Volubilis and Ahmed el Mansour's palace in Marrakesh, which Ismail had razed to the ground. The city was ringed by ramparts 15 miles (25 km) long. It included palaces with vast colonnaded courtyards, huge gardens, a zoo, stables for hundreds of horses, granaries, barracks for large numbers of troops, and of course a harem where his legitimate wife the Sultana Zidana, a giant negress, cracked the whip over hundreds of concubines.

Each time he granted his favours to one of the oiled and perfumed women she was paraded through the palace on a litter accompanied by singers and dancers. At the age of 30 she would be pensioned off and sent into limbo in Fez or the Tafilalt.

When Ismail visited the building sites he would personally run his lance through slave labourers if he thought they were shirking, or crush their skulls with bricks he considered badly made. The French diplomat Pidou de Saint Olon saw him dripping with blood after slitting a slave's throat.

The French remember the despot for his plan to marry the Princess Conti, illegitimate daughter of the Sun King Louis XIV, a proposal that caused hilarity in the Palace of Versailles and not a little bemusement in Méknès when Ismail was turned down.

Ismail's power rested on an army of blacks, the Abids, formed from the remnants of slaves brought into the country by the Saadians. They were placed in a stud farm at Meshra Er Remel on the Sebou river and

Far left, Moulay Ismail. **Left**, his heart's desire, Princess Conti, daughter of Louis XIV. **Above**, accounts of Christian slavery were graphic.

made to increase and multiply, all the boys being pressed into military service at the age of 15.

Considered more reliable than Arab or Berber warriors, the blacks were garrisoned in kasbahs built at strategic points around the country. They were also used to retake Larache and Asilah, to lay siege for years to Ceuta and Melilla, and to evict the Turks from Tlemcen. The English left Tangier of their own accord after occupying it from 1662 to 1684.

Ismail's death at the age of 81 in 1727 was followed by a period of chaos and famine such as Morocco has never seen before or since. His numerous sons and the Abids fought over the succession for 30 years. One was proclaimed and dethroned six times and in a generation there were 12 sultans. A contemporary wrote that in this period "the hair of babes in arms turned white" with terror.

In contrast, Sultan Mohammed ibn Abdullah (1757-90) left memories of a pious and peaceful man. He built Mogador (Essaouira), designed by the French architect Cornut of Avignon and finished by an English renegade named Ahmed el Inglesi. He forced the Portuguese out of their last stronghold at Mazagan, which he renamed El Jadida, but failed to evict Spain from Melilla. He was the first to recognise the infant United States of America and Washington called him "Great and magnanimous friend".

There was a bloody two-year interlude under his son Moulay Yazid, born of an English or Irish renegade mother, a sanguinary demon who among other excesses had Jews crucified in Fez by nailing them to the doors of their houses. Mercifully he was killed in 1792. He was followed by his younger brother Moulay Slimane (1792-1822) and Moulay Abderrahman (1822-59) who were pious and benign.

In the last half of the 19th century, Morocco isolated itself, became poor and weak, and was plagued by dissidence in the *bled essiba*, the parts of the country outside the *bled el-makhzen* controlled by the government. The last notable Alaouite sultan, Moulay el Hassan (1873-94), spent most of his reign in the saddle trying to subdue rebellious tribes while European imperialists began gnawing away at the country's fragile fabric.

EUROPEAN ENCROACHMENT

In the "last scramble for Africa" at the beginning of the 20th century, Britain, France, Germany and Spain vied with one another to dominate Morocco, one of the few remaining parts of the continent outside the colonial grasp.

It had escaped colonialism not because it was considered worthless—on the contrary, it was and remains strategically very important—but because it was an old independent nation with an organised society capable of resisting invasion. That made it different from the rest of the "Dark Continent" with its archaic tribal systems and maps featuring "elephants for want of towns".

Also, Morocco had existed as a Muslim nation for more than 1,000 years. It had a long history of dynastic rule, its own culture and civilisation, ancient cities such as Fez, Marrakesh and Tangier, and a record of fierce resistance to invasion.

Until the turn of the century, Morocco had survived by playing one European power off against another. But gradually the rivals were eliminated. In return for a free hand in Morocco, France agreed to let Italy colonise Libya and then, as part of the Entente Cordiale, struck a similar deal with Britain, which in return was given carte blanche in Egypt.

This left two contenders: Germany, whose Kaiser Wilhelm landed in Tangier and later sent a gunboat to Agadir to demonstrate its "interests"; and Spain, which, because of her centuries-long occupation of the Ceuta and Melilla enclaves on the coast, claimed "historic rights" in Morocco.

When European plenipotentiaries met at the Reina Cristina hotel in the Spanish seaport of Algeciras in January 1906 to discuss Morocco's future, Britain and Italy supported France. The Act of Algeciras proposed a plan of reforms and recognised France's "privileged position" in Morocco.

Germany withdrew as World War I loomed, after receiving from France the "gift" part of Cameroun in West Africa. Spain signed a secret accord with France delimiting their respective "spheres of influence" in Morocco. The European claimants to the Moroccan cake were reduced to two.

The Prodigal Son: This coincided with a crisis in Morocco. Sultan Moulay Hassan, a strong monarch who spent most of his reign in the saddle fighting rebellious tribes, had died suddenly in 1894. He was succeeded by his son Abd el Aziz, who emptied the

treasury with extravagant spending on frivolous pursuits. Unscrupulous Europeans sold him solid gold cameras, pianos no-one at court knew how to play, and a magnificent gilded state coach even though there were no roads.

To solve the financial crisis, large loans were contracted with a French bank consortium. To repay them, Morocco had to forfeit its customs dues, leading to revolts against the growing influence of the "infidels" and the encroachments by French troops in areas bordering Algeria.

One revolt, backed by powerful tribal chiefs of the south, resulted in 1908 in the

Left, conference members at the Reina Cristina hotel in 1906. **Above**, Abd el Aziz, one of the more profligate sultans.

overthrow of Abd el Aziz by his brother Hafid. But the new ruler was unable to assert his authority over a debt-ridden country assailed by external pressures and internal dissent. He was forced to sign the Protectorate Treaty in 1912, under which France became responsible for foreign affairs and defence and undertook to enact reforms. Hafid immediately abdicated in favour of his half-brother, Moulay Youssef. As the American historian Edmund Burke III remarked, "Morocco stumbled into the modern age."

France took over "useful Morocco", the main cities on the central plains and all the territory bordering on Algeria. Spain

international zone had its own currency, post offices and banks. The post offices later proved useful to independence workers from the French and Spanish zones, who used them to gain uncensored news of what was happening in Morocco.

Penetration of Morocco by France and Spain met with bloody resistance. As soon as the protectorate treaty was signed in Fez, the walled city was besieged by warrior tribes and it was not until 1934 that France was able to pacify the whole of its zone.

Spain's occupation of the northern zone was marked by the 1920 revolt of the "Emir" Abd el Krim, whose Berber warriors routed a Spanish army of 60,000 at the battle of

received the crumbs—the rugged Rif mountain area adjacent to its enclaves, and in the south the enclave of Ifni, the Tarfaya strip and beyond the Western Sahara, Rio de Oro.

Because of its strategic location, Tangier and its immediate vicinity became an "International Zone". For some time diplomats had been extending their influence in the town. They had been responsible for the building of the Cap Spartel lighthouse and had set up a sanitation programme. Good works, they thought, would foster good relations. No-one, and particularly Britain, wanted Spain to control both sides of the Straits of Gibraltar. Each nation within the

Anual. It was a remarkable achievement. Abd el Krim set up an independent republic in the Rif, with an education programme, a State bank and much of the administrative infrastructure of a modern country. He was finally defeated by a combined Spanish and French army commanded by the "saviour of Verdun" Marshal Philippe Pétain, and he surrendered to the French rather than face Spanish execution. He was exiled to the French Indian Ocean island of Reunion and later died in Cairo.

Lyautey's way: Marshal Hubert Gonzalve Lyautey, the first French Resident-General, or chief administrator, was an experienced soldier but also an audacious idealist. His "maxims" are still current in independent Morocco: for instance, "Not a drop of water should reach the ocean" and his warning, "Morocco is a cold country with a hot sun."

He believed the protectorate concept should be scrupulously respected: in other words, that all actions must be taken in the name and with the consent of the sultan in cooperation with the "makhzen" government, or traditional Moroccan élite. He insisted that the younger Moroccan generation should take an active part in all stages of the country's modernisation, otherwise they would become frustrated and rebellious. This proved prophetic.

Exactly as Lyautey had predicted, intellectuals formed a nationalist movement in Fez to spearhead resistance just as the "pacification" ended in 1934. Some of them were French-educated and inspired by "*Liberté, Egalité et Fraternité*", others, trained in Fez's old Kairouyine University, were strongly influenced by Middle-Eastern politicians.

The movement was amply fuelled by resentment over two grievances. First, the influx of French settlers (which Lyautey had opposed) took over the best farmland and monopolised the economy. Second, a heavy-handed bureaucracy (which had a mania for regulating everything, including even the

After Lyautey departed in 1925, succeeding Resident-Generals (there were 14 in 44 years) turned the protectorate into a virtual colony with direct administration that sidelined the traditional ruling classes and left few outlets for the talents of ambitious young Moroccans. As one of Lyautey's admirers remarked, the sultan reached the point where he had to read the French newspapers to find out what was going on in his own country.

Far left, European encroachment. **Left**, Marshal Lyautey. **Above**, the Rif presented the most determined resistance to France and Spain.

profession of snake charmer!) made sure that Moroccans were given only subaltern jobs.

Desirable property: While development of the Spanish zones was minimal because of the civil war and the fact that under Generalissimo Francisco Franco the Spanish economy was in dire straits, France poured resources into Morocco, building modern roads, railways and ports, laying out farms, opening up mines, and setting up education, public health and justice systems on the French pattern. This transformed the country. Ironically, in nationalist eyes, the French protectorate made Morocco even more worth fighting for than before.

When Sultan Moulay Youssef died in 1927, he was replaced by his third son Mohammed, who was 18 and had led a cloistered life. The French thought he would be more amenable to their interests. This was to prove a miscalculation.

What was later seen as a serious political mistake was the publication by the French of the Berber *Dahir* (decree) in 1930 to which the young and inexperienced monarch set his seal. The decree was intended to apply tribal custom law to the Berbers instead of traditional Islamic law. It aroused charges that it was intended to convert the Berbers to Christianity.

Disorders broke out and nationalist leaders such as Allal al Fassi, Mohammed ben Hassan Wazzani, Ahmed Balafrej and Mohammed Mekki Naciri were arrested. With many others, they were in and out of jail or in exile for the next 25 years.

In the Spanish zone, meanwhile, nationalists were tolerated—more to exasperate the French than out of idealism, since Madrid was still angry at being given the poorest parts of the country. The Franco regime encouraged rivalry between four nationalist groups in order to keep them busy with personal quarrels and divert attention from the fact that Moroccan troops had been recruited for the "anti-communist crusade" in the Spanish Civil War.

To counter nationalist agitation, the French enlisted the support of the "Grand Kaids" or Berber tribal chiefs of the south led by Thami el Glaoui, the Pasha or governor of Marrakesh, surnamed "The Lion of the Atlas", and other personalities with grudges against the sultanate. The religious leader Abdelhay el Kettani, whose brother Mohammed was flogged to death on orders from Sultan Moulay Hafid in 1909, was one.

Sultan Mohammed ben Youssef had espoused the nationalist cause by the time the nationalists who had formed the Istiqlal (independence) Party issued a "Manifesto" in January 1944 demanding for the first time not just reforms as hitherto but outright independence. This move was said to have been inspired in part by President Franklin D. Roosevelt's advice to the Sultan when they met at the Anfa conference near Casablanca during World War II.

Seething unrest: As agitation grew, the French reacted by arresting the ringleaders.

Riots and demonstrations followed, and finally the Sultan went "on strike" by refusing to seal protectorate decrees.

When General Augustin Guillaume, the 10th French Resident-General, took over in Rabat in July 1951, he found an uncooperative Sultan and seething unrest among nationalists. He also found a protectorate apparatus ready to defy the government in Paris and give in to the demands of the diehard leaders of settlers, who had grown to nearly half a million.

El Glaoui, Kettani and other Moroccan "collaborators" decided, in March 1953, that Sultan Mohammed ben Youssef must be deposed. The idea received active support

from settlers and their lobby in Paris, where ephemeral French governments of the Fourth Republic were coming and going at dizzying frequency.

In May Guillaume, accompanied by Marshal Alphonse Juin, a former Resident-General born in Algeria, reviewed tens of thousands of Berber tribesmen assembled near Azrou in the Middle Atlas mountains. Many were French army veterans who had served valiantly under Guillaume and Juin in the final stages of World War II. They were generally seen by settlers as "good Moroccans", in contrast to the "bad" ones represented by the urban nationalists. The latter considered the Azrou parade as a dress rehearsal for a march by massed Berber tribesmen on Fez and Rabat to force the Sultan off his throne.

French Foreign Minister Georges Bidault in April had told Guillaume clearly: "The French government will not accept being placed by anyone before a *fait accompli*...I ask you to oppose without hesitation any new progress towards a situation in which we shall have no choice but between deposing the Sultan and using force against our friends."

But El Glaoui and 300 of his fellow plotters met in Marrakesh on 13 August, 1953 (while Guillaume was in Vichy taking

ceremonies of Aid El-Kebir, due to start on 21 August that year, when the sultan would perform in public the traditional sacrifice of a ram.

The French founder: In an atmosphere of hysteria whipped up by the plotters and echoed in the colonial press, French Prime Minister Joseph Laniel gave the green light for the Sultan's deposition, apparently believing that the alternative would be civil war in Morocco. His Interior Minister, François Mitterrand, did not agree and resigned in protest.

A grim-faced Guillaume went to the palace in Rabat on Thursday morning, 20 August 1953 to demand that the sultan

the waters for his liver) and planned to depose Mohammed ben Youssef and proclaim Sultan Sidi Mohammed ben Arafa, an obscure 70-year-old who was a distant relation of the monarch.

Despite another Bidault message warning of the "incalculable consequences of such a *pronunciamento*", contingents of tribes began to march on Fez and Rabat, some of them doubtless believing they were on their way as usual to attend the Muslim feast day

Left, Thami el Glaoui, Lord of the Atlas, profiteer and friend of Winston Churchill. **Above**, money exchanges in Tangier in its international era.

abdicate in favour of his younger son, Prince Moulay Abdallah, whom the French thought would be a more "flexible" ruler than the elder son, Prince Moulay Hassan, the settlers' *bête noire*.

When the Sultan refused to comply, he and his sons and daughters were immediately whisked away in a fleet of black cars to the old Rabat airport, today the site of the Hyatt Regency Hotel, and flown into exile, first in Corsica and then Madagascar.

His departure was cheered by the Moroccan plotters and their settler friends of the "*Presence Française*" association, but their "victory" was short-lived. Only three

weeks later, on 11 September, puppet-sultan Ben Arafa narrowly escaped death when Allal ben Abdallah (after whom numerous Moroccan streets are now named) crashed an open car into a royal procession on its way to the mosque in Rabat, then tried to knife him.

This signalled the start of violent popular protests against the exiling of the legitimate sultan. It quickly snowballed into an urban terrorism campaign coupled with the emergence of a "liberation army" in the Rif and Middle Atlas mountains.

Resistance fighters, who were not necessarily controlled by the nationalists but were often small independent groups of patriots, shot French leaders and Moroccan "collaborators" and set off bombs in crowded cafés or markets. On Christmas Eve 1953, in Casablanca's central market, Mohamed Zerktouni (one of the city's main boulevards is named after him) planted a bomb in a shopping-basket that killed 20 people and wounded 28. The choice of the Christian holiday was symbolic: the Sultan had been exiled on a Muslim feast day.

The terrorists enjoyed the silent support of the population at large, some of the simpler people swearing they could see their Sultan's face in the moon or saying he was "*chez* Madame Gaspar" on that faraway Indian Ocean island.

Extremist French settlers reacted by organising terrorist campaigns of their own, at times shooting indiscriminately from cruising cars or murdering French personalities they suspected of pro-nationalist sympathies. There was evidence that they were being helped by the French police.

The campaign reached a climax on the second anniversary of the Sultan's departure into exile, on 20 August 1955, when tribesmen descended on the small farming town of Oued Zem, southeast of Casablanca, and savagely butchered 49 French people, including eight women and 15 children. The French Foreign Legion was sent in on a punitive expedition. According to Moroccan sources, 1,500 tribespeople were slain, raising tension at a time when the latest Resident General, the liberal civilian Gilbert

Grandval, was trying to solve the crisis while being physically attacked and insulted by outraged settlers.

In Paris, meanwhile, Prime Minister Edgar Faure called a conference of nationalist leaders in Aix-les-Bains, urged on by fears that a *jihad* (holy war) was about to be launched against France in Morocco and Algeria. The uprising broke out in the Rif mountains on 1 October when the "Moroccan Liberation Army" attacked three French outposts on the border of the Spanish zone.

The Aix-les-Bains conference was designed to form an interim Moroccan government and find a compromise solution

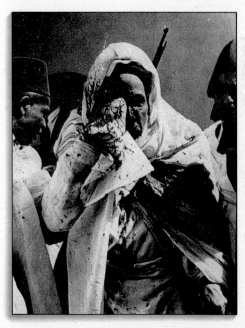

to the dynastic problem in the shape of a "Throne Council". But the Council formula was contested by none other than Thami el Glaoui himself, who astounded everyone by announcing on 25 October that the solution was to bring back Mohamed ben Youssef to his throne.

In the circumstances, France could hardly do otherwise. The legitimate sultan was flown back to Rabat on 16 November 1955 to receive a hero's welcome, whose scale and fervour has not been seen in Morocco since. He announced to massed crowds assembled in front of the palace that the protectorate had come to an end.

Left, Ben Arafa is installed as sultan by the French. **Above**, three weeks later he narrowly escapes assassination.

SINCE INDEPENDENCE

Sultan Sidi Mohammed ben Youssef changed his title to King Mohammed V in 1956 when Morocco regained its independence. The change symbolised the additional prestige acquired as an exiled national hero, "The Liberator" of the country. His great popularity, together with his religious prestige as Amir el Mumineen (commander of the faithful), enabled him to rule with uncontested authority during a crucial period when an élite had to be assembled to run a modern nation.

Although he had been humiliated by the French, he proved to be a moderate and magnanimous monarch. Foreigners were kept on to advise inexperienced Moroccan officials so that the transition would be fairly smooth. Many French settlers fled of their own accord, but others ran farms and industries until as late as 1973 when "Moroccanisation" measures were taken. This helped to save the economy from upheavals.

Morocco joined the Arab League, was a founder-member of the Organisation of African Unity (OAU), and cultivated cordial relations with France and Spain, who helped create the Royal Armed Forces and supplied aid for economic development. New industries sprang up based on agriculture and the phosphate industry, the mainstays of the economy.

Restive people: Gradually the number of schoolchildren grew from a few thousand to over three million in 25 years; at the same time improved health conditions stimulated rapid population growth coupled with the emergence of a restive urban proletariat. Providing work, housing and social services became and remains an arduous, uphill task.

A crisis erupted in October 1956 when the French in Algeria forced down the aircraft carrying Algerian nationalist leader Ahmed ben Bella and his associates from Rabat to Tunis. Rioters attacked French settlers in a violent protest organised by nationalists in support of the Algerian Front de Libération Nationale. Relations with France were

strained further because Morocco was channelling arms to the Algerian revolution.

The former Spanish and French protectorate zones and the Tangier international zone were quickly abolished, but it took several years to convince Spain to evacuate the Tarfaya strip and the enclave of Ifni in the south, in the latter case only after local tribes staged a revolt.

King Mohammed V's main domestic problem was dealing with the old-guard Istiqlal Party, whose leaders considered themselves the real architects of Moroccan independence, deserving to monopolise power in what they called "homogenous governments", i.e. excluding other political parties.

The Rif Rebellion: Istiqlal pretensions sparked revolts by other nationalist groups who felt deprived of the fruits of victory. One of the most serious broke out in 1958 in the Rif mountains after the Istiqlal ordered the arrest of Dr Abd el Krim Khatib and Mahjoubi Aherdan, two Moroccan Liberation Army (MLA) leaders who had led guerrillas against the French before independence but also contested the Istiqlal party's ascendance.

Left, King Hassan II, much pictured in public places. **Above**, literacy is becoming the norm rather than the exception.

Although the King ordered the release of Aherdan and Khatib, the Rif rebels defied Rabat until February 1959. There were heavy casualties when 20,000 troops commanded by Crown Prince Moulay Hassan were sent in to wipe out resistance. Nevertheless the King espoused the Istiqlal's territorial claims to large tracts of Algeria, the Spanish Sahara and Mauritania, claims which were soon to create serious diplomatic difficulties.

At the same time he tried to thwart Istiqlal attempts to dominate the government. Aherdan and Khatib were allowed to create a rival party, the People's Movement, representing the rural majority, which held office in all

tated for radical political and economic reforms, attacking the king's "personal power" and accusing the monarchy of being feudal or even fascist—views shared by the socialist regime in Algeria.

Newly-independent Algeria in 1963 rejected Moroccan claims to parts of its territory and a brief war broke out. Moroccan and Algerian troops fought over oases in a disputed area where the frontier had never been formally drawn. The conflict was halted by the Organisation of African Unity, but Mehdi ben Barka was sentenced to death *in absentia* for treason because he had taken Algeria's side in the dispute.

Just before the border war, Morocco's first

later governments, while by the end of 1962 the Istiqlal was eased out of power and went into the opposition.

King Hassan II ascended the throne in February 1961 on the death of his father. As he told King Juan Carlos of Spain 25 years later: "When I ascended the throne, people said I would not last more than six months."

By this time the Istiqlal Party had split. A radical left-wing, led by Mehdi ben Barka, emerged with distinctly republican leanings regarded by the palace as a serious threat to the throne. Ben Barka's break-away faction which came to be known as the *Union Socialiste des Forces Populaires* (USFP), agi-

constitution was promulgated. It outlawed the one-party regime, guaranteed basic democratic freedoms and provided for an elected parliament, but the king retained substantial powers. The first parliament elected in May 1963 was divided between five parties who spent their time in petty bickering.

The King dissolved it in June 1965 because of the "contradictory and irreconcilable demands of the parties" and he declared a "state of emergency". For five years he ruled by decree with a government of independence. He was the Prime Minister.

Plots and coups: Faced by what they saw as

the King's autocratic rule, left-wing militants resorted to violence. Many were arrested in connection with five plots against the monarchy between 1963 and 1977; on two occasions in 1965 and 1973 armed infiltrators entered the country from Algeria; in 1965, 1981 and 1984 there were serious street riots fomented by leftists.

The agitation was severely repressed and there were mass trials resulting in death sentences. Mehdi ben Barka, who had been living in exile and was suspected of inciting the agitation, disappeared in Paris in mysterious circumstances on 29 October 1965. He was certainly assassinated. General Mohamed Oufkir, Moroccan Minister of the

French financial aid began to flow again.

At about the same time cordial relations were established with Algeria and Mauritania after the King abandoned the Istiqlal's claims to their territory. He also convened Muslim leaders to a meeting in Casablanca where the Islamic Conference Organisation was created. This enhanced his own prestige and helped to forestall criticism from Islamic fundamentalists. It seemed that the King now had his hands free to return to more democratic rule.

He decided to rescind the state of emergency, and a second constitution was adopted by referendum; but it was boycotted by the parties, who complained it had been

Interior at the time, was convicted by a French court of master-minding ben Barka's abduction (he was in Paris at the time of the incident), and sentenced to life imprisonment in his absence.

France recalled its ambassador in Rabat and for three years relations were frozen as the King steadfastly refused to admit Oufkir's guilt, rejecting suggestions that the General be dismissed. Relations with France were resumed after De Gaulle's death and

Left, after the death of Mohammed V, mourners cover their heads in respect. Above, women queue to cast their votes.

drafted without their consent and was therefore an imposition, quite apart from their view that the new constitution still gave the King inordinately extensive powers.

The parties also boycotted the general election so that the second parliament was a colourless assembly with over 90 percent of its members so-called independents. The opposition claimed the vote was rigged. Elected for six years, parliament was a rubber-stamp affair plagued by absenteeism.

In an unsettled atmosphere, senior officers of the Royal Armed Forces staged an abortive *coup d'état* by storming the royal palace at Skhirate on the beach near Rabat on

10 July 1971 while the King was celebrating his 42nd birthday. Nearly 100 guests were gunned down by some 1,400 NCO cadets but the King escaped by hiding in a bathroom in a corner of the sprawling palace.

The army's motivations were mixed. Some coup leaders like General Mohammed Medbouh, Minister of the Royal Military Household, who was killed during the raid, were outraged by corruption and extravagance. They believed corrupt ministers should be brought to trial and made an example of and not just dismissed. Others were doubtless less idealistic and simply out to seize power in what would probably have been a right-wing military dictatorship, as most of the officers involved had great disdain for the factious political parties.

The Defence Minister, General Oufkir, had the rebels rounded up with the help of loyalist troops. Ten officers including four generals were summarily executed. Just over 1,000 of the troops stood trial in the following February, but only 74 were convicted.

The verdict appeared surprisingly lenient, but the King's contention was that the coup was the work of only a fraction of the armed forces and so it seemed politic to avoid alienating loyalist officers and troops. If this was in fact the royal thinking, it proved misguided because, on the following 16 August, the pilots of three Air Force jets tried to liquidate the King and his entourage by pumping cannon shells into his airliner as it was flying home from France.

Once again the King escaped unscathed. As he related later, he spoke to the fighter pilots on the airliner's radio in a disguised voice to tell them "the tyrant is dead", whereupon they called off the attacks.

General Oufkir's alleged suicide during the night after the attacks was at first thought to be the act of a dedicated senior officer who felt he had failed in his duty to protect his sovereign. The official version revealed days later was that he had master-minded the attack and was a despicable traitor who planned to rule Morocco using as a puppet the King's elder son, Crown Prince Sidi Mohammed, then aged nine. His original plan was to shoot down the royal airliner over the sea and camouflage it as an accident.

At their trial Air Force officers said Oufkir had persuaded them that the King had to be liquidated to save the country from chaos.

The truth is difficult to ascertain. The 11 ringleaders were all executed so that their real motives and the loyalty of other officers remain the subject of speculation.

In an apparent effort to defuse discontent, six former cabinet ministers and four accomplices were brought to trial for corruption. Eight were sentenced to prison terms ranging from four to 12 years for taking bribes totalling over $2 million, but three years later they were all released.

The two abortive military coups convinced many, including apparently the US Central Intelligence Agency, that the Moroccan monarchy's days were numbered. This may explain in part why in the follow-

ing year, on 3 March 1973, several hundred armed men infiltrated the country from neighbouring Algeria with the intention of touching off a "popular uprising" on the 12th anniversary of the King's accession.

The "uprising" also failed, reinforcing the popular belief that the King enjoyed *baraka*, or divine protection. Perhaps misled by their own propaganda which claimed that only a spark was needed to set off a revolution, left-wing USFP activists who led the infiltrators found that, instead of welcoming them as "liberators", peasants in border areas telephoned local security forces.

During the trials, at which 22 were sentenced to death, it was revealed that the plotters had also planted bombs at US offices in Rabat and Casablanca and at the main theatre in the capital. None exploded, apparently because the myopic activist who had made them got his wires crossed.

In 1974 the non-party government led by Prime Minister Ahmed Osman, the King's brother-in-law, decided to more than double phosphate rock prices to $64 a ton and borrow money on the strength of this to finance capital-intensive development projects. But the higher price held for only a short time because of a world-wide recession.

A sudden surge in the price of crude oil when Morocco had to import at least 75 ony internal autonomy and hold a referendum there, the King revived Moroccan historic claims to the territory and launched a campaign to recover it for the "motherland".

The Green March: Asked to decide whether the area was a *terra nullius* before Spain colonised it, the World Court found that West Saharan tribes had paid allegiance to Moroccan monarchs but that this did not constitute sovereignty, which should be decided by self-determination. The King interpreted this as vindication of Moroccan claims, arguing that in a Muslim society, and particularly in Morocco, allegiance to the monarch constituted sovereignty. With extraordinary speed and great efficiency he

percent of its energy, substantial increases in dollar and interest rates which imposed severe constraints on debt-servicing, and later a series of serious droughts which made it necessary to import millions of tons of grain, combined to place Morocco in an uncomfortable financial position.

But these problems were overshadowed, albeit aggravated from 1975 onwards, by the Western Sahara problem. When Spain announced she planned to give her desert col-

Left, anti-government demonstrators are rounded up and arrested. **Above**, the Green March into the Sahara Desert.

organised the spectacular Green March.

Some 350,000 unarmed Moroccan men and women were mobilised and on 6 November, led by Premier Osman, they marched south across the frontier waving flags and copies of the Koran. They camped for three days under the guns of the Spanish Foreign Legion, which held its fire, and then they withdrew when the King announced that they had "accomplished their mission".

The Green March succeeded mainly because Generalissimo Francisco Franco was gravely ill. In their disarray at the prospect of the dictator's imminent death, Spanish leaders were desperately anxious to avoid a colo-

IN SHA'ALLAH: YES, NO OR MAYBE

They tell the story of a poor father of a large family whose landlord ordered him out of his tiny house in the old city for non-payment of rent. Luckily, as often happens in Morocco, he knew a man who knew a man who knew an important dignitary who could intervene in his favour.

After weeks of patient contacts, he found himself in the august dignitary's presence. There were the usual courtesies over glasses of mint tea before he explained his predicament, pleading for an "arrangement" that would prevent him and his family from being thrown into the street.

On his return home, his anxious wife questioned him closely. The husband related the encounter in detail and told how he had asked respectfully for the favour. So what did the dignitary say? "He nodded his head and smiled and said *In sha'Allah*," the husband replied.

Immediately the wife burst into tears, and rolled about on the divan in great distress; because she realised that the dignitary had meant no, he would do nothing.

This apochryphal story illustrates the fact that *In sha'Allah* can mean many things: literally "If God wills" or "God willing", but also many nuances between yes and no, including possibly, perhaps, maybe, of course, absolutely, or why not?…if God wills it. The intended meaning can often be detected by the intonation.

Strictly speaking, the phrase is part of Islamic culture, where the name of God is constantly invoked. Before starting a meal or a journey, the Muslim will say *Bismillah er-rahman er-rahim* (In the name of God, the clement and merciful), which is a way of giving thanks for the meal, or praying for a safe journey. The King always pronounces it before starting a speech.

El-Hamdu Lillah (Praise be to God) is also heard frequently to express satisfaction, pleasure or simply give thanks to the Almighty for benefits such as good health, rainfall or prosperity. In times of trouble, the phrase used may be *Allah u Akbar* (God is great), the implication being that the deity is above human tribulations.

Thus *In sha'Allah* is primarily a devout religious invocation signifying that man's fate is in the lap of God and "the best laid plans of mice and men gang aft awry". In colonial times foreigners regarded it as an example of Muslim fatalism.

When in the early 1970s the state television network began broadcasting weather forecasts, they drew a protest from the *Ulema*, or doctors of Islamic law, who said it was outrageously pretentious, if not sacrilegious, to say it was going to rain tomorrow without adding the phrase *In sha'Allah*. Now all weather predictions are peppered with the phrase.

In sha'Allah is never contracted, each syllable is always pronounced clearly with varying degrees of emphasis, even by the Berbers who use it when they are speaking their native Shilha, Tamazirt or Tarafit dialects. This begs the question of what does it really mean in current Moroccan conversation. According to Abdullah Stouky, an author and publisher, "It means anything, everything or nothing."

Usually it means the speaker accepts a proposal, but if anything happens to prevent an agreement or a meeting "it is not my fault".

Another factor necessary in evaluating common Arabic expressions is what Abdullah Stouky calls "the phenomenon of ambivalence". For example, the word for blind man is *bassir*, which means literally "he who has lucid vision", and the word for kettle is *berred*, which means "the cooler". It should not be surprising, therefore, that *In sha'Allah* can mean the opposite of what one thought was intended.

Tourists need not venture much further into the intricacies of Arabic, one of the most complex and subtle of languages, unless they want to spend a few years learning it properly. But they can usefully remember handy phrases like *Allah y Jib* (God will provide) when accosted by a particularly persistent professional beggar, or *Allah y Henik* which literally means "May God give you calm", an approximate equivalent of goodbye.

The last word on the topic is from Godfrey Morrison, late correspondent in West Africa of *The Times* of London, who said, "*In sha'Allah* is rather like the Spanish *mañana*, except that it does not have the same sense of urgency.'

nial war at such a crucial juncture. Thus on 14 November they transferred the administration of the disputed territory to Morocco and Mauritania.

The Algerian President, Colonel Houari Boumedienne, who until then had supported Moroccan and Mauritanian claims to the Western Sahara, suddenly came out in open support of the Polisario Front—a group of left-wing guerrillas led by a former member of the Moroccan communist party, Mustapha el Ouali, who began campaigning for independence of the Spanish colony.

Algeria trained, armed, financed and gave sanctuary to the guerrillas, who proclaimed the Saharan Arab Democratic Republic

supporters to say there was a "world-wide communist conspiracy against Morocco".

In the event, the war took on some of the aspects of an East-West conflict, the Polisario were armed with Soviet weapons while pro-Western Morocco received military aid from France and the United States.

The Moroccan view was that Algeria was bent on creating a satellite state in the Western Sahara which would give it access to the Atlantic coast, that Polisario believed its guerrilla war would bring Morocco to its knees, and perhaps that the monarchy would eventually collapse—which, in fact, was one of the objectives voiced by El Ouali before he left Morocco. Algeria on the other hand

(SADR) just as the last Spanish troops withdrew at the end of February 1976.

The war dragged on for more than a decade and imposed a heavy burden on the Moroccan treasury while Boumedienne was able to finance it out of his petroleum resources. Aggressive Algerian diplomacy enabled the SADR to get official recognition from over 70 non-aligned or so-called "progressive" states, among them Libya and the communist regimes of North Korea, Vietnam and Cuba, prompting the King's

Above, in 1981 Morocco placed electronic sensors along its frontiers.

maintained it acted on the "sacred principle"of self-determination and equated the Polisario's struggle with its own bloody independence war against France and the Vietnamese war against the United States.

However, a major difference was that while the Algerian and Vietnam wars became increasingly unpopular in France and the United States, and ultimately forced political settlements, the Sahara war produced unprecedented cohesion in Morocco. Far from weakening the King as Algeria and the Polisario may have hoped, it created national unity as all political parties from left to right rallied around the King in the longest and most pervasive political peace the country had seen since independence. In this atmosphere, the King held new elections in 1984 in which the parties took part to produce a more credible parliament.

The small but vocal Party of Progress and Socialism based in Casablanca became the only communist party in the world to oppose the Polisario; leaders of the socialist USFP were even jailed briefly for criticising the King's decision to accept a self-determination referendum at a summit of the OAU in Nairobi in 1981. The irredentist Istiqlal Party not only approved the takeover of the Western Sahara but also continued to press Moroccan claims to various parts of Algeria and

the whole of Mauritania as well.

Finally, the King had to restrain his armed forces, many of whose field officers believed that the quickest way to end the war would be to launch a major strike across the frontier into Algeria and attack the Polisario's rear bases.

The King warned several times he would exercise the "right of hot pursuit" into Algeria as the guerrillas withdrew, but he never carried out the threat because of the risk of a devastating war.

The turning point came in 1981 when Morocco began building defence lines composed of ridges of sand and rock studded

with electronic sensors to give forewarning of guerrilla attacks. Gradually the lines were extended eastwards until they ran for 1,000 miles along the Algerian and Mauritanian frontiers. The army gained control of four-fifths of the territory and forced a military stalemate. By this time Algeria, where Colonel Chadli Benjedid had succeeded Boumedienne, apparently decided that the war could not be won and it was time for a political settlement.

Truce achieved: After mediation by King Fahd of Saudi Arabia, Algeria and Morocco restored their relations in May 1988. Morocco and the Polisario accepted a peace plan drafted by the United Nations Secretary General, Javier Perez de Cuellar. The plan proposed a ceasefire to be followed by a self-determination referendum, under international control, to give the people of the thinly-populated area a choice between independence or remaining part of Morocco.

The King said he was convinced the desert nomads would vote for Morocco, in which case it would seem that his policy of restraint would pay off, and he would earn his new title of "Unificator" of the kingdom besides that of "The Great Survivor".

The domestic stability engendered by the Sahara campaign also allowed the King to take several audacious initiatives, such as hosting a milestone Arab summit which produced a Middle East peace plan in Fez in 1982, signing a short-lived union treaty with his old enemy Colonel Muammar Gaddafi of Libya in 1984, becoming the first Muslim ruler to welcome the head of the Catholic Church when Pope John Paul II visited Casablanca in 1985, and arousing the ire of radical Arabs by holding talks in 1986 with Prime Minister Shimon Peres of Israel, the so-called "enemy of all the Arabs".

Finally the reconciliation with Algeria paved the way for realisation of the old North African dream of a union, "The Grand Arab Maghreb", composed of Algeria, Libya, Mauritania, Morocco and Tunisia. The link-up was conceived as a common market, a counterpoint to the European Community on the other side of the Mediterranean, and as an essential factor for the solution of the area's acute economic problems.

Left, traditional industries still thrive. Right, Islam and the monarchy, linked in lights.

THE SPANISH ENCLAVES

The Spanish do not hesitate to call **Ceuta** the pearl of the Mediterranean, but they should. One can think of few towns—Lima, perhaps, and Kinshasa—which have inspired more odium.

"Ghastly place," the writer Rupert Croft-Cooke was told in the 1970s.

The odium attracted him so much he decided to live there, in a flat on the Plaza de Africa.

Nor can the charges levelled against Ceuta be described as new. Not even Thornbury in his *Life in Spain* had a pleasant word to say. "I see nothing in Ceuta—the town of Seven Hills, the little decayed Rome from whence the Berbers shipped to conquer Spain, slay Don Roderick and furnish matter for that promising epic of Southey's—but rows and angles of decaying ramparts and a slope of houses which seem slipping off into the sea."

Ceuta is more interesting for its past than its present. With Gibraltar, which lies like a shark's fin opposite, it was one of the Pillars of Hercules—and the straits between them *finis terrae*, the end of the world.

But Ceuta was an important place 2,000 years before Gibraltar became a beam in Spain's eye. Abyla of the Phoenicians, Julia Trajecta of the Romans, Lissa, Exilissa, Septem, Septa, Cibta—it has changed names as many times as it has changed hands. It is also one of the sites claimed for the garden of the Hesperides, the seven daughters of Atlas whose task was to hang golden apples on the evening sky. Ceuta's history is chequered with this kind of legend. The first place in the west where paper was manufactured, goes one story. Another is that Ulysses drank its water for seven years when he felt himself captivated by Calypso.

The Moors won it from the Goths, who are meant to have bestowed the governorship on a woman with one eye. In A.D. 1001 another governor crossed the Gibraltar straits with his private army only to be strangled by his own eunuch at Jaen. But its importance as "the key to the whole Mediterranean" came in 1415 when it was seized by an expedition from Portugal which included Henry the Navigator. The capture of Ceuta from the Moors (who had used it as a point of embar-

kation for their conquest of Spain) took five hours, "to the amazement of all men", after which Henry was knighted by his father in the mosque they had just desecrated. Their expedition had been billed as a crusade against the Infidel, but it broke the geographic bounds of Europe. Its success not only encouraged expansion into Africa but also the expeditons that were to uncover India and the Americas.

Ceuta kept loyal to Spain when Portugal seceded in 1580. Most of the time was spent

in a state of siege. The first governor lived for 16 years inside a chain-mail coat in case of attack. One siege lasted 26 years.

A Spanish possession long before Morocco ever became a nation, Ceuta continues to embarrass both Morocco, which wants it back, and Spain, which doesn't want to give it but which also realises that its own continued presence there—and in Melilla, futher along the coast—rather erodes the argument for its claims on Gibraltar.

Such friction has meant that crossing into Ceuta can be an exercise in frustration. When, after the war, it belonged to the International Zone, it was not uncommon for passengers to be stripped and their cars taken apart. Then you would have to rely on the kindness of the Spanish governor's Titian-haired English mistress. Things are a little easier now.

As a rule, visitors to Ceuta do not stay more than a few hours. Most come from Spain on the ferry from Algeciras. Crossing the narrow straits like Yeats's heron-billed pale cattle birds, they flock to the duty-free shops. At night you can see their car headlights sweeping away from the port where

In the Plaza de Africa is the church containing the statue of the Virgin after whom the town is consecrated. The 15th-century wooden effigy of Our Lady of Africa was apparently found on the beach by a Portuguese sailor. The antique baton on her arm is borrowed sometimes when a dignitary takes up high position. She has several of these herself.

Apart from Patron Saint, the Virgin combines the role of Officer Commanding the Garrison and, oddly, Mayoress—this last

the poet meditated on death.

Nor is there much to keep them. In their architecture, the buildings resemble grey wedding cakes. The mountain where the Hesperides hung their evening apples, Monte Acho, is a military fortress and its slopes flap with garbage.

Hotels are few and expensive: the Ulysses, in Calle Camoes, which is like the inside of a marble stomach; the Pension Rosi, which looks over a small square with an alarmed statue of Ruiz, and the smartest of the lot, the Hotel Murilla in the Plaza de Africa.

Left, Our Lady of Africa. **Above**, Ceuta's harbour.

office granted in perpetuity by a unanimous vote of the 70,000 strong municipality.

A stroll about Ceuta relieves one of the desire to visit Spain's other enclave, **Melilla**, which lies half a day's drive to the east. Again, the character of a modern duty-free garrison town (Franco served here as a colonel in 1925) drowns out a proudly bugled past. Melilla was Spanish 192 years before Le Roussillon became French and 279 years before the birth of the United States. These years have condemned, not enhanced, the place. Apart from a few wider streets, a bull-ring and some gardens, it has little to offer.

Rupert Croft-Cooke liked it, though.

LES FEMMES

The wave of fundamentalism reported to be spreading through the Muslim world is not much more than a ripple by the time it reaches Morocco. King Hassan himself, who in the past liked to portray himself as a bit of a swinger, isn't keen to over-encourage the zeal of the Eastern mullahs.

From the start, he was keen to promote Morocco as a progressive state and, along with Tunisia, it has always been one of the more socially liberal Muslim countries. Alcohol is freely available, Western women's magazines are sold intact (without the rude bits cut out) and those who choose European lifestyles are happily accepted.

The many Moroccan women still wearing the *l'tam*, or veil (the Morocccan version covers the nose, mouth and chin), do so out of tradition rather than because they have been influenced by the born again Muslimism emerging in countries such as Egypt, where the grand-daughters of women who threw off the veil in the 1920s have reclaimed it as a political statement against Western imperialism.

Generally, in the north of Morocco, use of the veil is confined to older matrons and rarely do they wear the all-enveloping black *haik* as they do in the south. Frequently women attired in the traditional manner—*djellabah* or kaftan, often slit at the sides—will be seen with their jeans-clad, or even short-skirted, daughters. And men keen to marry a committed Muslim don't find it easy to find a young woman prepared to express devoutness in a covered face.

What's more, Berber women have always shouldered a great deal of the agricultural work—they are *under* those walking thorn trees you see in the Rif and Middle Atlas—and don't wear restrictive veils or *haik*. Increased modernisation means more women working in the cities—generally in factories, schools and offices.

Nonetheless, certain Islamic laws laid down by the Prophet in seventh-century Arabia still apply and King Hassan has

shown no intention of interfering with them. Polygamy, now prohibited in Tunisia and Algeria, is a case in point. Outside the Royal Circle it is not known how many wives King Hassan has. In theory, a man may take four spouses; he may also marry a non-Muslim: neither of which a woman is entitled to do. In practice, of course, things aren't quite as easy. A man who wishes to marry another wife must prove to the *adiil*, the Islamic judge in civil matters, that he follows the five requirements of Islam and is therefore en-

titled to benefit from Islamic law. This stipulation at least has logic. What it doesn't take into account, however, is the power of bribery, the concealed factor in Morocco.

The marriage ceremony itself underlines the chattel-status of women. Until quite recently it was common for a woman not to have seen her husband before the first stage of the wedding, a formal agreement signed a year or so before. Even now, arranged marriages, where there will have been negligible contact between the bride and groom, are frequent. During the wedding itself, a 15-day occasion of feasts and visiting regulated by strict protocol, the bride is like a motionless

Preceding pages: boys, still the favoured sex. **Left**, young women in Fez. **Above**, veiled threats, at least to outsiders.

doll; she does not speak, she barely smiles.

For two months prior to the wedding, she is attended by a *negassa*, whose job it is to enhance her beauty. Until a few years ago the most important function of the *negassa* was that she should be present in the room on the wedding night to ensure that the bride was a virgin. After she had witnessed blood and declared this important fact to the guests, everybody could then go home. This somewhat gruesome practice continues among the best and poorest classes, the most traditional sections of any community; but at least the *negassa* now has the decency to stand behind a screen!

The irony of all this is that when the

Prophet Mohammed laid down his laws on sexual and marital conduct, they were radical—far more so than Jewish or Christian precepts. For one thing, he recognised that women had a strong sexuality which needed to be satisfied—the very reason it also needed to be controlled. Otherwise, how could men ensure the legitimacy of their heirs? Jewish and Christian religious leaders had similar worries, but were less open about them. They preferred to instil the notion that sex was a distasteful duty even in marriage and that the best course of action for women was to lie back and think of Christendom or the Promised Land.

Morocco's feminist movement has been most feisty over issues relating to work opportunities, to most effect during the 1970s, the decade when women worldwide struggled to be heard. On the question of polygamy their approach is tentative—unsurprising when their organisation has been headed by one of the royal princesses—leaving it to the political Left to do the real chiselling.

The use of such pressure groups is in preparing a climate for change rather than producing change itself. They are helped by economics: fewer men can afford even one wife these days, and she will probably have to go out to work—the development most likely to produce dramatic change.

But to the casual visitor, Morocco seems very much a male society. The immediate impression of one first-time visitor was that it was a land peopled only by men.

Acceptable social behaviour has strict boundaries. It is, for example, perfectly all right for an older woman to take snuff, kept inside the neck of her kaftan, but positively indecent for a young woman to smoke in public. And the presence of three unchaperoned girls in one of the superior, *salons de thé* on the Boulevard Pasteur in Tangier, hardly the most conservative of Moroccan cities, was cause enough to prompt a discussion by three French-educated young men on the subject of female propriety. A woman's place, at least after dark and the market's closing-time is in the home. And at one time even there she was restricted. On the rooftop, among the washing, was the place where she was most out of the way of men.

Of course, strict Muslims would argue that Westerners apply Western definitions of "freedom" and "independence" when condemning women's roles in Islam. After all, is a person who works in a factory any less a slave than a person who works in a home? Doesn't a woman who wears a veil, protected from unwanted, possibly demeaning sexual attention, have greater diginity than a woman in high heels, tight skirt and makeup? But it should be remembered that, under the modest ankle-length robes and veil, this is exactly how many Moroccan women are dressed too.

Above, country women have always worked. Right, mother and daughters in Dades Valley.

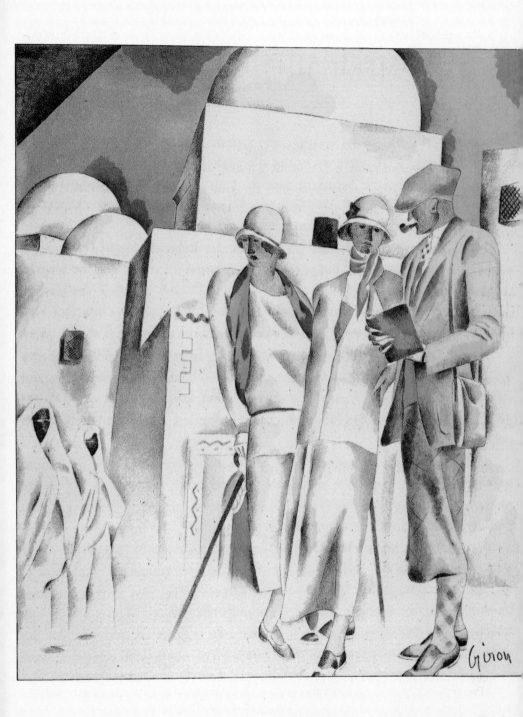

THE NOVELIST AS TOURIST

Paul Bowles, Tennessee Williams, Allen Ginsberg, William S. Burroughs, Joe Orton... Morocco has attracted more than its share of the 20th century's famous writers.

"Morocco appeared again in a dream one balmy night in May in New York just after the 1939-45 war," said Paul Bowles, the most long-standing, sympathetic and distinguished of infidels who have come to the royal desert jewel of North Africa to live. He had first been there in 1931, with Aaron Copland, with whom the young Bowles was studying music in Paris, and—we are, apparently, to believe—Morocco was never much more in his mind until it stole into his Manhattan dreams more than a decade later.

For such a romantic, of course, Morocco is going to come in a dream, and such a romantic American will also, of course, then immediately—or, at least, next door to immediately—pack a bag, kiss his pretty wife Jane goodbye and sail for dreamland. (In those days one still sailed across the Atlantic—it was half the cost of flying.)

Lucky, romantic Bowles: he found Morocco as dream-like in daylight as in the deep-sleep spring night-time of Manhattan. In fact, Morocco, the real thing, was better. There had been no scented desert winds in the dream. In the dream he had loved the noise of Tangier, and Tangier was indeed noisy and exotic. Fez was in her golden age—the traffic sounds of the 1940s were limited to the jingling bells on the horses (the horses and the carriages that now appear in the "Visit Old-fashioned Morocco" adverts in glossy magazines).

All the world, after 1945, had been rushing to New York City, the Imperial City of the new Atomic Age, but Paul Bowles sat in his room at Bab el Hadid in Fez and looked across the dusty valley of the Oued el Zitoun, listening to the wind rattling the high cane-brake. "The food was good," he said, in a matter of fact, dry New England Yankee manner, "and I began to write my novel."

Previously he had written only short sto-

ries; this was his first novel, *Sheltering Sky*, the first of many of Bowles's Moroccan novels and short stories. A new collection of his stories came out as recently as 1989, *A Thousand Days For Mokhtar*, and the best of these are about his adopted home.

Like all the great Arabists—like Lawrence, who spoke of the glamour of strangeness and turned himself into a sort of Sheikh of Araby, like the fun-loving Burton and even the indefatigable, bustling Victorian Doughty—there is a touch of the mystic

about Bowles, a Western man from a long line of Westerners who came by choice to live in the gorgeous cities of Islam.

It is surprising to learn from Bowles, an upright, energetic, old New Englander, a strange combination of aesthete and East Coast America prep school master, that the unusual title of his exotic first novel came from that jolly, old music-hall song, "Down Among the Sheltering Palms (Oh, honey, wait for me)". The idea was, Bowles said, that in the desert there was only the sky to give shelter.

How odd that such a tinny old turn-of-the-century song obsessed such a serious student

Left, the glamour of strangeness. **Above**, William S. Burroughs—with a drink, of course.

and composer of music; odd, too, that the non-European noise of Morocco should give such pleasure to Paul Bowles's musically-educated ears. In *Who's Who*, in fact, Bowles lists himself as a composer first, and a writer second. The music of Morocco had come to him in the big, life-changing dream, and, he claimed, the next day, while he was riding on the top of an open bus in New York, the actual plot of the Moroccan novel started to come to him.

What it is to be a mystic and have the music of Morocco come to you in dreams, and plots spring from the traffic's roar of New York City! No wonder Bowles loves Morocco.

But his Morocco is not all poetry and

not really play the piano, was setting industrial Manchester to music; indeed, he would seem to be inventing the jazz piano of the progressive school; round about the same time in New York, Thelonius Monk was also banging the piano with fist and elbow in order to make music out of the sounds of industrial society.

But what a treacherous lure the exotic is for the literary fish and how Morocco has reeled them in: Tennessee Williams, Gore Vidal, Truman Capote, Allen Ginsberg, Jack Kerouac and that great grey ghost of sex and drugs and bebop writing, William S. Burroughs. One is out of sympathy with them. They are the artist as tourist, the writer as

mysticism. In his autobiography he tells a funny story of a "musical evening" spent in the bosom of a Moroccan family which possessed an uncle who had, rare for this time, travelled to the north of England. Towards the end of the evening the Moroccan uncle sat down at the piano and proceeded to pound it with his fists and both elbows. This went on, according to Bowles's wristwatch, for a full 11 minutes, whereupon the musical uncle leapt to his feet and, beaming a big smile, announced that the title of the musical composition was "Manchester". Obviously the glamour of strangeness works both ways. The Moroccan uncle, who could

day-tripper. Morocco was that best of all combination, both chic and cheap.

Hadn't Barbara Hutton, the original poor little rich girl, the lady who owned all those five and dimes, set up house there? And hadn't smart, lavish, decadent parties been thrown there, with such a chi-chi number as the elegant Cecil Beaton himself giving a beach party by the Caves of Hercules, with one cave filled with champagne and another filled with hashish?

But the poor New Englanders. Unlike the old Englanders, they didn't have a Raj. They had to go to an old French colony. After all, they couldn't go to an English one: the

English would laugh at them if they picked up the wrong spoon. Besides, the Yanks never could understand the social rules by which the British played. They couldn't understand why an Englishman laughed at one thing and didn't laugh at another.

Morocco was French. The French were more free about everything. And the idea of French Morocco, the Morocco of Beau Geste and all those French Foreign Legion forts, how romantic it was. And when you had enough kif it got mystic.

They were also, in the main, homosexual. They came to Morocco for the boys. And the dope. Plus it was cheap, if you had dollars, if you had money from home.

The novels and stories of Paul Bowles give a truer image of Morocco, although when they first started to appear in the United States they were wildly misinterpreted. Libby Holman, the American singer who was married to Smith Reynolds, the American tobacco millionaire, told an amusing story of their precocious, teenage son Christopher being asked in 1949 what he wanted to do during his school holiday that summer. Christopher Reynolds's head was full of Paul Bowles's stories of wild, exotic Morocco. The archetypal New York rich kid, sounding like a brat in a *New Yorker* cartoon, said: "I want to go to Africa with Paul Bowles and have my tongue cut out."

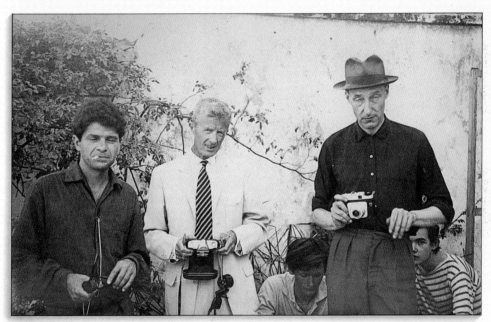

The exotic when Paul Bowles came to Morocco was far more exotic than it is today because you did not see it on television; and when you did see it at the cinema it was movie melodrama; not shot on location but done in Hollywood or Pinewood backlots. One thinks of *Casablanca*, with Humphrey Bogart, Ingrid Bergman and Claude Rains; and even the newsreels presented a bogus picture-postcard image.

Left, Bowles's novels, including *The Sheltering Sky* which attracted film-maker Bernardo Bertolucci. **Above**, Paul Bowles (centre) with Gregory Corso (left) and William S. Burroughs.

Morocco was a *Boy's Own Paper* story, full of adventurers, white men in pith helmets and devilishly dangerous but funny foreigners. It was, after all, the land of kif, the kasbah, old narrow-gauge railway lines with steam-drawn coaches marked *IVième Classe* travelling over the high plateaux between Oujda and Colomb-Béchar, where, completely astonishing the tourist, the line could be blocked by snow.

When Paul Bowles arrived, Morocco was, most of all, still a French colony, like its neighbour Algeria—like, indeed, Vietnam, which no-one actually knew as Vietnam but merely as French Indo-China. It was this

Frenchness of Morocco which Paul Bowles seems to love most of all, although he doesn't dwell on it. It appears merely as shading on the colourful native Moroccan backdrop before which Bowles's fictional characters play.

In his autobiography, however, Bowles lets slip that things have never been the same since the French left. At one point he speaks of the glamour of French Tangier and then says Tangier is now only "a vast slum". That seems unkind, and untrue. First-time tourists returning from contemporary Morocco speak of it in much the same way as Paul Bowles did in 1947.

In 1947, no doubt, there were Europeans,

old hands in Tangier, who spoke of the wonders of Morocco in 1937. William S. Burroughs, for example, a late arriver to the joy of Morocco by Paul Bowles's calendar, was able to find the same music in the street noises as Bowles had heard in 1931. Burroughs had come to Morocco because drugs were cheap, because he was less likely to be arrested for using drugs than he would be in New York or London at that time, and yet, however base these motives, he fell under the musical spell of Morocco. "The whole Muslim world," he said in an interview, "is practically controlled by music." Burroughs started recording the local street music.

Brion Gysin was another. He said he would probably have become a Muslim because of the music of Morocco, particularly the ecstatic music to which the secret brotherhoods danced. He opened a restaurant instead, the 1001 Nights Restaurant in the wing of a Tangier palace that belonged to a Moroccan friend. Gysin introduced the Rolling Stones to the ancient village music of Morocco. In 1971 Brian Jones made a record, *The Pipes of Pan*, at Joujouka.

Morocco, which was "very Sixties" as far back as the Forties, became a hippie heaven. There was all that music and *majoun*, cannabis jam, and, of course, there was Marrakesh, where all the terribly smart French dress designers from Paris now have homes.

Of the serious writers, only Paul Bowles stayed. Ginsberg blew in and out. Jack Kerouac treated Morocco like a day out at the seaside in Long Island. Gore Vidal, Tennessee Williams and Truman Capote were likewise on holiday. Silly as they might seem on the surface, underneath they knew that the exotic was for journalism and the ordinary for literature.

James Joyce, who lived most of his adult life surrounded by the exotically foreign and yet continued to write about the everyday life of ordinary Irish people, knew this. Paul Bowles seems not to have known it. Or perhaps he was too precious a New England flower, too mystic to remain in crass, commercial America.

All the writers used Morocco because it was a cheap place to live. Like some sort of wily old desert lizard or salamander, Bowles took on the protective colours of Morocco's Muslim world without being the thing itself. One wonders if he knows. In his 1989 collection of stories, there is one outstanding one, "A Distant Episode", in which a visiting American professor is captured by North African nomads and then displayed as a performing animal. The story ends with the professor, all decked out in beautiful, jingling ornaments, being led into the Sahara.

Perhaps Bowles, the novelist as tourist, has also been enslaved by the glamorous strangeness that first beckoned him in the dream.

Above, Brion Gysin and his Dream Machine. **Right**, Barbara Hutton, Woolworth heiress and the ultimate poor little rich girl.

A WILD TIME WAS HAD BY ALL

The Honourable David Herbert has lived through, and was a major protagonist in, what many have rightly or wrongly called Tangier's golden era—the time when the internationally famous and infamous descended upon the town to make hay while the sun shone and publicity blazed. Here he recalls the parties thrown by his friend Barbara Hutton, the Woolworth heiress.

Barbara's house was in an overcrowded part of the medina surrounded by small Moroccan houses. Originally it had belonged to the holy man Sidi Hosni, whose tomb is buried here; it had then become the property of Walter Harris, correspondent of the London *Times*; and after that the home of the American diplomat Maxwell Blake. Barbara's bid beat that of Generalissimo Franco.

It was actually more of a palace than a house, with a warren of staircases, rooms, mezzannines and terraces. As the parties took place on the terraces, we would be in full view to the outside world. The Moroccans of the neighbourhood enjoyed themselves just as much as the guests. They loved the lights, the music, the ladies' lovely dresses. They always stayed until the party ended.

The usual form was for Barbara to receive her guests seated on a gilded throne surrounded by Thai silk cushions. People were brought up to her as though she were a lady of royal birth. They would practically sit at her feet on the lovely cushions and worship at her shrine. Pretentious, perhaps, but for Barbara it was pure theatre, the staging of a tale from the Arabian Nights.

As soon as she had a large enough entourage, she would spring to her feet and dance the night away with all and sundry, and, this being the international era, that included cabaret artists, hairdressers, and pianists from the current nightclubs as well as the Tangier élite—in fact, *Tout Tanger*, as the French said.

Her most notorious parties, among the ones which attracted exaggerated headlines back in the American and British press, were those where

guests came dressed and behaving as members of the opposite sex. Straight-laced diplomats, bankers and respectable Moroccan businessmen would come in full make-up and decolleté, in spite of moustaches and hairy chests. Their wives, the elderly and the young, wore dinner-jackets or business suits and flattened their hair with brilliantine plastered over nets. In contrast to such spectacles, Barbara would come dressed exquisitely as a girlish Robin Hood.

There would be entertainment, including Flamenco singers and Moroccan acrobats. Belly-dancers would be hired from the Koutoubia Palace; and on special occasions, such as the annual ball when guests were invited from all over the world, the Blue People from the Anti Atlas Mountains would show in Tangier—on camels and carrying loaded rifles—to perform their ceremonial dances.

But although Barbara's parties were beautifully staged, to say they were always a success would be an exaggeration. If she was in a good and happy mood, Barbara was the perfect hostess. If she was tired or sad or had had too much to drink, they could be a disaster.

On these occasions she would not appear the whole evening. If she had sent a message saying, "I am not well, but do enjoy yourselves and have a lovely time," all would have been fine; but she didn't. The orchestra would play on in a dreary fashion, and there might be a little desultory dancing, but when we realised that Barbara would not emerge, the party died and little by little people drifted home.

Her parties generally finished late, usually at dawn. Then Barbara would say goodnight to her guests, looking incredibly lovely with her emerald tiara sparkling in the early morning sun. There was always a present for each one.

In Tangier Barbara remains a legend to this day. The poor Moroccans have no feeling of resentment against her or her wealth, or the fact that she had certain streets in the kasbah widened in order to accommodate her Rolls-Royce; they remember her kindness. Guides proudly point out, to tourists of every nationality, who have probably never heard of her and so do not know the difference, "You see over there, that was the Palace of the Woolworth heiress Barbara Button."

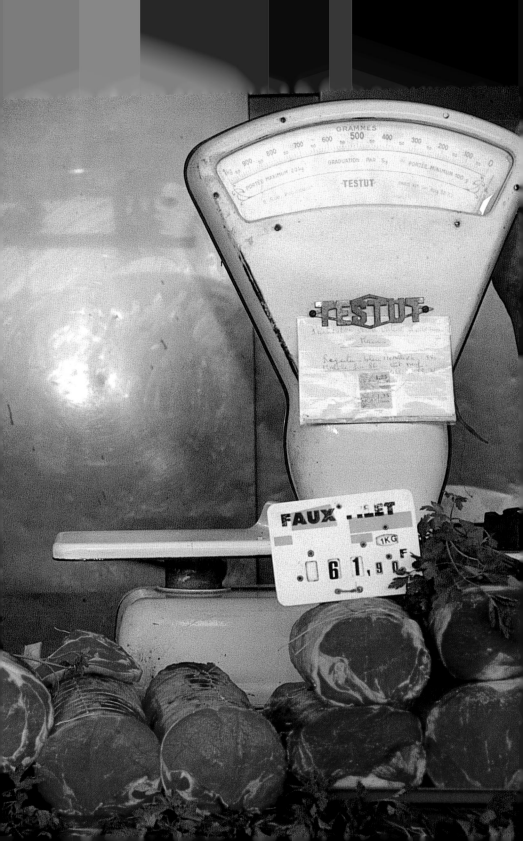

FOOD AND DRINK

No less an international culinary guru than Robert Carrier has pronounced Moroccan cooking one of the great cuisines of the world. Essentially it is a combination of the desert nomads' diet of sheep, vegetables and dairy produce and refined and exotically-spiced specialities—the latter of Syrian origin and introduced by Moulay Idriss along with the Muslim religion.

But it has incorporated other influences over the centuries: southern European (olives, olive oil, fruit, tomatoes); black African; and most recently French, particularly apparent in the country's restaurants. The cooking is neither over-oily nor heavy and the seasonings are a blend of sweet and savoury. Almonds, honey and fruit combine with spicy meats; *pastilla* (*bisteeya*), the famous Moroccan pigeon pie, is dusted with a generous layer of icing-sugar.

Home cooking: Allegedly, the best Moroccan food is found in the home. Certainly, many "restaurants" are of the humble kind, serving charcoal-grilled chicken or *brochettes* (kebabs of marinated liver or lamb), spicy sausages known as *merguez*, and *kefta* (minced lamb shaped into small cakes and served with a pepper sauce).

There are, though, excellent restaurants reflecting the rich range of Moroccan cooking and in the classier places it is perfectly possible to order specialities not on the menu if the chef is given prior warning. Something such as *pastilla*, for example, consisting of wafer-thin layers of *warkha* pastry filled, lasagna-style, with a mixture of pigeon meat and almonds, is a complicated dish requiring a full day to prepare. Locals and visitors alike tend to order and eat this dish in one of the restaurants across the country which has perfected the recipe. (L'Anmbra in Fez is one such establishment.)

Couscous, on the other hand, a base of steamed grain covered with steamed chicken, mutton and vegetables (usually carrots and courgettes), is usually cooked in

the home. Traditionally, it is served at the end of the meal to ensure that all guests have eaten sufficient. A sauce made from fried onions, crushed into the residue in which the chicken and meat were cooked, commonly accompanies it, and almonds and raisins may either be scattered over the couscous or added to the sauce.

Everyone makes this dish a mite differently. But even in Morocco convenience methods have evolved and pre-cooked couscous is widely used.

The ubiquitous *tajine* is a basic beef or lamb stew (sometimes just vegetables) simmered for hours in an earthenware dish covered by a cone-shaped lid, into which almost everything can go. There are very refined variations: *barrogog bis basela*, a lamb stew with prunes; *safardjaliyya*, a beef stew with quince; *sikbadj*, a lamb stew with dates and apricots; and *tajine bel hout*, a fish *tajine* containing tomatoes, ginger, saffron, and sweet and hot red peppers. Apples and pears may be thrown in when in season and black olives are invariably added to the honey-flavoured sauce.

One of the rewards of walking in the Atlas

Preceding pages: fish is plentiful; all meat is hallal. **Left,** A Ma Bretagne, probably Morocco's best restaurant. **Above,** street vendor during the period of Ramadan.

is to order a *tajine* from a Berber café before setting off and finding it cooked when one returns. Tourists often end up buying one of the glazed earthenware *tajine* dishes to try their skills at reproducing a *tajine* stew at home. In Morocco, though, *tajines* are usually cooked over the low, even heat of charcoal. When using a more direct heat such as gas or electric, a heat diffusing mat should be used. Also, just as one "seasons" a new frying-pan before using it, it is necessary to eliminate the flavour of earthenware from the tajine pot by doing the same.

The other popular everyday meat is chicken, *djej. Matisha Mesla* is an ancient Moroccan dish in which the chicken is

available for those unable to reach their home by the appointed hour.

M'choui, a whole sheep roasted on a spit and brought to the table for everyone to carve and dip into little dishes of cumin, is the ceremonial dish marking the end of the month-long fasting. Incidentally, Ramadan, when not even a drop of water should pass a Muslim's lips from sunrise until sundown, is still very much observed, though many modern Moroccans have come to regard it as a health programme.

Fish restaurants, established during the occupations of the French and Spanish, are to be found along the Mediterranean coast to Ceuta and on the Atlantic coast from Tangier

cooked in a sauce of tomatoes, honey, ginger and cinnamon; *djej bil loz* is chicken with spices and blanched almonds; and *djej mqualli* contains preserved lemons and olives. The mashed livers of the chickens add body to the sauces.

Ramadan: Even more than in most countries, special occasions in Morocco are celebrated by feasts and specially prepared foods. During Ramadan (although also served throughout the year in humble restaurants and by itinerant food vendors) *harira* is the traditional soup of beans, lentils and lamb with which Moroccans break their daily fast. Every café will have this soup

south. The most outstanding is near Casablanca—with the exception of Sam's, inside the harbour perimeter in Essaouira. Giant prawns caught off Agadir (where the country's fishing fleet is based), octopus, squid, boned and stuffed sardines (try those grilled at the open-air stalls on the corniche at Essaouira), sea wolf, skate and sole in all its international guises are available at the most modest quayside restaurant. Worth trying anywhere more upmarket is *samak mahshi be roz*, of Syrian origin, which is any large white fish stuffed with rice, pine nuts and almonds and served with a tamarind sauce.

Food to go: The Moroccan pleasure in food

is reflected in the amazing range of snacks sold by the great army of street vendors in every town—most particularly in those such as Marrakesh, Fez, Tangier and Rabat which attract farmers and travellers from the countryside around. These range from cactus-fruit sellers, who peel the fruit, said to settle upset stomachs, while you eat and charge you according to how many you consume, to men ladling snails, flavoured with cumin and rough salt, out of giant vats to homeward-bound office workers.

As in all restaurants in Morocco, the chances of food poisoning can be easily gauged. The busier the stall, the less likely it is. If you eschew all such food, you will

undoubtedly be missing out. A glass of freshly-squeezed orange juice from a stall on the edge of the Djemma el Fna in Marrakesh costs one-twentieth of the inferior carton variety served at La Mamounia Hotel.

Similarly, one of the pleasures of motoring in Morocco is the variety of produce to be bought along the way. In the north, Rif women hold out covered plates of tangy white cheese; in the south during the autumn, boys proffer baskets of freshly harvested dates. In the Atlas, dependent on season, you

Left, chicken and fennel tajine. **Above**, couscous, usually best eaten at home.

will find almonds, walnuts and lychees; and on the Atlantic coast, honeydew melons costing just three or four dirhams each.

A drop to drink: Alcohol is not used in cooking outside of French restaurants. Morocco does, however, brew beer and produce wine. The beer, light and Continental-tasting, comes in four varieties: Stork (the lightest), Flag Speciale (a favourite beer in squat green bottles), Flag Pilsner (more difficult to find) and Extra 25 (a popular new beer that comes in short brown bottles). All are produced locally by a Moroccan society of brewers.

The Moroccan beer drinker will invariably order all his drinks for the evening at the same time and then work steadily through them cowboy-style. At the Brasserie Excelsior in Midelt, where such serious drinking is done, you almost expect to find horses tethered outside and dancing girls on the bar.

Moroccan wine is beginning to find its way on to the shelves of Europe's supermarkets, mostly in the form of red wines, since the whites and the rosés do not travel well. The best known vineyards are in the Fez and Méknès region, and the wines most frequently listed on a hotel wine-list will be white Oustalet, Valpierre and Spéciale Coquillage, all three light and delicious and best served well-chilled. A rosé, Sidi Bouhai, has a greyish hue and is a good summer wine, while Vieux Papes, Cabernet-President, Club des Baillis, and Clairet Méknès Vins are top-class table varieties.

The tastes of Moroccan cowboys notwithstanding, the most common refreshment is, of course, mint tea. This is an infusion of mint leaves and either green or *nègre* (black) tea. A solicitous host will try to anticipate the preference of his guest. The mint leaves will be placed either in the glass or in the tea-pot. It is served throughout the day and after any meal, though since the French introduced the post-prandial cup of coffee some Moroccans feel it is more chic, being international.

Alternative drinks include apples and bananas liquidised with milk (an extremely good milkshake) and grape, orange, black cherry or pomegranate juice, dependent on season. In the afternoon it is usual to adjourn to a café and cake shop (they tend to operate as one unit) for tea and pastries. Almonds and honey are the most popular sweet combination; *cornes de gazelle*, almond-filled pastry crescents, a national sensation.

Moroccan architecture is dominated by Islam. But factors specific to the country—natural resources, European imperialism, climate and a tribal history—have all modified the Eastern stamp. Early Islamic influences had weakened by the time they reached the extreme west of North Africa, leaving many indigenous practices intact. And, as a staging-post on African, Saharan and Mediterranean trade routes, Morocco experienced a long and steady influx of various foreign styles.

High mountains separate desert conditions (in which unfired bricks and poor quality materials dictated a more rudimentary architecture) from damper, cooler coastal plains; they also support oak, pine and cedar forests—used lavishly in the internal ornamentation of larger houses and palaces. In the south, tribal warfare and the struggle of emerging dynasties have, without exception, determined defensive architecture: tall, crenellated *ksour* and kasbahs.

True believers: Nonetheless, the building of towns and villages presented an opportunity to express the ideals of the Islamic state. Islam touches every aspect of a Muslim's life, and architecture provides more than just a series of rules and customs laid down for religious buildings. Its emphasis on the community is reflected in the interlocked nature of housing. "Believer is to believer," said the Prophet, "as the mutually upholding sections of a building."

At the same time, Islam's asceticism is reflected in simplicity of form and respect for space. The Arabs of the seventh century, who had little architectural heritage, were never very far from the desert and its exceptional feel of expanse. Spaciousness and lack of distraction are suited to the observation of rituals and prayer.

The aesthetic role of buildings, important in the West, took second place to the practical function of defining a space, a purpose emphasised by dramatic gateways, enclosed

courtyards and enormous defensive walls. A small gate in a blank wall will lead into a beautiful courtyard, possibly containing a fountain, in which to rest or contemplate—within the communal whole an enclosed, personal oasis away from the heat and dust.

Because the Muslim religion forbids animate representation, the ornamentation of buildings reached a level of abstraction. While this rule was never totally observed and stylised plant and flower forms may often be identified, fine calligraphy is more usual. Kufic script is highly stylised—to the extent that, practically in cipher, it can be difficult to read even for a classical Arabist.

Gold and silver were similarly frowned on, so less lavish materials were used. Stucco, worked into delicate lace-like patterns, arrived in the 13th century while mosaic (or *zellige*) of green, blue, black and red tiling became popular in the 1300s. Both were Eastern techniques perfected in Andalusia and imported to Morocco by the Muslims of Spain, under whom the decorative arts flourished. Similarly in the Andalusian fashion, elaborate iron-work, which lends itself so readily to abstract design, was

Preceding pages: stucco, faïence and wood carving—the basics of Islamic decoration. Left, Medrassa el Attarine in Fez. Above, *ksar*, designed for defence.

used for the ubiquitous window and door grilles and for lanterns.

Building a religion: The mosque, the most important of religious buildings and the principal, though not the only, meeting place for prayer, formed a loose prototype for all Islamic architecture. Modelled on those of Cordoba and Kairouan of eighth-century Spain and Tunisia (at the time, the most important cities of Western Islam), which, in turn, were based on Damascene models, most Moroccan mosques are rather plain on the outside. A highly decorated entrance door and a minaret are the most notable external features, and the roof is usually of simple, often green, tile work.

washing, and the hall for prayer situated alongside, divided into aisles segregating the sexes. A niche in the wall (*mihrab*) indicates the direction of Mecca; and to the right of the *mihrab* is a pulpit called the *minbar*, often of carved cedar wood intricately inlaid. It is from here that the *imam* (priest) reads the Koran.

The religious buildings open to non-Muslims are the *medersa*, the schools where theology and Muslim law were taught and which served as early universities. While often attached to mosques, they developed from domestic buildings—sometimes the houses of the principal teachers—and were first established in the 12th century. Once

Early mosques did not include minarets; in fact, the earliest mosques were not even formally enclosed. Originally the faithful were called to prayer from nearby roof-tops. The square-shaped minaret of the Maghreb, unlike the circular minarets of the Middle East, corresponds to the bell-tower of a church (generally they are four times their width in height) and were copied from early Christian towers in Damascus.

The interior of the mosque, which, alas, is always out of bounds to non-Muslims in Morocco, though not in other Muslim countries, consists of a courtyard (*sahn*), with a fountain or basin for preliminary ritual

again, a central courtyard with a fountain, often cloistered on the ground floor, was flanked by a chapel for prayer, classrooms and library. The pupils' living quarters were situated above, on the first floor.

Many of the *medersa* were founded by sultans, in particular the learned Merinids in the 14th century. They are elaborately decorated with exceptionally detailed carving, mosaic tile and glass work, Kufic script and stucco. The most outstanding are the **Medrassa Bou Inania** begun in 1350 in Fez and **Medrassa ben Youssef** built in 1565 in Marrakesh.

In defence: As recently as the late 1930s, it

could be quite dangerous to travel in Morocco. The defences around many towns are immediately evocative of a warlord past. Within are all the necessary buildings for defence: vast stables, barracks, food stores, granaries, arsenals and water cisterns. What is remarkable about these tends to be their size rather than their level of architecture but the design of the *bab*, or gateway, is often the exception. Generally built of stone blocks and crenellated, two towers flank a central bay in which the gate is set. Above, its arch might be deeply carved in coloured stone like the **Oudaya** gate in **Rabat** or the **Bab Agenau** in Marrakesh.

Every dynasty left its stamp on the de-

defended. In the south these farms give way to the *ksour*, Morocco's most imposing architecture.

In effect, *ksour* are fortified villages, comprising a central square, granary, well, mosque and warren-type streets and housing, contained by high walls punctuated by watch-towers. Made of crude mud brick and rubble or split palm-trunk (a material known as *pisé*), they are permeable to water and can withstand only a very dry climate. Rain constantly undermines this form of architecture; the south is littered with abandoned and ruined *ksour* often only decades old.

Strictly speaking, the difference between the kasbahs and *ksour* is that the former

fences of the cities, often demolishing much of the work of its predecessor. The Almohads in Rabat in the 12th century and the Merinids in Fez and Chella in the 13th and 14th centuries were particularly industrious in this respect.

It wasn't only the towns and cities that were in need of fortification. Even the poor, flat-roofed, stone-built farms built on terraces in the Middle Atlas, homes of the Berber Cleuhs, were—and still are—well

Left, the "Mauresque" architecture of Rabat. **Above**, highly stylised script, in accordance with the Koran.

house individual families while the latter enclose a whole community. That said, in the rest of Morocco the noun kasbah refers to the defensive stronghold of a town. Most Moroccan towns possess one. It is in the south, however, along the Dadès valley, in particular (the scenic route of the kasbahs) that they are most evident. Square and built of crude brick, they show few openings on the outside. Yet their simplicity is often offset by geometric, positively African decorations carved into the mud bricks. Close to the desert, it becomes clear that another world, that of the Sahara, is beginning.

The palaces: Unlikely though it may seem,

such blank exteriors have contained some of Morocco's richest palaces. The sheer luxury, colour and decoration, and the quality of life within surpassed the comforts of Europe for many centuries. Once again, the central feature was the courtyard, around which were grouped suites of rooms in a symmetrical pattern. Service areas would often be built on particular sides, and these in turn might have their own central courtyard, as wealth and necessity dictated.

The most famous was El Badi, "the incomparable", in Marrakesh, built for magnificent receptions by Ahmed el Mansour in the 16th century. Its courtyard had five elaborate pools, lined with coloured tiling, whose

stricted area, had to be quite separate.

The **Dar el Makhzen Palace** in Fez is the finest palace in Morocco. Its courtyard is several acres in size and even contains a *medrassa* and a mosque. The decoration within these palaces employed the finest of the traditional skills of Moroccan artists, and while it is true that development and quality of style degenerated into showy exuberance by the 18th century, there are plenty of examples of good work preserved.

Nowadays many former small palaces house museums and hotels (e.g. the **Palais Jamai Hotel** in Fez; the **Dar el Makhzen** museum in Tangier, occupied by the deposed Sultan Moulay Hafid as recently as the

waters irrigated a series of gardens. Its marble came from Italy and its furnishings from as far as China. Its fabulous belvederes, kiosks, pavilions, towers and galleries made it a legend in Europe.

While the original structure of a palace was usually symmetrical, radiating from the courtyard, later additions were often haphazardly planned. Nonetheless certain essential features had to be incorporated. There was always a judgment hall and a *mechouar*, an open space to hold large audiences and dominated by a balcony called an *iwan,* where the sultan could receive homage from his tribesmen. The *harem*, which was a re-

beginning of this century, and the museum in the **Oudaya Kasbah** in Rabat) and as such provide an opportunity for tourists to view them at close hand. King Hassan II's palaces (there is at least one in practically every major town) are generally recent but traditional in style, enclosed by extensive gardens and strictly out of bounds. Some sense of their scale may be glimpsed from their perimeters or when approaching a city by air.

Historical perspective: Against any other architecture, that of Islam has remained comparatively static. After the fall of Rome, urban development in Morocco did not begin again until after the Arab conquest.

The Idrissid dynasty of the eighth to 10th centuries was the first to resume building, establishing Fez as its capital.

During the Almoravid dynasty of the 11th and 12th centuries, when many Muslims were expelled from Spain, the brilliant civilisation of Andalusia took root in Morocco. It is thought Abou Bakr founded **Marrakesh** and his son, Ali ben Youssef, built enormous fortifications at **Taza**, a city which, on the eastern approach to Fez, marked an important line of defence. Mosques were rebuilt, and domes, pillars and semi-circular arches, together with plaster sculpture, were introduced.

The Almohads of the 12th and 13th centu-

ries were prolific builders. Additions were made to Marrakesh, most notably the walls. The power of masonry was the symbol of the period. The mosques of **Koutoubia** in Marrakesh and **Hassan** in Rabat were commissioned at this time.

The Merinid dynasty of the 13th to 15th centuries was a period of increasingly sophisticated work rather than imposing building. The Merinids were responsible for most to the country's *medersa*.

Under the Saadians of the 16th and 17th

Left, public housing in Marrakesh. **Above**, traditional but not old houses in Tinerhir.

centuries Morocco became susceptible to foreign influences. The Portuguese took coastal towns and built fortifications at Asilah, Safi and El Jadida. Art and architecture then tended to repeat the styles of the past rather than innovate, but sheer scale was celebrated by Ahmed el Mansour, who embellished Marrakesh to a degree that impressed a decadent Europe.

It is the unflagging industry of the Alaouite Sultan Moulay Ismail of the 17th century that is often so evident today. He built and rebuilt constantly. Sixteen miles (25km) of wall was built around Méknès, and he achieved popular public works through the forced labours of slaves and Christian captives. In keeping with his personality, scale and grandeur took precedence over aesthetic considerations.

Modern architecture: There was little further development in architecture until the French and Spanish protectorates, when European styles dominated the northern and coastal cities. Marshal Lyautey, the first French Resident General, decreed that the new European development of towns, to house the great influx of European administrators, should be separate from the medinas in order to preserve the traditional civilisation. The new architecture, combining French civic pomposity and Moorish motifs, was known as "Mauresque". The 1920s even brought a smattering of Art Deco to Casablanca and Marrakesh.

Nowadays, the newest civic architecture reflects traditional Moroccan design rather than mimicking that of France. Other than in Casablanca, modern development has resisted introducing high-rise buildings. Tradition is for low buildings which the minaret of the mosque may dominate. Rabat's "skyscraper" is the "Immeuble Saidia", the low office block at the end of Boulevard Mohammed V, facing the medina.

Blocks of flats, the most common form of inexpensive housing, rarely rise above seven floors but, traditionally, it is the ambition of any well-off individual to have a house built rather than buy a property second-hand. This has introduced a non-traditional practice: mortgages and credit. The Koran forbids usury—which was why, historically, the Jews had the monopoly on money-lending—but modern pressures have dictated a modern compromise.

MAKING MUSIC

In the 1960s and 1970s right-minded liberals complained that the wildfire spread of Western rock music to Africa and Asia was another example of the corruption of the Third World by a decadent West. What they feared were worldwide, Coca-Cola drinking quasi-Americans dressed in Levis.

In fact, it was they who did the disservice to ethnic cultures—by underestimating them. By the 1980s, Western pop music, running out of new ideas, was turning to the Third World for inspiration. World Music, not least the music of the Maghreb, became a Western cult.

Whoops of joy: Wherever you go, you are likely to be assailed by wonderful rhythms, whether it's the most common musical phenomenon, the amplified voice of the *muezzin* calling the faithful to prayer, or the tinny sound of Egyptian taped music emanating from the doorway of a shop. Possibly it will be beating drums and the whoops of women celebrating a wedding long into the night which penetrate a hotel bedroom.

But what you should actively seek out—early evening is the best time—are impromptu sessions at music cafés (often identified by the musical instruments hanging on their walls). It is to these that local musicians will come to drink tea and then sing songs.

Chabbi, meaning popular, is the most common music played at these venues. Akin to the folk music tradition of Europe and North America, it started out as music performed by travelling entertainers, who would collect and compose songs along their way. Now, having received media attention, it has moved off the public squares and on to radio and television. Abdelwahhab Doukali and Hamid Zahir, two of the most popular singers of *chabbi*, began their careers, respectively, in Bab el Makina in Fez and Djemma el Fna in Marrakesh.

Inevitably, groups have begun to electrify traditional instruments (for example, the *buzouk*, a long-necked lute) and to add guitars and keyboards, but at local level it is still confined to the *l'oud* (11-string fretless lute),

Preceding pages: musicians at a *moussem.* **Left,** the drum, an essential accompaniment to many occasions. **Above,** street music.

kamanche (violin), banjo and assorted percussion. At the end of a song an instrumental section called *leseb*, twice the speed of the piece, induces shouting and dancing and syncopated clapping.

Classical roots: Interestingly, some of the complex traditional forms of Moroccan music—Andalus, now exemplified by the orchestras of Fez, Méknès and Tangier (towns which were most influenced by Moorish Spain), and *milhun*, an ancient form of sung poetry—have been combined with

chabbi to produce a mixture of sophisticated instrumentals and popular lyrics. In contemporary *rai* music, too, which originated in western Algeria (though, in the Maghreb, it is important to remember that borders are political rather than ethnographical), style and lyrics have come a long way from their Bedouin roots.

Rai's preoccupations tend to be sex, drugs and cars; and the instruments are now brass, accordions, electric guitars and synthesizers rather than flutes, violins and lutes. Naturally, lyrics such as "Hey, Mama, your daughter she wants me" or "Beer is Arab, whisky is European" have not endeared it to the establishment. Morocco's own *rai* stars include Chaba Zahouania (whose family insist that her cassette cover bares the photograph of a bikini-clad model rather than her) and Cheb Kader.

Rural rituals: Berber music, generally found in the country areas, is quite distinct from Arabic-influenced *chabbi* or rock-style *rai*. It includes ritual music, tied to the agricultural calendar or performed during exorcisms and purifications, and sung poetry called *tamdyazi* performed with just drums and flutes.

At one time it was common for towns and villages to be visited by professional musicians from the Atlas known as *imdyazn*, itinerant bands of four members, whose role was to bring news of world affairs in poem form. Using drums, double clarinet and *rebab* (a single-string flute), the musicians improvised as they went. This still happens, but now, outstripped by television, their function is to entertain rather than inform.

Outside of weddings, it is in the entertainment squares that one is also likely to witness the music of the *gnaoua*, whose wild drum rhythms induce states of trance. The *gnaoua* brotherhood has devotees all over Morocco but particularly in Marrakesh.

The *gnaoua* claim spiritual descent from Bilal, an Ethiopian who was the Prophet's first *muezzin*. Most of their ceremonies are held with the intention of placating spirits, good or evil, which have inhabited person or place. Undoubtedly, the origins of these rites are in sub-Saharan Africa and a black African influence is evident in the sounds and rhythms.

Music to take home: One thing immediately noticeable in any town is the number of tape stalls. Few copyright laws exist in Morocco. Unlike in the West where a performer is paid royalties, in Morocco, and most other African countries, an artist will be paid handsomely for the initial recording but little thereafter.

Tapes are copied shamelessly and sold legally for about 15 dirhams each. Don't be surprised if a tape ends abruptly; they're all like that. Tapes are of standard length and if the recording artist hasn't finished by its end, he is cut off in mid-flow.

Right, music festivals, the most celebrated of which is in Asilah.

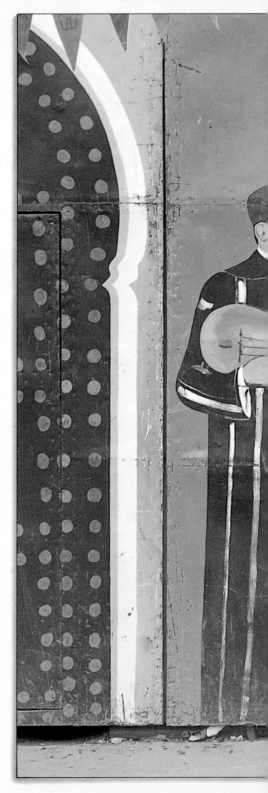

SKIING

It may be thought that skiing—an invention of the late 19th century imported from Scandinavia and developed as a pastime in the Alps— could have bypassed the hothouse of the Atlas. In fact, experiments in Moroccan *piste* skiing originated in the 1930s—before the winter sports fanfares of Courchevel and Val d'Isère could be heard.

During World War II expatriate Frenchmen installed primitive ski-tows in clearings of the Anti Atlas cedar forest and so set up the first equipped nursery slopes in the country. In 1942-43 the protagonists mounted several ski sorties into the Great Atlas; the spearhead was led by the now legendary André Fougerolles. By 1952 an 80-page guide to *piste* skiing and cross-country expeditions on skis had been issued, covering many ambitious projects—then achieved perhaps only once.

High hopes: Climatically, snow precipitations may occur in Morocco down to 3,330 ft (1,000 metres). Snow that may lie for more than two months raises the minimum level to 5,600–6,500 ft (1,700–2,000 metres). From an early date, *ski de haute montagne* was considered more rewarding than oscillating up and down short, sometimes artificially maintained, nursery slopes.

Multinational parties confirmed during the 1950s that the High Atlas was essentially a mountain skiing domain, and the specifically designed resort of **Oukaimeden** was conceived and completed in a few years. The modest weekend practice grounds at **Mischliffen-Jbel Hebri** on the west rim of the Anti Atlas remained fairly basic.

Nothing much has changed at Mischliffen in 40 years. Skiers generally commute to the three lifts from agreeable amenities in Azrou and Ifrane, 10 to 12 miles (15 – 20 km) away. Equipment hire is a hit-or-miss affair. In a poor year the season is short—maybe only five weeks, though usually extending to eight with runs falling through a modest vertical interval of 330 – 660 ft (100 – 200 metres). Obviously, Mischliffen is not a package-tour destination. Adherents are invariably the resident hoi-polloi of Fez, Méknès and Rabat. Youngsters and school groups, with amateur instructors, are much in evidence.

To widen the horizon, bolder skiers persuaded the authorities to open up **Bou Iblane** in the Anti Atlas as a high altitude resort. A road was pushed beyond the Taffert forestry hut to a site at the foot of the mountain, where an initial ski-lift was built. However, the car-park here, about 85 miles (140 km) from Fez, often cannot be reached in late winter because the road is not kept open by snowploughs (a case of economic viability versus the small number of participants).

Those attending sleep rough at the hut. There is no accommodation or restaurant—or indeed any other services—at the "resort". *Dortoirs* (self-catering flats) are on the drawing-board.

Across the quite suitable north-facing slopes and hollows of the several Bou Iblane summits, from 10,200 ft (3,100 metres) downhill sweeps of 2,300 ft (700 metres) are possible. The main problem is that good snowfalls may not last long. With a deteriorating surface, the skiing soon becomes of poor quality and, in the absence of waymarks, eventually a hazardous slalom among boulders. So here, too, one must count the season as short.

Oukaimeden, 47 miles (75 km) from Marrakesh, ranks as the premier ski-station in the country. The road is normally swept clear of snow and the season lasts from mid-December until early April. Now 30 years old, this resort has had Alpine-type trappings grafted on to it, though long spells of winter drought during the 1970s have taken their toll on Oukaimeden activities.

The chair-lift to the top of Jbel Oukaimeden (3,273 metres), the highest cableway in Africa, may be closed by mid-March. Its operation is not justified for spring and summer visitors, who mostly congregate at Imlil. Five ski-tows supplement the main lift; accessible beginners' slopes use portable drags. The graded runs are rather limited unless one is prepared to use skins and make out of bounds circuits.

Accommodation is available in two

hotels, four skier-chalets, various apartment blocks (including some for renting), and hired private chalets.

There are general food shops for self-caterers; equipment hire; but no garage repair. A splendid French Alpine Club establishment, with low charges, vies with the best commercial chalets for standards of comfort, but the *après-ski* of noise and "party games" lacks the sophistication of Alpine resorts.

Youth clubs and schools are encouraged by a government-sponsored national body (FRMSM) to assemble parties to train at Ouka for competitive downhill and cross-country skiing. Special firms now aspire to

summits and a party proceeds on foot using climbing techniques as conditions dictate. Mount Toubkal itself is an exception, though even here skis are removed by most parties 30 minutes from the top.

One for the professionals: The outstanding expedition ski ascent in the area is Tazaghärt—coincidentally offering the best winter gully climbs as well—but it is very serious stuff, helped along by the strong Berber backup available at Imlil.

The high level routes of summer become popular ski tours in winter, threading the high valleys and crossing passes to reach their ultimate destination. The rigours of these excursions undoubtedly demand a

arrange ski journeys supported, below the snowline, by mules and porters.

In the **Toubkal massif**, British parties have excelled in formulating tactics for unique long-distance experiences on skis. *Ski-mulet* is a description that figures prominently in holiday brochures of the 1980s. As an explanation of the term, some indigenous cartoonists have depicted mules wearing the skis and sweat-soaked tourists in tow behind carrying bags marked "hay".

Spurious, misleading claims abound about ski climbs in the Toubkal massif. Most of the desirable peaks cannot be reached on skis; they must be shed some way below the

brand of enthusiasm usually confined to mountain skiing fanatics.

Ambitious plans exist for turning the **Bou Guemez valley** in the Central High Atlas into a skiing paradise. Specifically, a consultative document has been produced detailing certain options. A fundamental disagreement between the promoters pivots on downhill infrastructure—lifts and tows, chalets and shops, or a chain of huts, to link up with other valleys, for touring.

Another scheme, favoured by ecologists and environmentalists, would have the district preserved altogether from pylons and cables, and allow only wealthy heli-skiers to be flown in from Beni-Mellal hotels and collected the same way. Clearly, the Berbers are totally opposed to this idea. Finding the funds to realise any of the grand designs published so far will hinder advancement, but by 1990 Azurki and Izourar huts should be open for business.

A lot of skiers already make the rough journey to **Azurki** mountain 12,000 ft (3,677 metres). As long ago as 1950, this huge smooth-sided mass was pronounced potentially the finest skiing location in Morocco—coupled with its equally bulky neighbour Ouaoulzat. Skis have glided over every facet, spur and depression where trails of 1,000 metres can be plotted. Snow retention

objective. This has been accomplished many times, but it is strictly the province of the well-trained alpinist and is avalanche-prone in some prevailing conditions.

Close to Midelt, the gigantic **Ayyachi** will tax the fittest exponent. Doubtless a gratifying feat, incredibly it has half a dozen ascent-descent routes described in specialist publications, with a preciseness suggesting scores of ascents have been made. In fact, some of these are believed to have been helicopter-assisted. Air charter is a growing business in Marrakesh and Beni-Mellal and the demands of skiers have been making a significant contribution.

In the skiing season, daily forecasts of

on mountains round the Bou Guemez is traditionally good and skiing in favourable years continues to mid-May.

Skiing further east enters the realms of wilderness exploits, in which the *ski-mulet* recourse might be essential to success and perhaps survival. Pre-planning, organisation and local knowledge will mentally defeat many hopefuls.

Jbel Masker, near Tounfite, has been singled out as a solitary noble ski ascent

<u>Left</u>, Oukaimedan Lake, close to Marrakesh. <u>Above</u>, Oukaimedan, which has yet to become a Moroccan Val d'Isère.

weather and ground conditions for Mischliffen and Ouka are available in towns and cities all over Morocco. Based in Marrakesh or Méknès, one can go at short notice to either in a couple of hours. Personal, portable rescue beacons—small battery-operated radio transmitter/receiver devices, worn by cross-country and touring skiers in Europe—cannot function in the Atlas mountains where rescue services are distant and have no compatible electronic receiving equipment.

Final word of advice: Make certain you have adequate rescue and air repatriation insurance for skiing in the Atlas.

PLACES

Travel in Morocco has come a long way since the days when Europeans needed to disguise themselves in *djellabahs* and veils in order to penetrate anywhere beyond Tangier. Dusty old tomes on Morocco all contain photographs of their authors in native dress—though Wyndham Lewis seemed to think this had more to do with a childish desire to "dress up as Arabs" than any real fear of attack.

In fact Berbers, being naturally resourceful, have proved the very opposite of their famously violent image; they have welcomed tourism and at a local level, particularly in the Atlas, have been quick to profit from it, often undermining the government's broader attempts to capitalise on big spending by foreign visitors.

Some hotel development has spawned on the Rif coast, especially south of the Spanish enclave of Ceuta, but, amazingly for a country so close to Europe with sandy beaches and reliable sunshine, it has largely escaped the type of concrete monstrosities that mushroomed on the southern coasts of Spain, Turkey and Portugal. The Moroccan government, showing uncharacteristic foresight, is seeking a better class of holidaymaker. The southern valleys, long favoured territory of middle-class French motorists, have been earmarked for upmarket tourist development, with well-hidden traditionally designed luxury hotels proliferating yearly. Even Agadir, where Morocco strives to achieve the image of a "playground resort", is not entirely without attractive qualities.

But, despite long blonde, blue-skied beaches, fortified Portuguese fishing towns, green oases in pink desert plains, mountain ranges offering walking, climbing and winter skiing, the extraordinary attractions of Morocco are still the imperial cities of Fez, Méknès and Marrakesh. Founded in the Middle Ages and expanded by succeeding dynasties, they contain some of the best examples of early Islamic architecture; even more remarkable, the trades and practices of their medinas still function much as they did in medieval times throughout North Africa and the Middle East.

Morocco's capital, Rabat, though having similar historic claims, seems European by comparison: the French-style cafés and "Mauresque" architecture on the verdant Boulevard Mohammed V reflect an urban style not confined to the down-town area. Here, more than anywhere, is a reminder that a large part of Morocco was governed by the French. If Rabat seems somewhat bourgeois, Azrou and Ifrane, south of Fez in the Middle Atlas, with their steeply-roofed Alpine-style architecture, would not be out of place in a Disney version of Switzerland. Incredible, then, that just 200 or so miles (320 km) away, radiating from the foothills of the Atlas, lie the deserts and palm oases of the south—landscapes that helped win acclaim for David Lean's *Lawrence of Arabia*.

Preceding pages: winter in the Dades Valley; darkness falls over Fez; the ferry from Rabat to Salé. **Left,** the whitewashed streets of Chaouen, in the Rif.

200 km

CANARY ISLANDS

LA PALMA
TENERIFE
GOMERA
GRAN CANARIA

LANZAROTE
FUERTEVENTURA
ESPAÑA
(SPAIN)

Atlantic
Ocean

Essaouira

HIGH ATLAS
Ouarzazate
Zagora

Agadir
Taroudant

Tata
Akka

Goulimime
Foum-
el-Hisn

Tarfaya
MOROCCO
Al Mahbas
Tindouf
Hawza

Lemsid
Smara

Tangier

Asilah

Larache

Ksar el Kehir

Dakla
Bir Enzaran

Bfr. Mogrein
Galtat Zemmour

Ain Ben Tili

ALGERIA

Kediet ej Jill

Techlé

MAURITANIA

Atlantic
Ocean

O. Sebou
Sidi-Slimane
Kénitra
Sidi-K
Salé
Rabat
Mé
Khemisset

Mohammedia
Casablanca

El Jadida
Berrechid

Benahamed

Settat

Khouribga
Oued Zem

Oualidia
Sidi-Bennour

Safi
Youssoufia
Skhour-des-
Rehamna

El Kelâa
des Srarhna

Marrakesh

Essaouira
Chichaoua
Aït-Barka

Smimou
Sebt-des-
Aït-Daoud
Imi-n-Taoute

Ijoukak

Tamri

Taroudant
O. Sous

Agadir

O. Oum er Rbia

PAYS ZAËR ZAÏNE

Rommani

Kenifr

Fkih Ben Salah

Beni Mellal

Imilc

Azilal
Aït Mehammed

Tilmi

ATLA
Ti

El Kelâa
des Mgouna

O. Dades
Ait

Ouarzazate
Barrage d'el-Mansour-
Eddahbi

Taliouine
Tazenakht

O. Tensift

O. Tessaout

HIGH

Ceuta
(Sp.)

Mediterranean Sea

an

El Amria

Bou Hamed

Al Hoceïma

Melilla
(Sp.)

Beni Saf

Chechaouèn

Nador

Marsa
Ben Mehidi

Midar

ERRIF

(RIF)

zane

Tlemcen

Taounate

Aknoul

Oujda

Taourirt

O. Sebou

Guercif

Oued Za

ALGERIA

El Aricha

Taza

Fez

Âin Benimathar

Abdelmoùla

ATLAS

PLATEAU
DU REKKAM

Sefrou

AL-MAGREB

Zerouilet

O. Charef

(MOROCCO)

u

Outat Oulad
el Haj

Matarka

Borj de Trarite-
Rhars-Allah

Enjil

Missour

Tendrara

Ghedir Draa
El Rich

DDLE

Midelt

Anoual

Bouârfa

Moulouya

Talsinnt

PLAINE DE TAMLELT

Mengoub

Amouguèr

Aït Krojmane

Figuig

udal

Er-Rachidia

Lahmar

Boudenib

O. Guir

Goulmima

Ksar-el-Azoudj

Touroug

Béchar

Asrir

Erfoud

Rissani

HAMADA

O. Zousfana

DU

Abadia

ALGERIA

Hamaguir

GUIR

Morocco

S A H A R A

100 km

115

TANGIER

"That ragamuffin city" was Truman Capote's affectionate description of Tangier in 1949. It's a strange fact that the rich and famous, who could be up among the stars, never mind looking at them, often prefer the frisson of the gutter.

In its heyday, Tangier was there with Cannes on the international set's calendar. It was frequented by Tennesse Williams, Cecil Beaton, William Burroughs and Tallulah Bankhead. Brion Gysin, Paul Bowles and the Honourable David Herbert, younger son of the Earl of Pembroke, lived there, and Barbara Hutton, fabulous hostess and Woolworth heiress, owned a house in its medina.

Its tax-free status attracted world bankers and unscrupulous profiteers. In its squares, the Grand and Petit Soccos, whose very names reflect the town's hybrid character, anything, absolutely anthing, could be found and purchased. It was truly an international zone.

Until, that is, six months after Morocco's independence in 1956, when its international status was revoked and the administrative infrastructure dismantled. It was typical that Tangier, a city of indulgence, should be granted these few months' grace. Nonetheless transition was a shock to a city whose prosperity was based purely on its freeport status. It underwent a sharp decline from which it only steadily recovered.

Vestiges of its former character survive. There are still retainers from the international era; David Herbert and Paul Bowles have stayed, and been joined by younger writers and artists, such as Gavin Young. The famous bars it used to boast have nearly all closed, but there are others and Tangier remains a late-night city, much more so than Fez, Marrakesh or Rabat.

The homosexual mecca that it became in the 1950s still to some extent pertains. And around mid-afternoon **Café de Paris** in the **Place de France** continues to attract a sprinkling of genteel old men wearing white linen trousers and shaded spectacles.

Covetable asset: Tangier has excited a long history of foreign interest—hardly surprising, considering its strategic value at the mouth of the Mediterranean. The Carthaginians were the first to realise the site's potential and it was they who established a trading port, then called Tingis. Next came the Romans; followed by the Vandals, Byzantians and the Visigoths (when Christianity gained a foothold). By 705 the Arabs had arrived.

Tangier prospered under the Berber dynasties until the 14th century, when internal order in Morocco broke down and the whole of its north and northwest coast became infested with pirates. This prompted Portugal to intervene in North Africa, and, having already captured Ceuta, they eventually managed to seize Tangier.

Mosques were destroyed and churches were built. But Berber resistance was determined, and after two centuries the Portuguese finally passed

Tangier to England as part of Catherine of Braganza's dowry on her marriage to Charles II in 1661.

England deemed Tangier a covetable asset. Even Samuel Pepys, who loathed Tangier and described it as an "excrescence of the earth", reckoned it would be "The King's most important outpost in the world". Unfortunately for England, it could not resist the constant Berber attacks. The British withdrew in 1684, first destroying the principal improvements they had introduced.

From then on, Britain's prime objective in Tangier was to uphold the authority of the sultan and keep any single European power from colonising it. Britain had held Gibraltar since 1713 and it was vital to have a close, cooperative source of food and supplies for her tiny island. Other powers were equally jealous of Tangier, and by the 19th century the town was overrun by diplomats.

Foreign control: Europe tightened its hold on the town by making various improvements: a lighthouse was built at Cap Spartel (by then treacherous rocks,

not pirates, were the main hazard along the Strait), and in 1872 a Sanitary Council was formed in response to outbreaks of plague. But European influence was also exerted in a less noble way; certain privileges were granted to natives working in the legations and consulates. They were exempted from sultanic taxes and justice—a privilege Jews found particularly valuable—and before long the consulates were selling "protection" for exorbitant prices.

By the signing of the Treaty of Fez in 1912, which established the French and Spanish protectorates, Tangier was already virtually an international zone; the Treaty of Algeciras put it on an official footing; and in 1923 another statute handed Tangier to the victors of World War I: France, Spain, Britain, Portugal, Sweden, Holland, Belgium and Italy.

Tangier today: Following independence, and the collapse of Tangier's spurious economy, the town that had been so coveted was left to recover. Then closely situated around its cor-

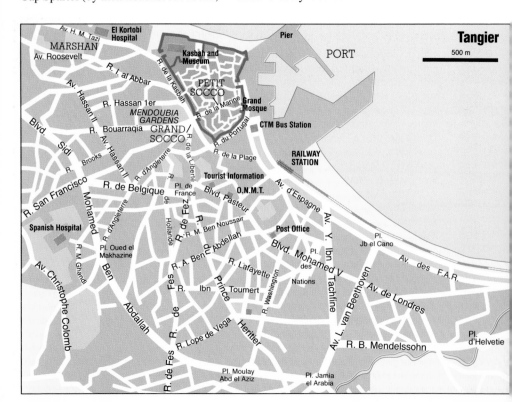

niche, medina, Boulevard Pasteur, Marshan and The Mountain (the latter two a couple of manicured hills populated by the villa-owning classes), it has since expanded into a large town boasting suburbs and an industrial region to the south. Food and textile manufacturing apart, tourism is its biggest industry.

Even in the l9th century, Europeans visited Tangier for its weather, and climate is supposed to be one of the town's enduring attractions. In the summer, it rarely becomes unbearable. It is warm well into October, even November, and in mid-winter, when it is often cold and wet (a fact emphasised by the complete absence of any heating in most houses, and some hotels), there are always some hours of sunshine during the day.

However, the *chergui*, an eastern wind, bearable in the town, seems always to be at its most violent on the beach. It guarantees business in the serried ranks of beach clubs, sometimes the only convenient respite.

Tangier's low cost of living and proximity to Europe accounts for its popularity as a package-tour destination—witness the large number of medium-priced hotels, nearby holiday complexes, and Club Mediterranée in Malabata over the bay. The town attracts a large number of British (pleased to discover it is one of the few places in Morocco where English is widely spoken), some of whom are on day trips from the Costa del Sol and Gibraltar.

However, Tangier is primarily a summer resort for Moroccans. Any summer evening the streets between Boulevard Pasteur and the Grand Socco are solid with freshly-dressed families *"faisant le boulevard"*. Often they are Fassis—and inspiration for many jokes among the Tanjaouis sitting outside the cafés.

Around the town: Boulevard Pasteur, running up from Boulevard Mohammed V and the central post office, is Tangier's High Street. To its right, on the ocean side, streets containing small hotels wind steeply down to the bay; behind it on the left are shops, restaurants, nightclubs and bars. The large

Tangier has expanded considerably since independence.

banks, the **tourist office** (29) are here, plus the **Librairie des Colonnes**, a European bookshop run by a bouffant-haired madame, invaluable to the expatriate writers in Tangier.

The Boulevard's cafés and *salons de thé* are the kind of slightly upmarket establishments to which a Moroccan man might take a woman. (Café La Colombe, by the way, at its eastern end, serves the best coffee and croissants in town.) It runs down to a paved platform, with a view over roofs and tree-tops to the harbour, and joins **Rue du Mexique**, the main shopping street, in the **Place de France**—an animated circus containing the famous Café de Paris.

From here **Rue de la Liberté** curls down to El Minzah Hotel and the Galerie Delacroix, while the **Rue de Belgique** leads to **Rue d'Angleterre** and the English church. Following either route you can find your way to the **Grand Socco**, a large sloping square overlooked by the coloured, tiled minaret of the **Sidi Bouabid mosque**, the first to be built outside Tangier's old walls. Directly opposite the top of the square is the main, horseshoe-shaped gate to the medina.

The **El Minzah Hotel** is the classy hotel in Tangier. Previously it was the residence of a wealthy British gentleman, but its design reflects traditional Moorish architecture: a discreet entrance off the street precedes an elegant lobby leading to a tiled open courtyard overlooked by the hotel's upper storeys. An exit on the opposite side of the quadrangle leads to a terrace, small swimming-pool and gardens. On a particularly hot day afternoon tea in the gardens can seem like paradise; especially compared with the pandemonium on the street outside, not that dissimilar to hell.

The **Galerie Delacroix**, part of the **French Cultural Centre** directly opposite the Minzah, is a small gallery containing not work by Eugène Delacroix, the French painter who toured North Africa in 1832, but the art of aspiring Moroccan artists and images of Morocco by foreign painters (entrance

The Grand Socco.

is free). The French Cultural Centre is extremely active (check noticeboard for forthcoming events), and the French Lycée, off Boulevard Pasteur, contains the **Salle Bastianelli**, venue for good French theatre and international films.

Oddly enough, the English do not have a cultural centre in Tangier (the Spanish provide Ramon Y Cajal, the Lycee Polytecnico Espanol, also excellent), obviously thinking it more profitable to establish a church with a proper English graveyard. The **English Church**, St Andrew's, built to serve the expatriates, close to the British Consulate in the Rue d'Angleterre, contains an incongruous mixture of styles. Inside, Islamic features—delicate stucco tracery, thin pencil pillars, Kufic script and keyhole arches—combine with village-church trappings: pews and hassocks; cross and chalice, organ and pulpit.

Near the entrance are copies of the Book of Common Prayer and on the wall the flower-arranging rota. In the graveyard, the venerable Moustafa, the Church's enthusiastic, and Muslim,

caretaker, will point out Walter Harris's grave. Harris, famous correspondent for the London *Times* and devoted Arabist, wrote many revered tomes on the country, including the classic *Morocco That Was*, every guidebook writer's bible.

Downhill of the church is one of Tangier's main market areas. Small shops, not much larger than cupboards and selling everyday items such as *babouches* (the open-backed leather footwear, traditionally in yellow or red), earthenware and clothing, extend to the edge of the Grand Socco. Halfway along, through a gap flanked by Riffians crouched over bunches of mint or flat-leafed parsley and fattened hens, is the market proper—spice, vegetable, cheese, olive, and grisly butchers' stalls—fulfilling every touristic expectation of a Moroccan souk.

The **Grand Socco**, where Rue D'Angleterre and Rue de la Liberté converge, is a large irregular-shaped area, ringed by cafés, that used to be the main market square. It is still a gathering point,

where women come to sell their bread. Directly opposite is the gate leading into the medina.

Rue es Siaghin, to the right as you pass through, leads to the **Petit Socco**; **Rue d'Italie**, a steep, flagged street with broad steps on either side, leads directly up to the **Kasbah**, passing on the way the old **British telegraph office**. During the international era all the European powers had their own communications systems, and it was through the telegraph and post offices that the Moroccan nationalists gleaned news of what was happening in the French and Spanish zones.

The other route, **Rue es Siaghin**, meaning silversmiths' street, cuts deep into the medina. It was to the right of here, in the *mellah*, that the Jews lived, the traditional dealers in silver in the town. Some jewellers still trade, but most Jews have moved on. Also on the right is the long disused **Spanish mission**—a bone of contention between those who feel it should be commandeered for other purposes and those who believe that Muslim use of Christian premises would offend Allah.

Such caveats never used to exist. The **Grand Mosque** at the end of **Rue de la Marine** (reached by walking straight on) was built by Moulay Ismail in the late 17th century. It occupies the site of the Cathedral of the Holy Spirit, built by the Portuguese. Incidentally, the **Spanish Cathedral** in **Avenue Hassan II** used to be the tallest building, dominating the view of Tangier from any approach by sea. Now a new mosque, in honour of Mohammed V, has been built just behind it in **Place Kuwait**. This now claims to be the tallest sight.

The **American Legation**, also off the beginning of **Rue es Siaghin**, in the Rue d'Amerique, is less easy to find, and consequently rarely visited by the droves of tourists heading for the Petit Socco. Although the building has served the Americans since 1684, the sultan gave the Legation to the US in 1821. Morocco was the first country to recognise US sovereignty. This legation was the first American government

The Sea Gate.

property held outside the United States.

Today the elaborately decorated 17th and 18th-century interior (in one room the decoration of the ceiling, floor and shutters all match) is used for concerts and exhibitions. Its permanent collection contains some of the best paintings, lithographs and photographs in Morocco, including work by Delacroix and contemporary Moroccan painters such as R'bati and Hamri; one by Yves St Laurent; and various naive and impressionist works.

The Legation is in one of the poorest parts of the medina, in fact the red-light area. The **Petit Socco** at the end of Rue es Siaghin also verges on the louche. It was here that much of the bohemian lowlife that so attracted the likes of William Burroughs and Brion Gysin happened. It still has a seedy atmosphere.

The cafés here are very different to those on Boulevard Pasteur. Most are packed with men seemingly watching television. Watch them, however, and you will notice individuals sidling in to whisper in an ear or beckon. This is where "business" is done. Sit for long enough and you are bound to be hustled to buy hashish and told of "upstairs rooms".

From the Petit Socco, **Rue des Cheratins** and **Rue Ben Raisouli**, positively festooned with kaftans, handbags and toy camels, meander up towards the Kasbah. This used to comprise the sultanic palace (now a museum) and administrative quarter. Within its walls is some of the most sought-after property in Tangier. Barbara Hutton had a house here and so did Richard Hughes, author of *A High Wind in Jamaica*. The palace itself was occupied as recently as 1912 by the abdicate Sultan Moulay Hafid, though by all accounts he found it uncomfortable.

Tangier's prison used to be here, and locals like to relate the story of the time its prisoners escaped, all of them except one. Asked why he'd remained, the man apparently replied that the prison provided all his needs—food, shelter and company—so why should he leave? When the escapees had been caught and

Tangier's bay, often prone to east winds.

returned, the man was made a warden of the prison.

In the *mechouar*, the large court outside the prison, originally used as an assembly place for public pronouncements and as an arena for story-tellers, you are likely to catch snake charmers or musicians laid on for the coaches.

Like most Moroccan museums, the **Palace Museum**, on the west side of the *mechouar*, is well designed—the original Arabesques, *zellige* and marble providing a stylish context for the artefacts. But typically, too, it is short on relevant literature. Exhibits, arranged in rooms lining the sides of two courtyards, include carpets, ceramics from Fez and Méknès, costumes, musical instruments, household implements and jewellery. The kitchen quarters house an **archaeological museum** containing a Roman mosaic from Volubilis.

North of the *mechouar*, the **Rue Riad Sultan** curls left round the ocean side of the Kasbah to pass a door leading to an upstairs café called **Le Détroit**. Music, sometimes traditonal, often a Moroccan rendering of a Western hit, either tempts or repels. This used to be the most exclusive restaurant in Tangier, where owner and writer Brion Gysin entertained the privileged. Now custom is reduced to package groups in the afternoons; it affords exciting views, though, with a clear sight of **York House**, the machiolated residence of the English governors in the 17th century and now a private house owned, reputedly, by Givenchy.

A short walk further west along **Rue Assad ibn Farrat** and **Rue Mohammed Tazi**, or else reached by taking a number 1 or number ll bus from the centre, is the **Forbes Museum of Military Miniatures** in the Tangier home of American millionaire, publisher and Arabist Malcolm Forbes. His house is the large white villa smothered in purple bougainvillea. There is no admission and to visit is exactly like entering a private home.

His own tastes are much in evidence—two huge BMW motorbikes flank the hall, the gardens include a

The courtyard of the Palace Museum.

swimming-pool. Exhibits—war memorabilia, depictions of a soldier's life, war posters and photographs, as well as huge models of famous battles, many relating to Moroccan history—are well worth seeing.

Turn left as you leave the Forbes Museum and left again after the hospital and you will discover a terraced cliff-top café, peaceful and secluded, with views over the ocean.

Life after dark: Perhaps more than any other Moroccan town or city, Tangier has the most concentrated nightlife and it certainly keeps the latest hours; many restaurants and clubs don't open until 9 p.m. and stay open until 4 a.m. It was once famous for its bars: in particular the Safari, Les Liaisons and The Parade, none of which remain.

A bar's success depended upon the personality of its owners and in the late 1940s and early 1950s Tangier attracted its fair share of charismatic hosts and hostesses. **Dean's bar**, at one time more a fashionable club than a bar, remains (behind a shabby, nondescript door in **Rue Amerique du Sud**), but Dean himself, who began his career as the lover of a rich and titled English gentleman, has long gone and nobody who's anybody goes here any more.

The **Koutoubia Palace**, also a discothèque, offers kitsch Moroccan decor, belly-dancing and girls. For lowlife, **Churchill's** in **Rue Moutanabi** still attracts a certain *demi-monde*, but now the arty and the crafty tend to go to the smart, new establishments that have opened—even if they do have to rub shoulders with par-boiled English tourists in the summer months.

The **English Pub**, 4 Rue Sorolla (with higher than English prices and a restrictive door policy), is popular, as are **The Wine Bar** (formally the far rougher Carousel) in **Rue Khalil Metran**, and the wine-bar of **El Minzah Hotel**. For inexpensive drinking in a convivial, if overridingly gay, atmosphere, **The Tanger Inn** in **El Meneuria Hotel** (writing retreat of William Burroughs), **Rue Magellan**, is certainly worth finding.

The beaches to the east of Tangier are the best.

There are also some excellent restaurants: **Restaurant Hammaq** at the foot of Rue d'Italie is the best known Moroccan restaurant in Tangier, but the one preferred by most Tanjaouis is the Italian **San Remo** on **Rue Murillo**. Expatriates, on the other hand, frequent **The Marquis** on **Rue Tolstoy**, where prices match elegance; or, famous in the international era, **Guitta's** in **Place de Kuwait**, with its huge garden and garrulous hostess. **Coeur de Tanger** on **Boulevard Pasteur** (again expensive) is another option; and for less extravagant occasions **La Grenouille** on **Rue Rembrandt** is outstanding value.

The beach bars: Although rentals are renewed at the start of each season, bars only occasionally change hands and each bar has developed its own character. Some are 100 percent gay (**Miami Beach** and **Macumbu**, for instance); the **Yacht Club** (belonging to the port Yacht Club) is private; **BBC Emma's Bar** is popular with Europeans, expatriate or not; the **Chellah Beach Bar** and the **Golden Beach** are expensive (they

serve mainly residents from the Chellah and Solazur hotels) and the **Costa del Norte** is notorious for its prostitutes and fights.

During the day they provide changing facilities, sunbeds and a place to buy refreshments (all for around 20 dirhams a day) and many are open until the early hours of the morning, **Trés Caravelas** and **Sun Beach** being the liveliest.

Sea air: To the west of Tangier, **Cap Spartel** offers alternative beaches to Tangier's decent (but in summer well-populated) sands. The interesting route leaves Tangier on the S701 (the Mountain road), passing Tangier's most exclusive properties, including the King's mother's house, a residence of the King of Saudi Arabia, and what used to be the Governor of Tangier's house but which is now being renovated for use by the Crown Prince, Mohammed.

Just off the road at the bottom of the far side of The Mountain is the **People's Dispensary for Sick Animals Rest Home**, in fact a dogs' graveyard and a reminder, if any was needed, of the sentimentality of expatriates. The road then loops the headland, passing the Cap Spartel lighthouse, erected by foreign diplomats in the 1870s, and the **Caves of Hercules**, natural rock chambers inhabited in prehistoric times and in the international era used as an off-beat party-venue. En route, there are several small bays to adjourn to, and south of the Caves an Atlantic beach which stretches 30 miles (45 km).

A little further on, you pass the ancient Roman ruins of **Cotta**, dating from the second and third centuries, which include a small temple and a bath-house thought to be evidence of a factory for the production of *garum*, a fish extract used in Roman cooking. A turning left before the road to Rabat leads back to Tangier via the town's prison and the Coca-Cola factory.

Alternatively, east of Tangier, there is **Cap Malabata** (also with a lighthouse), now an upper-middle class residential area; **Ksar es Seghir**, with its tiny jetty and excellent beach; and quietest and most perfect of the lot, **Dalia**.

Left, inevitably many prefer the hotel pool. **Right**, a more artful display of flesh.

THE RIF

"A naked, steep, savage-looking wall" was how the German explorer Gerhald Rohlfs described Morocco's **Rif** in the middle of the 19th century. The reputation of its people, too, is for ferocity. Blood revenge used to be a serious cause of population depletion and possibly deforestation, since trees and property as well as life were destroyed in a feud. It was said that a male Riffian who had not taken a life before he was married was not yet considered to be a man.

The mountains rise sharply from the Mediterranean. East of Tangier their foothills begin close to **Tetouan**. Here, contrasting strongly with the low hills and gentle colours of the Tangier hinterland, the landscape is impressively rugged.

Soaring cedars: To the immediate east trees begin to cloak the craggy limestone peaks and as you climb into the central section of the Rif dominated by the often snow-capped **Mount Tidiguin** (on which, myth has it, the Ark rested), squat holm-oak trees give way to soaring cedar forests and the kif plantations of Ketama.

The further east you travel, the redder the hue of the mountain range becomes, a change that strikes the traveller on the road to **Al Hoceima** where the terrain becomes denuded and barren. From Al Hoceima to **Oujda** on the Algerian border, south of a fertile coastal plain, the land is desolate, crossed by cracked riverbeds.

More inviting, on the Rif coast directly below the range, are some of the finest sands in Morocco, a fact which has led to a number of package-tour type hotels and imitation "Club Med"-style holiday villages, fed by the airport of Tangier. (Ironically, beaches are now being named after hotels.)

But it is still possible to find unspoilt secluded sands between the pockets of development, and some of the best fish restaurants in Morocco are along this shore. The "resorts" include **Restinga**

M'diq, Cabo Negro, Martil and **Amsa**.

For a spectacular view of the coastline and mountains, it is possible to fly by small plane from the old airport, established by the Spanish just outside **Tetouan** (toward Ceuta), to the tiny but modern airport in **Al Hoceima** for around 200 dirhams. Trips to **Gibraltar** by catamaran from the port in M'diq run several times a week.

The people: The area has for centuries been influenced by Spain, as an Andalusian style of architecture in the towns, a common fluency in Spanish and the consumption of foods such as paella and tortilla and the serving of *tappas* testify. Many of the Andalusian Muslims who fled Spain in the 15th and 16th centuries settled here; and from 1912 until 1956 the Rif, plus the short stretch of Atlantic coast to just north of Larache but excluding the international zone of Tangier, formed the bulk of the zone governed by the Spanish—what, in fact, in the scramble for Moroccan territory, France had wisely left them.

Until this time, the Riffians had existed outside authority in what was known as *bled es siba* (land of dissidence), or those parts of Morocco where the recalcitrant inhabitants refused to pay taxes to the sultan or accept his garrisons. (Strictly speaking, the term Riffian applies only to the tribes of the middle Rif around Ketama; the J'bala, Arabic rather than Berber-speaking tribes, inhabited the extreme western Rif close to Tetouan. But the general term Riffian refers to inhabitants of the whole of the mountainous area in the north.)

The Rif tribes were a force for the Spanish to reckon with. The Rif Rebellion of 1926, led by Abd el Krim and finally quashed by the Spanish but not without help from France, was the antecedent to nationalist demands in the rest of Morocco. And since independence the Riffians, disappointed by what has been accomplished for them, and still having something of the *bled es siba* attitude, have been the most irksome to the Moroccan government. In December 1958 a rebellion stirred near Al Hoceima, which the then Crown Prince Moulay Hassan was sent to quell.

Despite illegal kif plantations, illegal smuggling of goods from the tax-free ports in the Spanish enclaves of Melilla and Ceuta, the creation of a new steel plant at Nador, and a developing tourist industry, the area remains poor. Its inhabitants still complain of economic deprivation and neglect by central government.

Heading east: By Moroccan standards, the P38 from Tangier to Tetouan is a busy stretch of road. As part of the main thoroughfare from the densely populated northwest of Morocco to the Spanish enclave of Ceuta, it is used by people heading to buy the cheap electrical goods and garments smuggled out of Ceuta to Tetouan. Consequently it is lined by Riffians intent on selling the motorists their produce too.

Women dressed in the typical pompom sombreros, red and white striped skirts and what can only be described as bathtowels (often rigged into a papoose

Left, elaborately tiled Tetouan townhouse. **Right**, hunting—a popular sport.

to contain a baby) and looking positively Peruvian, hold covered dishes containing the crumbling, white cheeses (either salted or unsalted) or honey of the region. Men tout amethysts and pottery.

The flying customs officers and police, who also populate the lay-bys and verges, are looking for motorists' less innocuous purchases, but it is on the other side of Tetouan and Chaouen, towards the kif-growing areas of Ketama, that the road-blocks and customs checks start to get really tiring.

Tetouan, flanked on all sides by ragged limestone mountains whose lower reaches are forested, is a surprising sight worthy of its name—meaning in Berber "open your eyes". In autumn it is prone to rain and low cloud, and in the winter to snow. It isn't until you arrive that you appreciate the town's situation and realise how high the road has climbed.

Its past importance as the capital of the Spanish zone, where the Spanish High Commisioner lived, is immediately apparent in its civic architecture. Imposing bow balconies beneath tall windows and curlicued grille-work are reminiscent of those in Seville. **Place Hassan II** (where, incidentally, a new royal palace is being built on the site of the old Caliphate palace), with its sweep of old market buildings, looks distinctly Andalusian. But more interesting is some of the older domestic architecture. The large, old mansions at the lower end of the *mellah* at the foot of **Rue Luneta** are in a state of dilapidation but even so the intricate, enamelled tiling and fancy wrought-iron work decorating their exteriors demonstrate a difference between Spanish and Moroccan styles of building; on Moroccan houses adornment is all internal.

Tetouan was a busy trading centre even before the Spanish protectorate added to its importance. At the beginning of the 16th century, the Jews and Muslims who arrived here from Spain practised an old maritime profession, piracy. They made slaves of passengers and crews then extracted fabulous sums

Tetouan's bus station: a Moroccan experience.

KIF GROWING IN THE RIF

The road from Chaouen to Ketama is one of impressive beauty. It switches back and forth through the rugged heights of the Rif. As it approaches Ketama, it is flanked by cedar and evergreen-oak woodlands and the landscape feels more like the Black Forest than Morocco.

None of the inhabitants of these parts, though, believe for one moment that visitors are there to appreciate the scenery. From out of patches of low cloud and from behind rocky outcrops youths loom brandishing lumps of cannabis resin pulled from their *djellabahs*, or miming a rolling movement with their fingers (rolling a joint) and gesticulating at all cars to stop. The rule is, don't.

Foreign embassies warn against travelling along this route. Most Moroccans, too, are wary. Horror stories propagate as abundantly as the plant itself. Everybody knows somebody whose vehicle was halted by a fallen tree trunk, who was then hauled out and forced, some say at knifepoint, to buy hashish. The nightmare never ends there. A few miles up the road, the story goes, the innocent traveller is stopped by the police—who are in the drug hustlers' pay—and the hashish is discovered.

The cultivation, sale, use and transport of hashish (or kif as it is called before it is processed) is

illegal. Nevertheless, it is smoked openly throughout Morocco, often in upstairs rooms above cafés and bars, and the plantations on the hill terraces around Ketama are clearly visible from the road: a dense, head-high crop with spear-shaped leaves.

The Koran, which clearly prohibits alcohol, is ambivalent about kif. Wine is taboo because it is an intoxicant; kif, some say, was not banned by the Prophet precisely because it is not an intoxicant but a suppressant.

In Morocco, kif was grown for many years for local purposes, but it was in the 1960s that the expertise for turning it into a resin (hashish), a much stronger and more concentrated product easier to transport, was introduced, reputedly by the French. It was no coincidence that Morocco

quickly became a draw on the hippie trail. Suddenly, the poor Riffian farmers, who until then eked out a subsistence living, had the means to become rich. Not rich by Western standards, of course—that was the privilege of the trafficker—but rich enough to afford new divans and a TV set.

The process for turning the kif seeds into hashish is simple: they are sieved, and then pushed through a muslin filter. The fine brown powder that emerges is pressed into bars. This is hashish resin. The more the powder is sifted, the smoother the end-product. Kif, on the other hand, is the cut and dried leaves of the plant. This is smoked in a long-stemmed kif pipe, or *sebsi*, containing a clay filter, and the effect is far milder.

These days it's the older generation who tend to use kif; the younger generation prefer the effects of hashish. Until recently, it was common for the wealthier households, desiring a convivial atmosphere, to lace the family tea with an expensive hashish preparation called *gaouza*. And *majoun*, jams with a kick, is traditionally home prepared (beware the cheap, street-touted variety).

The price of the resin quickly escalates the further one travels from Ketama, a town with a couple of buildings and a lot of expensive Chevrolets. There, anyone stopping is assumed to be on "business". A few inches of resin in Ketama will cost as little as 10 dirhams. By the time it reaches Tangier the price will be six or seven times that.

The Rif is ideally situated for export purposes. The quiet, quaint fishing villages east of Tangier—such as Dalia and Oued Dalian—are fronts for more lucrative business than sardine-fishing. From these it is a short sea-crossing to Spain. The international airport of Tangier and the port of Casablanca are also within a few hours' drive.

In line with international pressure, the Moroccan government claims to be phasing out the cultivation of kif. This is partly why tourists caught dabbling in hashish smuggling are dealt with harshly: it is a way of demonstrating an intention to clamp down. In reality, the region is one neglected by the government, and the industry has become economically indispensable; the large-scale smuggling behind the café façades of Ketama continues unabated.

of ransom. Ships were attacked indiscriminately, but those of Spain particularly suffered, and Philip II closed down Tetouan's port on the river Martil. Under Moulay Ismail the town's economy prospered again.

Nowadays Tetouan is a strikingly spirited town, a fact stemming perhaps from its history as the focus of political resistance in the Rif. It was here that in 1954 a rally of 30,000 tribesmen protested about the deposition of Sultan Mohammed V. It doesn't feel like a town willing to hang around.

As recently as 1984 Tetouan experienced bread riots, demonstrations against the high prices of basic foodstuffs. Even the café life is not as totally idle as elsewhere. During the afternoon and early evening its numerous cafés resound to the slap of draughts being played.

Shopping is another cause of activity. Visiting Moroccans interested in buying cheap smuggled electrical goods and inexpensive clothing head for the **souk Nador** in the west of the town, its entrance marked by a stall selling huge televison sets. (Like many other occupations in the Rif, this trade is illegal but tolerated by the state.)

The souks within the medina, entered through the **Bab el Rouah** on Place Hassan II, are more geared towards tourists—who are numerous, since Tetouan is a common first stop for those expelled by the Algeciras and Malaga ferries at Ceuta—but the **souk el houts** behind the Spanish Consulate is local in character.

Turning right at this souk leads to the **Bab Oqla** and an excellent **Museum of Moroccan Arts** containing examples of Riffian and J' bala traditonal crafts. In the **Place el Jala** there is an **archaeological museum** displaying Moroccan artefacts from the Roman and Phoenician periods.

Picturesque town: Chaouen, south of Tetouan, stacked into the hills, belongs to the higgledy-piggledy, whitewashed, cobbled places, from the Devon town of Clovelly in England to the Greek island Poros, that merit the description pictur-

esque. Chaouen has the sort of houses that look as though they have been sat upon: their walls bulge, the tiny windows look squashed. It is startlingly clean and white; contours, worn smooth, are whitewashed or painted blue and the effect is reminiscent of the penguin pool at a zoo.

Women wear the white, rather than black, *haik* (unless they are in mourning when the reverse is true); in winter the town is visited by snow. Colour comes from the trellises of violet clematis, the red roofs and the tiled lintels around the doors.

Chaouen was founded in 1471 by Moulay el ben Rashid as a base against Christians, though the kasbah was built in the 17th century by that great gratuitous builder in Moroccan history Moulay Ismail. Christian invasion didn't, in fact, happen until 1920 when the Spanish finally managed to conquer the town. When they did, they discovered Jews, descended from the first refugee settlers, speaking 10th-century Castilian, a language extinct in Spain for over 400 years, and leather craftsmen working in tanned and decorated leather as their ancestors had done in 12th-century Cordoba.

The P28 leading to the town arrives just below the old walls. By climbing up through the market place you reach a brown gate called **Bab el Ain**, overhung by one of the town's typical wrought-iron lanterns. This leads to the main square. The cobbled **Plaza Uta el Hamman**, shaded by trees, strung with lights and lined by bowed cafés, is an excellent place to sit, appreciate the light and inhale the mountain air (not to be confused with the scent of kif emanating from the cafés' upper storeys).

It was here that until 1937, when the practice was outlawed by the Spanish, boy homosexuals were auctioned. The Riffian tribes were staunchly anti-homosexual—Abd el Krim, leader of the Rif Rebellion, made homosexuality illegal—but the J'bala, Gomara and Sehhadja tribes, who populated this area in the western Rif, didn't share their aversion.

Left, a surfeit of whitewash. **Right**, Chaouen's steep and winding streets.

In glowing sandstone on the opposite side of the square, in vivid contrast to the tiled-roofed, sugar-cube housing, is the ruined **kasbah** with its quiet gardens. It can be visited for a few dirhams. To the right of this are the cells where Abd el Krim was eventually imprisoned in l926.

By following the main throughfare to the back of the town, through the **Place du Makhzen** and its cluster of pottery and gemstone stalls, past the succession of tiny shops opening directly on to the steep, cobbled street, you reach the point under the mountains where a waterfall hits the river. Here women wash clothes and sheep's wool. A new car park and tourist facilities are about to do their worst, something the town has generally managed to avoid happening until now, despite having more than its quota of day-trippers from Tangier and the northern resorts.

The Berbers of this region are renowned for their reverence of *marabouts* and it is an area with many religious associations. Chaouen is considered a holy city, as is **Ouezzane**, on the P28 travelling southwest, just brushing the gentlest hills of the Rif on the boundary between the old *bled el makhzen* and the *bled es siba*. It was chosen by Moulay Abdullah, a descendant of Idriss II, to found the Taibia brotherhood in l727.

The *zaouia*, or centre, prospered. Its *shereef*, who lived in a sanctuary separated from the town, was—and some might say still is—considered one of the holiest men in the land. While the authority of the sultans didn't extend to the *bled es siba*, that of the shereef of Ouezzane did. Pilgrims from all over Morocco came for his blessing and criminals sought immunity here.

The sanctuary, surrounded by gardens, was supposed to represent the Islamic paradise. In reality, it had at least one foot in hell. Wine, spirits and kif were sold along its approach and the shereefian family had its share of mortal troubles, caused by congenital insanity.

Sidi Mohammed, shereef in the middle of the l9th century, had a psy-

A *moussem* in Ouezzane.

chopath and a kif-addict among his sons. And he, at the least, was eccentric. Admiring all things European, he decided to marry an English governess called Emily Keene. The marriage was not a success, washing up in a surfeit of drink and womanising. Nevertheless the Englishwoman was calculating enough to extract a large payment from him which lasted the rest of her life.

The *zaouia*, with its distinctive octagonal minaret, attracts people today. The shereef of Ouezzane is still a person of moral influence consulted on matters of religious philosophy. Pilgrims are particularly visible in the spring when they arrive for the annual *moussem*.

In character, the town is rather like Chaouen: dazzlingly clean and pretty; its white houses climbing up the mountain Bou Hellol. Again, there is a strong Andalusian flavour. The larger houses are faced by decorative tiling and fronted by wrought-iron balconies.

Switchback ride: Ouezzane, some would argue, does not really fall in the Rif at all. Below it stretches a fertile plain and the heavily-populated triangle of Souk el Arba, Rabat and Méknès. It formed part of the French zone during the protectorates and it was one of the places where French troops rallied in order to help Spain defeat the Rif Rebellion. The Rif proper continues along the P39 to Ketama.

This journey along the spine of the range passes through the most spectacular scenery in the region. Each switchback reveals a new panorama or unexpected scene, such as a whole village celebrating a wedding on an otherwise deserted mountainside, bride and bridegroom carried shoulder high. Driving is slow, but the road is wide, and outside of winter the route is safe enough.

Vegetation is a strange mixture of holm-oak, pine, gorse and cactus. **Ketama** is heralded by cedar and kif plantations and a large number of Berbers, looking like Franciscan monks in hooded brown *djellabas*, attempting to persuade drivers to stop and buy hashish. The town has little to recommend it apart from its location, though the

The hills above Chaouen.

Tourist Office plugs its virtues as a boar-hunting and [doubtful] skiing centre.

East beyond Ketama, trees become fewer, and the red sandstone of the mountain a more violent colour. **Targuist**, the last stronghold of Abd el Krim and from where the Rifians' ammunition was distributed on muleback, is a gritty, workaday place situated on a small plain. Its streets are laid out in grid fashion. Perhaps for this reason it has a touch of a small North American steel town, though its importance is administrative rather than industrial.

Al Hoceima to the north, on the other hand, reached by taking the P39a from Ait Yussef ou Ali (birthplace of the Abd el Krim brothers), is a seaside resort popular with Moroccan tourists, though it's seen more exciting visitors in its time. It was at Al Hoceima that King Hassan, then crown prince, emulating Spanish tactics in the capture of Abd el Krim, landed with his troops in smuggling boats and a rented British-owned ferry to surprise and defeat the small-scale Rif rebellion of 1959.

The town, on the west side of a large crescent-shaped bay, has a noticeably large number of small hotels. A hotel complex, with the full-range of amenities, appears to take up most of the beach and gives the impression of owning it (after all, possession is nine points of the law); in fact, it is perfectly possible to bathe here.

For a real bargain, and character, **Hotel Florido**, unmistakable in **Place du Rif**, offers a double room for 35 dirhams. It is a round, tiered, 1930s building whose rooms have elegant, French-windows; the ground floor is a popular café, but the tobacco-haze and animation make it feel more like a saloon. Hotel Florido would be perfect in a Hollywood Western.

To the Border: From Al Hoceima to Nador, the landscape changes from the fertile Nekor River plain to virtual desert just south of the Spanish enclave of **Melilla**. **Nador**, below Melilla, is known particularly for its steel plant, an industrial scheme, promised in the

Arcadian idyll.

wake of independence, which took a long time to materialise. The government had planned to develop what was then a village into a regional capital. Consequently many poor mountain Berbers descended on Nador, expecting economic prosperity.

It is also a university town which, along with Oujda, draws all students from the eastern Rif (in the west they go to Tetouan), but can't be the most stimulating environment for the young. Along with Tetouan and Marrakesh (also a university town), Nador experienced riots in 1984.

Beyond this, it is a cultivated plain, watered by the **River Moulouya**. This river, whose Barrage Mohammed V has greatly aided irrigation, marked the boundary between the French and Spanish protectorates. Historically, it has helped form a barrier against Algeria. However, the Beni Merin tribe, the seed of the Merenid dynasty, entered Morocco at this point by taking control of the river valley, then cutting a route through the Taza Gap. The leader of the tribe, Abou Yahya, captured Fez in 1248.

Borders in the Maghreb are determined by politics rather than differences, and an Algerian influence in **Oujda** is instantly felt. The language is similar to Algerian Arabic and many women have adopted an Algerian style of dress (the veils of Algerian women are tiny, covering only the nose and mouth, not extending to the chin and neck—a fact that surprises in view of Algeria's conservative reputation).The music of Oujda, too, is more in tune with Algeria. The type known as Andalusian, which forms the classical music of Northern Morocco—Tangier, Tetouan, Fez—evolved from that of Seville and Cordoba. The Andalusian music of Oujda and Algeria, on the other hand, has its origins in Granada and is more structured in style. Modern *rai* music, fashionable in Europe as well as the Maghreb, developed in the brothels of the border towns of Oujda and Algeria's Oran.

Owing to its strategic importance,

The beaches are excellent.

Oujda has always been fought over. Since its founding in 994, it has passed through many hands: those of the Almoravids, the Almohads, the Merinids, the Saadians, the Alaouites, not to mention the Turks whose empire didn't penetrate much further west than this. It was also the first town to be threatened by the French, who were on the Algerian border long before their protectorate was agreed in 1912.

Apart from the hardcore rucksack contingent and French Jeep drivers planning to plough on to Algeria, comparatively few Western tourists venture as far as Oujda, for despite its turbulent history there is little to see. Most of the bustle is caused by visiting Algerians who holiday on the coast at **Saidia**, just to the north.

Sidi Yahya, however, a lush spot four miles (six km) on a minor road southeast, is an eerily fascinating excursion. The body of Sidi Yahya, reputed to have been John the Baptist, is said to be buried here, and Jewish, Muslim and Christian pilgrims gather. It is a strange place, associated with hermits and steeped in religious rites.

Pieces of coloured cloth are hung in the trees; in the domed tombs animal sacrifices are made, and women seeking fertility wash in the streams (a sight reminiscent of the John the Baptist scene in Martin Scorsese's film *The Last Temptation of Christ*). There is also a grotto called the **Ghar el Houriyat**, or Cave of Houris, the handmaidens of Paradise whom Muslim men wistfully hope await.

Since 1988, political tensions between Algeria and Morocco have slackened—though it's sensible to discover whether there have been any further political conflicts to date. Travel across the border to the towns of picturesque **Tlemcen**, perhaps to see the Almoravid mosque, and **Mansoura** for the Merenid ruins, should be straightforward.

One advantage to such a trip is the opportunity to enter the mosques: the Moroccan exclusion of non-Muslims to these most interesting of Islamic monuments is guaranteed ultimately to be a frustration.

Natural assets: The road from Nador to Oujda skirts the **Beni Snassen** mountains. If the Rif hasn't produced an aversion to any landscape much above sea-level, an agreeable detour might be to visit the richly cultivated **Zezgel gorges** via **Taforalt**, a small village with a Wednesday market, and the **Grotte du Chameau**, a cave which, as its name suggests, contains a stalactite shaped like a camel. Less obviously, it is reputed to cure sterility.

Routes through the Rif: There are three main passages through the Rif. The **P26** from Ouezzane skirts the grander peaks, and for those wanting only an impression of the range, with less tricky mountain driving, this is the best route to Fez.

A more spectacular way, however, is the **S302** from **Ketama**. This is known as the **Route de l'Unité**, which was built along the old caravan passage to Fez by voluntary national effort after independence. Initiated by Mehdi ben Barka, a prominent figure in the nationalist left before his radical, verging on republican, views prompted his exile and later disappearance in Paris, it was intended to link the French and Spanish zones. Like "Operation Ploughing", a scheme to cultivate over 300,000 wasted acres (120,000 hectares), it was as much a public relations exercise as useful development of the country.

Nevertheless, begun in 1957 when the country was still enjoying the euphoria of freedom, this was the first road to be built from north to south in the Rif—the Spanish never having been very enterprising in the development of their zone. The other main throughfare through the Rif is the equally beautiful **S312** off the P39 at **Talamagait**. Both are punctuated by villages containing petrol stations.

The advantage of the latter route is that it leads to **Taza**, an important town strategically and the capital of Morocco at the beginning of the Almohad, Merenid and Alaouite dynasties—hence its impressive fortifications. It was through Taza that Moulay Idriss, founder of the first orthodox Muslim dynasty, came.

THE NORTHWEST COAST

The triangle of land delineated by the main roads connecting **Souk el Arba du Rharb**, **Fez** and **Rabat/Casablanca** is the most densely populated in Morocco. The P2 from Tangier, therefore, is one of the busiest stretches of highway. It links the rest of Morocco, and indeed Africa, to the point of closest contact with Europe.

Along here the migrant workers ferry. Roadside stalls, selling anything from melons to pottery, are many; and "meat-sandwich" cafés, all looking identical, their smoking braziers casting a veritable cloud over the road, abound—Moroccans being frequent stoppers and constant eaters on any journey.

The coast along this Atlantic stretch has been heavily effected by Spain and Portugal. In the 15th and 16th centuries the Moroccan ports were regularly besieged, and one by one they fell under Spanish or Portuguese rule. The area, along with Tangier, Ceuta, Tetouan and Rabat, also formed part of what was known in the 17th century as the Barbary Coast, monopolised by corsairs, many of whom, contrary to popular belief, were not Muslim pirates at all, but European.

Asilah, lying 30 miles (46 km) south of Tangier, and **Larache** (54 miles/87 km distant) are most reminiscent of Portugal and Spain, having been colonised by both intermittently until 1691 and 1689 respectively. These early influences were compounded by the Treaty of Fez in 1912, when both towns fell under the Spanish protectorate. They contain large populations of Spanish origin and Spanish rather than French is the second language.

Asilah, a favourite excursion from Tangier, is a model town. Citrus trees and good, informal fish restaurants, with outdoor tables sporting check tablecloths, line its streets, and its medina looks positively vacuumed, such is the conspicuously high level of hygiene. Like Essouiara, in the south, it draws artists and many of the white houses of its medina are enlivened by brightly-painted murals.

Every August a music festival attracts popular, classical, jazz and folk performers from all over the world, and any time of the year its cafés are good places to experience live Moroccan music—usually in the late afternoons.

Its walls, punctuated by vantage points from which you gain a view of the excellent beach and the harbour (where they are now building a marina), were originally built by the Portuguese. The **Palace**, where the music festival is held, is more recent. It was built in 1909 by the infamous **Shereef Ahmed el Raisuni**, a self-styled leader credited with considerable *baraka* by the J'bala tribesmen in the hills around Tangier. He achieved fame through a series of kidnappings, most notably of the London *Times* journalist Walter Harris, who, though imprisoned with a headless corpse, was forgiving enough to befriend his captor and later invite him to his villa in Tangier.

Preceding pages: wall painting in Asilah. Left, villa-fringed Atlantic coast near Rabat. Right, fishermen inspect their catch.

El Raisuni's relationship with the Spanish protectors was more equivocal, and out of fear rather than admiration they made him governor of the region. Revelling in his new-found grandeur, he established his palace in Asilah. The peasants forced to build it called the palace "The House of Tears", alluding to the hardship of their labours. Being a man of spirit, however, Raisuni was not content to languish in splendour and was soon in revolt again. He fought the Spanish sporadically for a further eight years. An Englishwoman, Rosita Forbes, visited Raisuni in 1924 and recorded his biography, a classic work on Morocco.

Larache, on the mouth of the Oued Loukos, is more Spanish than Portuguese in character. **Stork's Castle**, the fortification overlooking the bay, was built by its 17th-century Spanish masters. The **Place de la Liberation** (previously Plaza de España), the main circus, was built during the time of the protectorate, when Larache served as the chief port for the Spanish zone. Hotels, bars and restaurants—many serving excellent fish—all reflect the Spanish influence, though the blue and white paintwork is badly peeling and the stucco embellishments a little knocked about. Larache's charm is one of decayed elegance.

The best view of the town is from its beach on the far side of the **Oued Loukos**, approached by a circuitous route following the turning off to Lixus, a kilometre or so to the north of the town, or after crossing the estuary by boat. A foreground of moored fishing vessels is backed by the fortified walls of Stork's Castle and the medina's houses rising in a higgledy-piggledy crown.

The Roman town of **Lixus**, its remains scattered over a hill on the right-hand side of the road which leads to the beach, was in fact founded by the Phoenicians in about 1100 B.C. It is one of several claimants to the site for the mythical Garden of Hesperides containing the golden apples sought by Hercules in his penultimate labour.

Moonrise over the ramparts of Asilah.

Apart from some megalithic stones, built into the acropolis and oriented towards the sun, few remains pre-date the Roman period. At the top of the hill there are foundations of temples, a theatre and amphitheatre, ramparts and houses and, near the bottom of the hill, the remains of salt and *garum* (anchovy paste) factories.

Further south, the road passes the now functionary **Ksar el Kebir**, once an important power base coveted by the Spanish and Portuguese in Larache and Asilah, but which British playwright Joe Orton more recently described as the "Leicester of Morocco". Beyond, outside Arbaoua, is the old **protectorate border**—the former checkpoint gathering weeds. During the French and Spanish protectorates, passports had to be shown in order to pass this point. After independence, Mohammed V made an ceremonial visit to the spot to declare the point closed.

Beyond is the turning to **Ouezzane** (a rewarding detour: see the chapter on the Rif); and the road to the resort and holy village of **Moulay Bousselham** across a large lagoon. A *moussem* is held in the village every summer, when pilgrims visit a cave, apparently—though hard to credit—to suck a sacred stalactite.

Back on the P2, the surrounding hills begin to level into a rich agricultural plain whose focus is the market town of **Souk el Arba du Rharb** (*rharb* meaning west). Its industrial centre is **Kenitra**, a large town founded by the French in 1913 which used to lodge a US military base. This is now defunct but more than compensated for by Moroccan forces.

Kenitra is not particularly diverting, but the **Kasbah de Mehdiya** seven miles (11 km) to its south on the mouth of the Oued Sebou is impressive. The Spanish who captured the point in 1614 built the fortress upon a prototype conceived by Louis XIV's military engineer. Moulay Ismail, however, with his usual vigour, drove the Spanish out and established his own man there, the Caid Ali er Rif, the governor responsible for the Moroccan gateway and palace.

Donkey and trap: common transport in the west.

RABAT

The town of Rabat was founded in the 10th century near the ruins of the Phoenician and later Roman port of Sala Colonia in the mouth of the River Bou Regreg. This first *ribat*, or Islamic military community, later became the capital of the great 12th-century Almohad conqueror Yacoub el Mansour, who ruled from Tunisia to northern Spain. Ribat el Fath, the Fortress of Victory, was the assembly point for his armies, which bivouacked in the shelter of three miles (five km) of massive walls.

With the death of Yacoub el Mansour, Rabat lost much of its importance and was not to become the capital again until the French occupation in 1912. By then the town of Rabat—the present medina—was one of five separate entities: the medina itself; the adjoining Kasbah of the Oudayas; the *mechouar* or palace complex situated some distance away; beyond this the ruins of Chella; and finally, across the Bou Regreg from the Oudaya, the old town of Salé. The centre of the modern town was then grazing land between the medina and the *mechouar*, still partly enclosed by the ruins of the Almohad walls. Horsemen galloped across this plain in the traditional fantasia to pay homage to the sultan on his infrequent visits to his Rabat palace.

Now all is engulfed in the Rabat-Salé agglomeration of over a million inhabitants, due to reach one and a half million by the end of the century. Modern **Rabat** is staid, heavily policed and respectable, with its poor areas well out of sight or camouflaged by "walls of shame". Casablancais may call it provincial, but by Moroccan standards Rabat is a tolerant and (unlike Salé) a Westernised city. The *ville nouvelle* or New Town built during the French Protectorate has filled up the space between the medina and the Almohad walls and spilt over into other *quartiers*.

Despite the overflow, seen from the outside, these ochre walls still seem to encircle the town. From the great gate of **Bab Rouah**, finest of the five city gates and now an art gallery, they run down past lawns and orange-trees to **Bab el Hed** at the corner of the medina, where the **Marché Central** stands. It was at Bab el Hed that the last pre-protectorate sultan exhibited the heads of defeated rebels. Now for most of the year, swifts and martins flock there at dusk, nesting in the regular holes in the masonry (designed to support the crossbeams of small mobile platforms for repairwork to the walls).

On the other side of the town another well-preserved section of Almohad wall encloses the palace area and, beyond the palace, Chella overlooks the valley.

Principal sights: Following the road round above the valley, one comes to the principal Almohad site in Rabat, and the city's invariable symbol, the **Hassan Tower**, magnificently situated on the crest of a hill commanding both Salé and Rabat. This is the unfinished

Preceding pages, the Hassan Tower and unfinished mosque, Rabat. **Left**, guarding the mausoleum of King Mohammed V. **Right**, downtown Rabat.

minaret of the great Hassan Mosque, constructed by Yacoub el Mansour in the last five years of his reign after his victory over the kings of Castile and Leon at Alarcos .

At his death in 1199 work seems to have ceased, but the main structure of the mosque was well advanced. The design was monumental: 21 east-to-west aisles in the prayer-hall, with space for 40,000 worshippers (double the Karaouyine in Fez) made it the largest mosque in the west and the second in all Islam. El Mansour, it is said, wanted his whole army to pray together.

The shell of the mosque was destroyed at the same time as the city of Lisbon in the earthquake of 1755. Many of the 400 columns have now been re-erected upon a foundation of modern flagstones. Parts of the mosque's outer wall survive, and a large sunken water-tank near the tower, which was to have fed the fountains in the ablutions court, has been converted into a monument to the victims of the independence struggle. But the site of the mosque is really no more now than a great white open space between the modern mausoleum on one side and the Hassan Tower on the other.

The tower, designed by the same architect as the Giralda in Seville and the Koutoubia in Marrakesh, rises to only 165 ft (50 metres), (the height of the Koutoubia) out of its projected 265 ft. Within the tower's eight-foot-thick walls is an internal ramp up which mules carried building materials and which (intermittent restoration permitting) is usually open to visitors. The climb itself and the spendid view from the top convince one of the real height of the truncated structure despite its stocky look.

With its 16-metre-square cross-section, as against the Koutoubia's 12 metres, the Hassan Tower would, if completed with its upper ranges of tilework and its lantern, have appeared more slender than either of its sister towers. But the harmonies of its decorative carving (different on each face at the lower level, the same on three

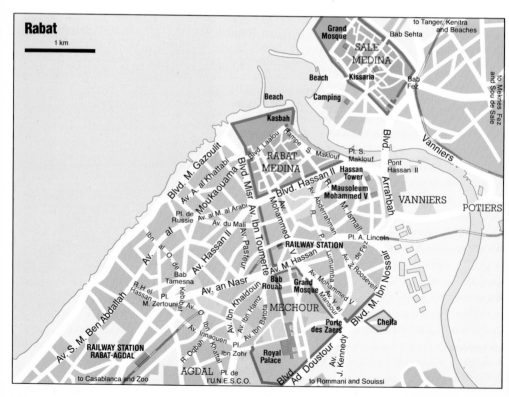

152

faces at the upper), the magnificence of the site and the rich ochre of its stone (though sadly discoloured in places by restoration) make it one of the most memorable buildings in Morocco.

It is, however, towards the latterday kitsch of **Mohammed V's Mausoleum**, on the other side of the rows of columns, that the busloads of visitors prefer to direct their attention. The main building, housing the tombs of the late King and of his youngest son, is flanked by a sunken mosque beyond which is the structure of another mausoleum, as yet unoccupied. All are the costly but uninspired products of architectural and decorative styles unchanged in 400 years.

But the mausoleum is redeemed by the genuine popular piety of its many Moroccan visitors. To the traditional religious veneration paid to a sultan is added respect for a hero of the independence movement and an affectionate memory of the first king in Moroccan history to have ruled unselfishly.

From the Hassan Tower, roads lead down to the rather seedy **riverside** where fishing boats dock and a large fleet of rowing-boats carry passengers across to Salé. In earlier times lighters discharged cargo from ships moored outside the river mouth at these wharves. And it is from here, looking towards the sea, that the **Kasbah of the Oudayas** can be best seen.

Built by Yacoub el Mansour on the site of the original *ribat*, in former times the fortress of the Oudaya, itself a small town, also contained the sultan's residence in Rabat.

In the 17th century, the period of the corsair state known as the Republic of Bou Regreg, the Kasbah's inhabitants lived by piracy. Their captives used to be sold in the **Old Wool Market**, a triangular space now surrounded by souvenir shops, facing the Oudaya entrance on the medina side of the road.

Moulay Ismail, whose reign spanned and paralleled that of Louis XIV, put an end to the vicious little republic, took over the corsair business himself and

The mausoleum of King Mohammed V.

constructed a new palace within the Kasbah, which is now the Museum of Moroccan Arts. He also installed in the Kasbah the warlike Oudaya tribe whom he charged with the tasks of subjugating the equally fractious Zaer tribe south of Rabat and keeping the corsairs in line.

Approaching the main entrance, the **Oudaya Gate**, you are well advised to purchase half an hour's peace and quiet by engaging one of the many freelance guides. Thus protected, you can begin to take in the façade of this superb Almohad gate, with its extraordinary superposition of arch around arch, working outwards from the basic keyhole profile of the entrance to the massive square block of the whole gate. Contemplated at length, the façade begins to shimmer and dance with the tension between inward and outward pressures around the arch and the interplay of different geometrical motifs.

Pass through the angled entrance in the side tower and you find yourself next to the interior face of the gate and in the main street of the Kasbah. Halfway along this street on the left is the **Oudaya Mosque**, rebuilt in the 18th century by the renegade English architect Ahmed el Ingles.

Any turning to the right off the main street followed downhill will bring you to the **Café Maure** on the ramparts overlooking the river, which connects with the Andalusian gardens and the **Museum of Moroccan Arts**. This not only contains a fine display of jewellery, costumes and carpets, but is of interest in itself as a handsomely decorated royal residence, with elegant reception rooms opening on to a central courtyard.

The Oudaya Kasbah stands at the northwest corner of Rabat **medina**, the four sides of which run first along the river, then past the cemetery on the coast, down the Almohad walls running from the lighthouse in to Bab el Hed, and finally along the Andalusian walls on Avenue Hassan II. When in the 17th century the last wave of Muslim refugees were expelled from Spain, many of them settled in Salé and Rabat.

They found the latter in ruins and almost deserted and the area within the old Almohad defences far too large for their needs. So they put up the Andalusian walls to contain the part they settled, and this—the present medina—they rebuilt in the style of their Spanish homeland.

When in 1912 the French made Rabat the protectorate capital, Marshal Lyautey, in a pattern later followed in all the old towns of Morocco, forbade the development of the medina by European builders and ordered the creation of a new town outside its walls. The first consequence of this policy was urban segregation, but in the long run it has preserved the traditional Moroccan towns better than any others in North Africa.

Carpetbaggers: One enters the medina a little downhill from the Oudaya Gate by the Rue des Consuls, the only street in which foreign consuls could formerly set up shop, and today largely but not exclusively a tourist shopping street. The first section is occupied by carpet, rug and wool merchants. Popular types of carpet include the Ribati, with gaudy reds and blues in geometrical patterns, and the generally smaller Taznacht with their softer-hued vegetable dyes and cruder patterns often including animal forms (never as strictly taboo here as elsewhere in the Muslim world).

Most of the big carpets are now produced by sweated labour in carpet factories, but private carpet-makers sell in the souk held in this street every Thursday morning.

If buying a carpet, bargain for yourself. For a given size and type and quality of carpet (knots per square cm), test the price in a shop first, but don't buy there. Ask the dealer's price and, when pressed for *your* price, name a figure a bit over half his. Always remain courteous and friendly, and admire the carpets.

The price the first dealer stops at is the price to try and beat in the next shop. If speaking French to him, asides to a companion in English (which the carpet-seller will understand) can be a

<u>Preceding pages</u>, all tombstones point towards Mecca. <u>Below</u>, to the Andalusian gardens in the Kasbah of the Oudayas.

156

useful tactic. But remember that what for you is a game is the dealer's livelihood.

Lots of leather: Halfway up the Rue des Consuls, side by side on the left, are two old *fondouks* (inns for travelling merchants and their pack animals) which now house leather workers. A few yards further up on the left a more modern *fondouk* has become a cloth-sellers' *kissaria* (shopping arcade), arranged round a small garden. The street continues with leather and clothes shops until you come to a small crossroads.

Ahead and on the left is the former Jewish quarter, or *mellah*, while to the right the road leads through a covered market (jewellers—closed on Fridays—and shoeshops) and past the medina's **Grand Mosque**. On the corner of the sidestreet beside the mosque is a 14th-century Merenid fountain, a survival of pre-Andalusian Rabat now incorporated into the façade of a bookshop.

The covered market leads straight on into the **Rue Souika**, the medina's main shopping street, which emerges at the **Marché Central**. While the Rabat medina is too Westernised to have preserved the strict street-by-street trade groupings, there is still a tendency for sellers of roast sheep's heads and cows' feet to cluster in one stretch and those of lingerie, spices, ironmongery or cassettes in others.

The area behind the Marché Central is veined with *derbs*—those narrow cul-de-sacs between windowless walls leading off the main thoroughfares. Within the *derb* massive iron-studded doors open, through the traditional blind entrance-way with a right-angle bend, into the courtyards of private houses. These old-style, inward-turned houses were described by Leonara Peets in 1932 as "lidless clay boxes in which the Moroccan man hides his women and his home life...a rectangular well of two storeys, with all the windows directed onto the internal patio." It was on the roof terraces of such houses that the womenfolk, who

Left, light and shadows in the souks. Right, selling babouches, the popular open-backed shoes.

otherwise never went out except to visit the baths, were allowed to emerge in the late afternoon, when men were banished from the rooftops.

Behind the Marché Central, to the left as one faces the medina, there is a small **flea-market** in which interesting oddments are sometimes to be found.

Government property: The Marché Central faces the **Boulevard Mohammed V**, which runs through the centre of the New Town shopping area before broadening out into an elegant palm-lined promenade, scene of the evening walkabout, past the **modern Parliament** building and straight on up to the 18th-century **Grand Mosque** (cathedral mosque) of Rabat at the top of the hill.

Do not, like many tourists, take the school entrance next to the mosque for that of the **Palace**, which is actually 200 yards further to the right, halfway between the mosque and Bab Rouah. Visitors are allowed to walk or drive through the archway into the *mechouar* (Palace area, containing **Dar El Makh-**

zen—the House of Government).

Here one enters a town within a town, containing the modern palace, the Prime Minister's office and the Ministry of Religious Affairs. The resident population of 2,000 includes extended branches of the Alaouite ruling family (others are distributed among the palaces in other towns) as well as retainers serving and retired, a guards regiment and cavalry. The complex also contains a mosque, at which the King, when in Rabat, leads the midday Friday prayer on feast days. These occasions are accompanied by a great deal of ceremony, including impressive processions both to and from the mosque.

Burial of the dead: The central road through the *mechouar* brings you out through the Almohad walls on the far side, just 10 minutes' walk (towards the left) from the **Chella Necropolis**. The walled area of Chella, stretching down the hillside almost to the level of the valley, was for 1,500 years the site of the port—Phoenician, Roman, Berber and then Arab—of Sala, until in the 13th century its inhabitants took themselves and the name of their town across the river.

But Rabat remained the assembly point for armies bound for the Spanish wars, and the first three Merinid sultans in the 13th and 14th centuries used Chella as a burial place for their dynasty. (The other Merinid necropolis is outside the walls of Fez, their main capital.)

You pass through an unusual gate (more ornamental than defensive—Muslim graves contain no treasure) with stalactite corbels surmounting the gate towers like hands upraised in Muslim-style prayer. This gateway, whose style is positively sprightly after the massiveness of the Almohad gates, must once have blazed with colour from its now lost tilework.

Inside, paths lead down through half-wild gardens and scented trees (notably the huge white trumpets of the hallucinogenic *dattura* or belladonna tree) to the cluster of domed saints' tombs to one side of the ruined Merinid

A favourite nesting spot for storks.

mosque and *zaouia*, and over on the left, the excavations of the Romano-Berber town. These remains of **Sala Colonia**— or what was left of it after the Merinids had quarried it for their own buildings—can be viewed from the outside only, but visitors can walk all over the ruins of the mosque and the royal tombs behind the mosque.

This is, incidentally, the only mosque in Morocco apart from Moulay Ismail's tomb in Méknès that non-Muslims may enter (following the ban imposed by Marshal Lyautey). One feels here, even more so than elsewhere in Morocco, the haunted charm of ruins which are not sterilised and minutely patched but intertwined with fig-trees, overgrown with flowers and grazed by sheep— much as the 17th century discovered Italy. Tomorrow's loss is today's gain.

The doorway into the mosque leads first into what was the ablutions court, and then into the prayer-hall, behind the rear wall of which were the burial chambers. Ahead and to the right is the **tomb of Abou el Hassan**, known as the

Black Sultan, with part of a richly decorated wall still standing behind it. His wife, the former Christian slave Shems Ed Duna (Morning Sun), whose saintliness is commemorated in local legend, is buried to the far left (the sexes being segregated in death as in life). This mosque was built by Abou el Hassan's grandfather, Abou Youssef Yacoub, the "King of the djinns", who is believed to have buried his gold nearby and set the djinns to guard it.

To the left of the mosque stand the ruins of the Black Sultan's *zaouia*, a place of religious retreat and study. Small cubicles surround a courtyard with a central pool, beyond which a small prayer-hall culminates in a *mihrab* (niche pointing towards Mecca) encircled untypically by a narrow passageway, now blocked with thorn branches and rubble. Legend has it that walking seven times around this *mihrab* is as good as a pilgrimage to Mecca— perhaps the reason why it is now blocked up.

At the other end of the central court,

The ruins and wild gardens of Chella.

down some steps beside the minaret, are the old latrines with accommodation for eight (generous provision, surely, for the occupants of only 16 study cells). The inmates would, of course, have slept in dormitories above the cubicles. The minarets of both *zaouia* and mosque, as well as some of the plane-trees and saints' shrines, are hosts to that bringer of good luck, the stork's nest.

Emerging again from the mosque on the side opposite the Roman remains, you find the ground slopes down to the ruins of a *hammam* (steam bath), in which a sunken pool now houses a colony of three and four-foot eels. Fed with hardboiled eggs on sale from helpful children, these sacred creatures confer fertility upon women and aches and pains upon those who doubt their power or seek to harm them. They are ruled over by a giant eel with long hair and golden rings, and draw their magic from the saintly Shems, as does the small spring rising in the gardens below the ruins.

Archaeological finds: Those disappointed by the ruins of Sala Colonia should console themselves with a visit to the **Archaeological Museum**—by no means the least of Rabat's splendours. A five-minute walk from the Grand Mosque, in a sidestreet next to Radio Télévision Marocaine, this collection is notable for the superb bronzes recovered from the excavations at Volubilis, the Romano-Berber capital of Mauritania Tingitana.

When Rome ordered the evacuation of Volubilis in the third century, the citizens, expecting to return shortly, buried their works of art outside the city, where they were to remain undisturbed for 17 centuries. These pieces are kept apart in the **Salle des Bronzes** (tip required).

In addition to many charming small Graeco-Roman statuettes, there are three or four pieces of such grandeur that one wonders at most visitors' neglect of this museum: the Guard-Dog (centrepiece of a fountain); the ivy-crowned Youth (the Ephebus, copied from Praxiteles); the Rider; and above all the busts presumed to be those of Cato the Younger and the young King Juba II of Mauritania Tingitana. The Head of Cato, not unlike Sir John Gielgud in its austere and fastidious attitude, is entirely convincing as the enemy of Octavius Caesar who killed himself for a principle.

The Head of Juba, however, is the *pièce de résistance* of the collection— the product of *"pays berbère, occupant romain, esthétique grecque"*.

Undoubtedly a Berber youth, it could easily have been a sculpture of their king. The short *retroussé* upper-lip is characteristic and seen all over Morocco. It is the Chaplinesque appearance (all moustache and front teeth) seen hunched over the wheel in all Rabat taxis as they edge their way through the traffic, cautious and scrupulous, and unlike any other taxis in the country.

The historical Juba, a famous scholar of his time, was a protégé of the Emperor Augustus, and married Cleopatra Silene, the daughter of Anthony and Cleopatra. He reigned for 45 years. Their son Ptolemy, summoned to Caligula's games at Lyons, was murdered by the mad emperor, allegedly for wearing a more brilliant purple toga than Caligula himself. (Apart from animals for the amphitheatres, indigo dye and wheat were ancient Morocco's main exports.)

From Roman games to modern: King Hassan is a keen golfer and the **Royal Golf Club**, on the outskirts of Rabat off the Rommani road, comprises two excellent 18-hole courses to which visitors have access as temporary members.

Capital restaurants: Eating out in Rabat is no problem, even if the choice is a little limited for a capital city. A traditional Moroccan restaurant off the Place Piètry in the New Town, **L'Oasis** serves moderately priced formal meals in a traditional setting. An excellent and very cheap Lebanese restaurant in an arcade opposite the Hôtel Terminus by the station serves good meat and vegetarian dishes (but no alcohol).

Perhaps more typical of local taste in

eating out are the Spanish-style fish restaurants. Cheapest and most Moroccan is **Le Mont Doré** in l'Océan (the quarter next to the medina). Others include the beach restaurant on the lighthouse side of the Oudaya and the **Miramar** on the beach at El Harhoura, on the coast road just south of Rabat.

There are also good Chinese restaurants—for example, **La Pagoda** behind the railway station, and **Le Dragon d'Or**, slightly out of town, next to Supermarché Souissi. Good pizzerias include **La Mamma** behind the Hôtel Balima in the town centre and the **Sorrento** in the Place de Bourgogne. There is a pancake restaurant called **Le Crépescule** near the curiously appealing Maghrebin-Gothic cathedral in the town centre, and French cooking is to be had in all the main hotels.

Twin city: Crossing the main Hassan II bridge over the **River Bou Regreg** (Father of Reflection) brings one directly to the centre of Rabat's twin city. It is hard to believe that **Salé** and Rabat are nowadays part of a single conglomeration. Crossing the river is a journey in time and certainly in moral space. For Salé, despite its prodigious current growth, remains strictly Muslim (a dry town), culturally resistant and (theoretically) maintains an anti-European tradition going back to the last wave of Andalusian refugees from the Spanish Inquisition and the tradition of the corsairs, who were active well into the 19th century. But the Slawis' courtesy today compares well with most, and foreigners have no hassles here.

The town of Salé has been so called since 1260 when, following the sack of the former town on this site by Alfonso X of Castile and the enslavement of most of its inhabitants, the population of Chella (Sala) crossed the river to settle here and rebuild the town. For the next six centuries Salé's economic importance was greater than that of Rabat.

From the 13th to the 16th century it was Morocco's principal trading port

Rabat's beach.

and when, after the last wave of Andalusian resettlement in the early 17th century, Rabat and Salé formed the short-lived corsair state of Bou Regreg, Salé was predominant. The hero of Daniel Defoe's story *Robinson Crusoe* was captured and sold into slavery by the Sallee Rovers.

From the Salé end of the Hassan II Bridge, the first town gate you see is the unusually tall **Bab Mrisa** (Port Gate), built by the Merinid sultans to admit sea-going boats by means of a now-vanished canal to a dock within the town walls. Following the outer walls up to the left brings one to a crossroads (Bab el Haja) in front of the Town Hall. Turn right here and take the left-hand side of the square ahead of you.

Straight ahead and bearing left, you enter the main trading streets of the **medina**. Here craftsmen and shopkeepers flock together by trades, grouped guild-like in their own narrow streets. This is very much a traditional Moroccan town, visited by few tourists and entirely free of hustlers.

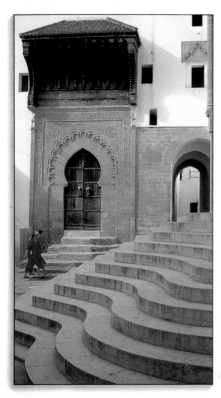

The long straight road up to the left (Rue de la Grande Mosquée) takes you to the area of merchants' mansions and religious centres (*zaouias*) around the Grand Mosque. Behind the mosque to the right is the **Medrassa el Hassan**—a lovely little Merinid religious college, just as finely wrought and well preserved as the great Bou Inania *medersa* in Fez and Méknès, but much smaller. There is the same ubiquity of decoration—first *zellige* (faïence mosaic), then incised stucco, and finally carved cedar-wood. Visitors are admitted to the dormitories in the upper storey and even to the roof, with its view across the river to Rabat.

Beyond the Grand Mosque on the seaward side lies the shrine of **Sidi Abdallah ben Hassan**, a 16th-century saint revered by the corsairs. His cult survives in an annual procession on the eve of Mouloud (the Prophet's birthday) in which men in period costume carry large lanterns, intricately made of coloured wax, from Bab Mrisa, up to the saint's shrine, where they dance and sing.

Away from the town, there is a thriving cooperative of **potteries**, on the Salé side of the river, beside the airport road out of Rabat. Salé pottery is marked by delicate economical designs in white and pastel shades, often including the Roman *fibula*, or brooch fastener—a traditional motif in Berber decoration. Unfortunately this faïence work chips easily, unlike the hotter-fired Fez stoneware with its characteristic scrollwork and resonant blues and whites.

Six miles (10 km) north of Salé on the Kenitra road, recognisable by the coloured sun-hats for sale on racks outside an arched metal gate, are the **Jardins Exotiques**, a botanical adventureland with liana bridges and winding jungle paths. Designed by a French conservationist to illustrate a variety of ecosystems, the gardens are now rather run down, but the obstacle course is still fun.

Four miles (six km) further north there is a turning off to the five-star Hôtel Firdaous and the attractive sandy

To the Grand Mosque.

beaches of the *Plage des Nations* (where the sea is dangerous).

Rabat to Casablanca: Many of the Atlantic beaches are subject to currents which make swimming dangerous. But a number of small sandy bays between Rabat and Casablanca are both attractive and safe. Six miles (10 km) south of Rabat on the coast road brings you to **Temara Plage**, with a series of beaches—Contrebandiers, Sables d'Or (Sidi el Abed) and Sehb ed Dahab. Around Sables d'Or there are several restaurants and discos, also sports facilities, while Sehb Ed Dahab boasts a new marina. In summer, however, these beaches are appallingly crowded.

Temara Ville, a couple of kilometres inland, has Morocco's only zoo, a well-maintained collection (originally the King's own) in extensive grounds.

A little further south, where the coast road crosses the small Oued Ykem river (by the Ain Atiq motorway exit), two campsites and two restaurants cater for visitors to the attractive **Plage Rose-Marie**. The Hôtel Le Kasbah hires out horses which you can ride along the beach, has a good pool and, in summer, a nightclub. If camping in summer, be warned: in the holiday season Moroccan campsites are often chock-a-block with semi-permanent tent cities, and camp life is far from restful.

At **Skhirate**, 19 miles (30 km) south of Rabat, the King's seaside palace—scene of a bloody attempted coup in 1971—is flanked by excellent beaches and two hotels.

Forty-four miles (70 km) after Rabat and 19 miles (30 km) before Casa lies the long thin coastal strip of **Mohammedia**—a town with a split personality: on the Casa side, an oil port, industry and poor districts; on the Rabat side (described as East Mohammedia), a playground for rich Casablancais, with hotels, nice beaches and sports facilities that include an 18-hole golf-course, a marina, water sports, riding (Hôtel Samir), a casino and a racecourse. It's a relaxed sort of place and has two excellent Spanish-style fish restaurants.

The world goes by.

CASABLANCA

To most English speakers, the name of **Casablanca** evokes good living, romance and adventure in a tropical setting. This was the Sin City image that the 1943 Bogart film conveyed to cinema-goers in the drab war years. It has long been associated with brothels. More recently, it gained notoriety as a centre for sex-change operations.

But nothing could be further from the prosaic reality of Morocco's economic capital. For many fun-seeking Gulf Arabs (known to Moroccans as "penguins"), Casablanca may have replaced Beirut, but it is still a city that shuts down before 10 p.m., and from which Moroccans and foreigners escape when they want to enjoy themselves. It is also a city of extensive poor areas and sealed off *bidonvilles* which have been the scene of murderous bread riots twice in the last decade. The first *bidonvilles* sprung up as long ago as the 19th century; they mushroomed in the Post-War years; and still little has been done to address their problem.

The original Berber town of Anfa was destroyed by the 1755 Lisbon earthquake. Rebuilt as Dar El Beida (the White House, or Casa Blanca), its population by the turn of the century had barely reached 20,000—not a tenth of that of Fez at the time. Since then, however, it has risen to be the main port and industrial powerhouse of Morocco, with a population variously estimated from the official figure of nearly three million up to an unofficial five million. This makes it Africa's second city after Cairo.

At the centre of Casablanca there are two large squares, the Place des Nations Unies and the Place Mohammed V. From the latter, a road runs down to the port entrance and Casa-Port railway station. This road marks the eastern edge of Casablanca's small and rather dull **old medina**, at the lower end of which, facing the sea, stands the 18th-century fort, the **Borj Sidi Mohammed ben Abdullah**, built to resist Portu-

guese raids. The only reason for visiting the medina is to go shopping in Derb Omar, in which, the Casablancais boast, "you can buy anything"—its only resemblance to Harrods. On the other side of the Place Mohammed V there is a modern pedestrians-only **shopping precinct**, between the Place d'Aknoul and the Boulevard de Paris.

Architectural attractions: Around the **Place des Nations Unies**, on the other side of the Place Mohammed V from the medina, stand four monumental public buildings from the protectorate period—very much the sort of thing that Moroccan visitors to the city come to see: the **Grande Poste**; the **Wilaya** (Prefecture), with its clock tower, the **Palais de Justice** with elaborately tiled courtyards; and the **Banque d'Etat**. The first three are in the neo-Mauresque style cooked up by French architects in the 1920s and 1930s.

Other examples of the exuberant exploitation of exotic themes by European architects, combined with local craftsmanship, are seen in particular

Preceding pages, Casablanca, Morocco's high-rise city. **Left**, the Royal Mansour Hotel. **Right**, Casablancan elegance.

along the **Boulevard Mohammed V** and in the surrounding streets, where carved façades abound, often with decorative tiles or *zellige* mosaics, ornate entrance-ways and some remarkably elaborate wrought-iron grilles on doorways.

A 10-minute drive from the centre takes you to the **new medina**, alias **Quartier Habbous**, a French orientalist folly built in the 1930s. This charming but totally spurious complex, in which a whole range of Hispano-Mauresque styles are represented, is now a shopping district (not primarily for tourists) specialising in Arabic bookshops and utilitarian objects of a traditional nature. It's a Disneyland medina, fun to walk around and agreeably hassle-free. Worth visiting here is the famous **Patisserie Bennis** in the Rue Fkih El Gabbas.

From the entrance to the port, the **Corniche** leads westwards along the shore to the fashionable beach clubs (admission DH 30 and upwards) and restaurants of **Ain Diab**, a rich residential area of Saudi palaces, bikini-clad girls and veiled domestics.

Along the Corniche one passes the **Hassan II Mosque**, the gift of a grateful nation to its sovereign on the occasion of his 60th birthday in 1989. This costly building (complete with library, museum, steam baths, Koranic school and conference facilities) is built on the seabed with water on three sides, and was financed by universal voluntary subscriptions. Its position complies nicely with a Koranic saying:"Allah has His throne on the water."

The money was collected by various means. Officials called on every home in the land, and some employers deducted a percentage from their workers' wages in order to contribute to the coffers. The King's highest officials are said to have fallen over themselves to be generous. In all, more than £325 million was collected, but then such an ambitious mosque wasn't likely to come cheap.

The prayer-hall, with an electrically-operated sun-roof over the central

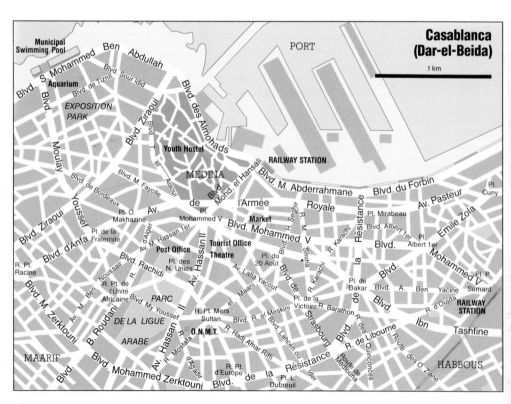

court, has space for 20,000 worshippers while another 80,000 can pray on the surrounding esplanade. The minaret is 82 ft (25 metres) square and 575 ft (175 metres) high, which makes it the tallest religious building in the world, beating the Great Pyramid of Cheops by 98 ft (30 metres) and St Peter's by 131 ft (40 metres).

A 20-mile-long visible laser beam, *Star Wars*-style, is also planned. Its purpose will be to point, like a giant finger, from the top of the minaret towards Mecca. If it becomes a reality, it should prove an interesting aeronautical hazard. Visible for hundreds of miles out to sea, this is the largest mosque in Africa and the westernmost monument of Islam. Unlike El Mansour's Hassan Mosque in Rabat, this one is earthquake-proof.

Where to eat: The gourmet is well served in Casablanca. Moroccan-style restaurants include the pleasant and reasonably priced **Ouarzazate** (Rue Mohamed El Qorri, off Boulevard Mohammed V), the **Bahj** (Rue Colbert, also off Mohammed V), or the more up-market **Al Mounia** (Rue du Prince Moulay Abdallah, off the Boulevard de Paris) and the **Sijilmassa** (Rue de Biarritz—an extension of the Corniche at Ain Diab). For the latter establishments, arm yourself with a copious supply of 10-dirham notes to tuck into the girdle of the *shikha*, or bellydancer, when she comes and wiggles at your table.

Good fish restaurants are plentiful around the Corniche, but for atmosphere and quality at modest prices go to the **Restaurant du Port de Pêche** (through the port entrance, immediately left and straight on to the first restaurant you come to).

Vietnamese and even Japanese and Korean restaurants are to be found at Ain Diab and among the eating places clustered around the left-bankish Rond-Point de Mers Sultan, five minutes' walk from the Place des Nations Unies. Finally, for lovers of up-market French cooking, the **A Ma Bretagne** in Ain Diab is reputedly the best restaurant in Morocco.

Casablanca contains Morocco's best selection of shops.

SOUTH OF CASABLANCA

Atlantic Coast: This coastal strip is served by two roads: the busier (and therefore not necessarily faster) **P8**, and the **S121**, the more scenic coast route (without the attendant poor surface the description usually implies). The scenery, though, is not as obviously dramatic as elsewhere in the country.

To the west vast stretches of Atlantic breakers are intermittently hidden by sand dunes, still lagoons or long lines of wind-breaking sugar canes sheltering tomato plantations. To the east is a still and stony plain populated by grazing sheep and scattered farm buildings.

Occasionally the melancholy character of the region is relieved when the road sweeps within feet of an unexpected and inviting sandy cove. Mules *and* carts (complete with number plates) suggest a more affluent peasantry than that of the south. Even the occasional horse is spotted.

Fifty miles (80 km) south of Casablanca at the mouth of the **River Oum Er Rbia** (Mother of Spring) the main road passes the little town of **Azemmour**. The view of the town from across the river is one of the most memorable in this country of set-piece, almost contrived, painterly views. The white of the square buildings stacked up behind the walls is set off in this case by the astonishing colours of the river—reds or greens depending on whether it has rained in the hills or not.

From within, the town is unspectacular but pleasant. One can walk round the Portuguese ramparts and reflect on the extraordinary energy of that small country in the 14th and 15th centuries, when at one time or another it held most of Morocco's Atlantic ports.

The annual *moussem* in Azemmour commemorates a Jewish holy man, but the Jewish population, like most Moroccan Jews, fled to Israel in 1967 fearing reprisals for the Six-Day War. The *mellah* is now in ruins, but the rather plain little synagogue is opened up for determined sightseers.

Sixty-three miles (100 km) south of Casablanca is the seaside resort of **El Jadida**, a refuge in summer for Marrakshis fleeing the suffocating heat of the *chergui*, the east wind. Its miles of sandy beaches (often obscured by mysterious hot fogs), its carefree atmosphere and the interesting old **Portuguese Town** make it a pleasant stopping place, though usually it is crowded in summer.

The Portuguese held the town, which they called Mazagan, for 250 years and built the fortified and moated medina adjoining the harbour. The most remarkable Portuguese relic is the underground cistern, pillared and vaulted like a church crypt, and astonishingly lovely with oblique shafts of sunlight reflected in the shallow water. Orson Welles filmed part of his *Othello* here. Round the corner the old church, now restored, stands in a quiet square in the centre of the Portuguese Town. The minaret of the nearby mosque was once, as you can see, the Portuguese lighthouse.

Fifty-six miles (90 km) further south,

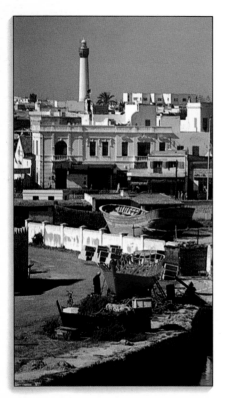

past a series of coastal salt-marshes, you come to the charming little bay of **Oualidia**, famous for its oyster-beds. There are two hotels with good seafood restaurants, two campsites, a 17th-century kasbah and a royal villa. Though also crowded in summer, especially at weekends the atmosphere is pleasant and the swimming excellent.

Safi: Ninety-four miles (150 km) south of El Jadida is an important phosphate and fishing port with a thriving and very smelly chemical industry south of the town. Its two main monuments were left behind by the Portuguese, who occupied Safi briefly in the early 16th century.

The **Dar El Bahr** (Château de la Mer), on the shore below the medina, is well preserved. The different origins of the cannon on its ramparts reflect the European competition for commercial influence after the Portuguese were driven out. In the 17th century Safi was Morocco's chief port.

Up on the hill behind the medina, another Portuguese stronghold, the **Kechla**, was later beautified and added to by a spendthrift son of Moulay Ismail, who, inheriting the extravagant tastes but not the industry of his father, squandered the money the Sultan intended for military purposes on high living.

Incongruously, in the middle of the medina, the Portuguese **St Catherine's Chapel**, once part of a now-vanished cathedral, bears the arms of King Manuel I and is an attractive blend of Gothic and Renaissance elements.

On the hillside to the north of the medina are the Safi **potteries**, which turn out brightly coloured earthenware plates and vases with distinctively bold geometrical patterns. Naturally, these are sold at the numerous roadside stalls along this stretch of coast.

The road up to the clifftop north of the town brings you to the village of **Sidi Bouzid** with its *zaouia*, good restaurant and magnificent view of town and port. One can watch the long procession of sardine boats returning to port from their night's fishing and sample the deliciously spiced sardines that are the local speciality.

Preceding pages, El Jadida; baskets to sell. **Left**, El Jadida harbour. **Right**, pausing in Azemmour.

174

THE IMPERIAL CITIES

Before the Arabs arrived in Morocco in the seventh century, communities were organised into small but numerable Berber settlements and a few trading ports. Not since the Roman era had anything much resembling towns existed. But the Arabs—an urban people whose religion emphasised the communal benefits of the city, exemplified in the holy city of Medina—were quick to build more central communities, where trade could develop, Islam flourish, and from which they could effectively govern. Moulay Idriss I, the father of the first Arab dynasty in Morocco, established the city of Moulay Idriss close to the Roman city of Volubilis, and then, in A.D. 789, founded Fez, which was to become the political capital of the whole of the Western Maghreb and southern Spain.

The pre-eminence of Fez wasn't challenged until the Almoravids developed Marrakesh in the 11th century. From then, the two cities vied for supremacy. The Almohads raised the status of Rabat but still sultans chose either Fez or Marrakesh as their capital. Until European encroachment and the eventual shift of power to Rabat, only the Alaouite sultan Moulay Ismail departed from this pattern. He ruled a strong and prosperous Morocco from Méknès (60 km to the west of Fez), no doubt preferring this city partly because its relatively limited architecture presented more scope for the notoriously egocentric sultan to express his large personality.

When Rabat became the French capital in 1912, Fez continued to boast an intellectual and cultural superiority (a claim staked long ago by the Merenid dynasty, responsible for many of the city's *medersa*, or theological colleges). Even today, Fassis are proud of this heritage. Fez contains an abundance of impressive architecture, but the old city, Fez el Bali, is more than fine buildings. It is a medieval city in motion; it offers the last chance to witness a 12th-century lifestyle other than in a museum. Marrakesh has its architectural sights—the Koutoubia, the palaces, the Saadian tombs, the Ben Youssef Medersa among them—but what most excites here is the Djemma el Fna, the market *cum* circus *cum* fair which evolves each afternoon outside the medina and expires late in the night. The purists may complain that the buildings around the square are now modern and dull in character (following a fire at the beginning of the 1960s) but it is still an evocative reminder that Morocco is in Africa.

Both Fez and Marrakesh are surrounded by lush countryside, a reason for escaping the cities' summer heat, which even in Fez can be ferocious. From Marrakesh it is easy to travel into the Atlas mountains or west to Essaouira on the coast. Fez, Méknès, Moulay Idriss and Volubilis are close to the fertile lowlands south of the Rif and the lakes and the cedar forests surrounding Azrou and Ifrane. Just a few miles from Fez there are the hot springs and cool sources of Sidi Harazem—where the ubiquitous bottled water comes from.

Preceding pages: relics of an imperial past; Fez from the old wall near Bab Guissa. **Left,** a *fantasia* rider.

FEZ

High up by the fort that dominates the two cities that comprise Old Fez, students in their *djellabahs* sit in the evening sun surrounded by Coca-Cola cans and test each other for their university exams. Below them in the valley lies their past: the old medina, with its domes and minarets, embraced by high walls behind which hooded figures move swiftly down narrow streets, trains of heavily-laden donkeys with baskets full of rubble pass through the crowds, and beggars crouch by the gates of the mosques.

Two miles (three km) to the right, up on the plain that is bitterly cold in the winter but full of summer breezes, stretch the boulevards and squares which could belong to any one of a hundred old French colonial towns. The *Tricoleur* flies above only the French Embassy now, but for all the world this is France, with its cafés and institutions, cinemas, and villas for the city's middle classes.

For the students, this land of bougainvillea and comparative Western plenty holds the promise of the future. The medina—the hotly debated, anachronistic, wholly impractical, decaying yet treasured, lauded and always loved medina—represents everything that made Morocco.

For the casual visitor, Fez is the past—mysterious, exotic and, for all the warmth of the people, a hidden place. Once the poets praised it for the beauty of its mosques, the quality of its water and the palms that lined the banks of the sweet river which flowed through its centre.

But where rulers once fought for it and craftsmen gave their lives to adorn it, today politicians and historians fight to preserve this chipped and battered jewel of North Africa. In places the river now runs fetid and the palaces are falling down, but the world watches to see if it, along with Venice, can survive the ravages and pressures of an industrial world.

Motorbike escort: There's no need to look for Fez. If you arrive by car, you'll be flanked at the first traffic-lights by motor-biked guides offering to lead you into the city. It will cost you a few dirhams. The route to the New Town, where the majority of hotels are, or to Old Fez (Fez el Bali and Fez Jdid) is clearly marked, but it's a question of keeping your nerve. The boys will drop back quickly if you look as though you know what you want and where you're going. All Moroccans watch carefully the movements of newcomers; after a few days the hassle-patter is likely to be replaced by a wave.

If you are staying in the **New Town** (most hotels are here), it is easy to find your way around. Built by the French after World War I on a simple grid system, it doesn't have the charm of Rabat (and Casablanca to a lesser extent), where the French incorporated their design into the Moroccan structure. The streets here are plain and wide. Lots of cafés, restaurants, banks and shops but not much atmosphere and not

Left, Fez el Bali. **Right**, a glimpse inside the Kairouyine Mosque.

even a very exciting nightlife. Old Fez has much more to offer after dark.

Marshall Lyautey declared Fez el Bali and Fez Jdid, which make up the medina, a historic monument and slapped a preservation order on it. New Fez was built some two miles away as the industrial and colonial centre. The administrative buildings are here, and ironically, so is the centre overseeing the preservation of Old Fez. Transport between the new and the old town, though it is quite possible to walk, is frequent and easily available (buses and taxis from the main squares).

A panoramic view: The best way to get your bearings and a feeling of the size and complexity of the **Old City** is to take the route **Tour de Fes**. It circumvents the city walls, taking you first to the west of the Palace and up to the **Merinid** tombs on the hillside.

There is some mystery attached to the tombs, mausoleums of the last Merinid sultans; it is not known exactly who is there. Described in the chronicles as beautiful white marble with vividly coloured epitaphs, they are now a crumbling ruin, more a landmark than of any particular architectural interest. If the King is in residence, the tombs are guarded and you can't clamber among them, but you are still allowed on the hillside.

The view is sensational. Once you are in the Old City, there is seldom an opportunity to see the overall structure and dimensions of the mosques and *medersa* to such an advantage. From here you can appreciate the structure of the town and the scale of its finer buildings. The view is best at dawn and dusk; then the light is magical.

At the foot of the hillside **Fez el Bali** stretches out on both sides of the river. The quarter on the west bank dates from about 925 when over 2,000 Arab families from Kairouan in Tunisia came as refugees to Fez. The Andalous quarter on the east bank had been established 100 years earlier, when 8,000 Arab families settled here, expelled from Andalusia by the Christians. With them came skills and learning which were to

Selling candles outside the *zaouia* of Moulay Idriss II.

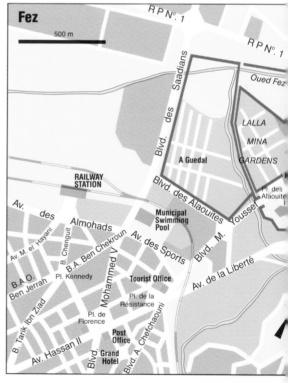

make Fez an outstanding centre of culture and craftsmanship.

As Arab rule in Spain drew to its end, further influxes of refugees from Cordoba, Seville and Granada arrived. They introduced the mosques, stucco, mosaics and other decorative skills and a variety of trades that are still central to the medina's economic survival.

The strategic division between the two quarters was used by warring factions through the centuries until Youssef ben Tashfine of the Almoravid dynasty took control in the 11th century. Although Marrakesh was his capital, he did great things for Fez. He began by demolishing the wall dividing the two quarters and building a bridge across the river; this helped, but even today you are aware of the distinction between the two.

His greatest contribution was the rerouting of the river. Engineers were instructed to create an elaborate system of channels and by the late 11th century every mosque, *medrassa*, *fondouk*, street fountain and public bath, as well as most of the richer households, had water. The system included a successful method of flushing the drains.

Mosques were built in each quarter and, seen from above, the quarters appear to form a kind of amphitheatre around the **Kairouyine Mosque** (Fez's most important building), the green tiles marking out its total area.

To the right of the Kairouyine as you look down on Fez, a thin minaret marks the other great religious monument of Fez, the **Zaouia of Moulay Idriss II**. **The Andalous mosque**, a similar focal point, is on the east bank.

To the right of the two minarets you can see the vast area of **royal palace and grounds**, with Fez Jdid (Fez the New) beside it. Built by the Merinids in the 13th century, Fez Jdid primarily provided a superior royal residence for the sultan and those connected with the palace, the administration and the army. The *mellah* is at the east end. With the emphasis on grandeur and open space, Fez Jdid contrasts strongly with Fez el Bali.

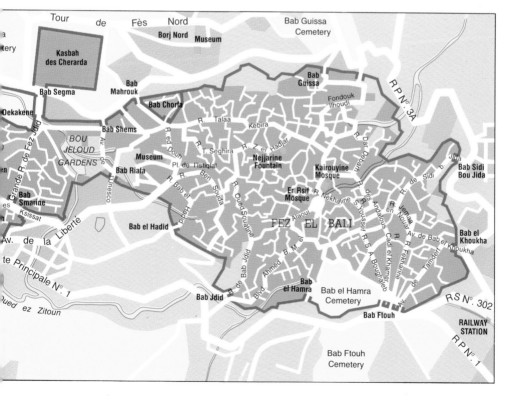

The two parts of the Old City are linked by the **Avenue des Français**, which borders the peaceful and attractive **Boujeloud Gardens** on one side. The walls between the two were joined at the end of the 19th century and some of the buildings around this area date from that time.

This is probably the clearest view you will get of the layout of the city. Once down in the medina there are no vistas and it's only by design that you can get a glimpse of a minaret or a roof top. Most of the *medersa* have good views from their roofs, if you are able to reach them. The carpet emporiums frequently use their roof-top views as a bait to entice tourists!

Behind the Merinid tombs is the five-star **Hotel Merenids**, an ugly but brilliantly positioned hotel, not surprisingly a matter of contention when planned. The **Borj Nord**, a fortress dating from Saadian times is just below the hotel and houses a collection of arms, a large number of fairly uninteresting muskets. Its opening times are erratic—not really worth making a special journey for unless you're particularly interested in weaponry, but if you're up there and it happens to be open, why not?

On the opposite hillside the **Borj Sud** stands sentinel amid olive trees and grave stones; there are plans to build additional housing around this area. Many of the hillsides surrounding Fez are dotted with white stones—the cemeteries have to be outside the medina as there is no room for graves in the city. The Tour de Fes takes you on from the tombs and Borj Nord past the Bab Guissa to the Borj Sud and then sweeps back to the New Town, leaving Fez Jdid on its right.

Fez is the medina: Within the city walls everything and nothing is revealed. At street level in the non-souk areas plain walls are continuous and blank except for dark doorways. Each of these opens into a darkened passage which in turn opens into the centre of a house, its beauty invisible to passers-by. Its centre is the courtyard, often paved or tiled in

Among the Merenid tombs.

mosaics, with walls and pillars supporting a gallery in carved stucco or wood; the courtyard is open to the sky and all the rooms look on to it.

The houses are part of the city but at the same time closed off from it. Unless you're lucky enough to be invited to join a Moroccan family meal, the nearest you'll get to seeing the design is from the old houses that have been converted into carpet co-operatives, or in snatched glances through briefly-opening doors.

Getting around the medina is a challenge. It is a good idea to get a guide at the beginning. He can take you to all the main sights, which can serve as landmarks on your own excursions later. Fix a price to begin with. This is important, although at the end he will disarmingly suggest you pay what you think he's worth. Don't get drawn into that—your evaluation and his may radically differ and it can then get complicated and unpleasant.

There are fixed rates for official guides so work on that basis,plus extra for qualifications, language skills, etc. You can arrange an official guide through your hotel, an unofficial guide will find you. Students are many and some much more interesting company than a rather bored official guide.

Another warning: the close relationship between the people and their city means that everybody knows somebody with something to sell—and a sale helps the community. Part of your tour will inevitably include a visit to a carpet emporium or co-operative. If you have absolutely no desire to buy and are short of time, try and make this clear to your guide at the outset, although he won't believe you. If you *do* find yourself being sucked into the sales patter, retreat politely as soon as you can; the longer you're there the more difficult it becomes.

If you are guideless and taking your chance alone in the medina, remember that any young lad will guide you out (for a few dirhams) should you get hopelessly lost. Contrary to some first impressions, it isn't a frightening city.

The distinctive green-tiled roofs of the Kairouyine Mosque.

THE FUTURE
OF THE MEDINA

All Arab cities with some history have their medina. The Prophet founded the first Islamic community in a city named Medina, which was second in importance to Mecca, and it became the pin-up prototype for every other Islamic town.

To a follower of the Islamic faith the pursuit of this ideal of the just and ordered city was (and in theory still is) obligatory. It is believed that on the Day of Judgment men and women will be assessed not only on their own merits but also on their performance in society.

The design of the medinas, therefore, reflected communal values. Each quarter contributed to the benefit of the whole. Even during the French and Spanish protectorates, the integrity of the medinas was respected. Marshall Lyautey, the first French Resident General, decreed that new developments to serve the influx of European administrators should be set apart from the medinas in order to preserve the old towns' way of life. In the long run, such good intentions have created their own problems. Yes, many of the medinas are intact and in some cases still function much as they did in medieval times, but equally they have lost their administrative and political importance to the new towns. After independence richer, influential families often moved to the more modern quarters vacated by the Europeans, leaving the medina to the powerless and populous poor.

Fez is the archetypal example illustrating the medina's crisis. For centuries it was the political and cultural capital of Morocco. In fact, it is still seen as the home of intellectual values in the country. But its 1,000-year-old medina relies upon the interdependence of industries and social structures for its continuing efficiency and survival and this is gravely threatened. Contrary to some visitors' impressions, it doesn't exist as a museum for tourists, its souks do not stock merely the tourist trinkets; the Fassis rely on their industries, and their leather goods, silverware and cedarwork are sold throughout the country—to Moroccans. Over 20,000 people live and work in the medina in Fez and it's clear to anyone wandering through the packed souks that tourists are irrelevant to most of the inhabitants.

Old methods are still used by the dyers, tanners and the brass and silver craftsmen. There isn't room in the city to introduce new technology, open new factories and streamline production, even if they were wanted. So far only potteries have been moved out of the centre of Fez to hillsides close by, where new technology could be introduced. But such progress is beset by problems: break a part of the vast structure of the medina and it all might crumble.

Overcrowding is the main cause of Fez's ills. Over the past 50 years people have been moving into the town from the countryside to find work and fulfil the dream of prosperity. This has put Fez under severe strain. Certain public infrastructures, such as water supplies and 13th-century sewage systems, are at breaking point. There is no new housing available and shanty towns have been spawned on the hillside near Fez. The different quarters of the city, once so well defined, are slowly losing their individual functions.

Sadly, demographic, social and economic constraints have had detrimental effects on the city's architecture. Fez's ancient mosques, *medersa*, palaces, *fondouks* and houses—only a fraction of which the tourist sees—are crumbling. Toxic waste is being poured into the rivers and sewers; the small but numerous machines that are used by the craftsmen produce damaging vibrations.

In 1980 Unesco launched an appeal and introduced a programme of works. Their plans make both optimistic and tragic reading. The task is enormous and would seem impossible, but work has started. The objective is to keep the medina as a working structure—reinforcing its foundations both physically and administratively. But it is difficult not to be pessimistic when the office dealing with restoration works has moved to the new town where services are more efficient.

To survive, the medina has to take account of progress. The task of "up-dating" may be impossible, but the most urgent objective is to lighten the pressure within the city walls and let it breathe.

A tour: One of the main entrances to the medina is through the **Bab Boujeloud** to the right of the Palace area. Cars are not allowed in the medina but parking is easy around the gates. Expect to pay a small sum for a "*gardien* of the car*", who will appear as you draw up. Buses or cabs can be taken from **Place Baghadi** just by the gate.

As dusk falls this area is thronging with people. A dusty flea-market stretches out across the waste ground just outside the city walls, with frequent buses passing and turning.

The Bab Boujeloud, built in 1913, is one of the most recent *babs* but traditionally tiled and decorated: blue and gold outside, green and gold inside. Inside the gate the square splits into the two main streets, **Talaa Kebira** (or Grand Tala), the upper one, and the less interesting **Talaa Sghira**, running parallel below it.

Just off the square is one of the most remarkable sights in Fez, the **Bou Inania Medrassa**, an exuberant example of a Merinid monument. The *medersa* used to play an important role in Morocco. Essentially urban, these buildings were used as lodging houses for students who were strangers to the town; the idea was that the isolation would help them concentrate on their pious studies. *Medersa* were supported by endowments from the sultans and revenue from local inhabitants. For convenience, they were built close to the mosque where the students went for their lessons.

Similar in structure to the mosques and private houses, they are all based around a central courtyard and highly decorated with mosaic, *zellige* (elaborate tiling) and stucco. Students often spent more than 10 years at university, so places to live were at a premium.

Sultan Abou Inan commissioned the Bou Inania, built between 1350 and 1357, and the cost is legendary. The story goes that he threw the accounts into the river when it was finished— beauty is unaccountable. It was a surprise to his contemporaries that he built one at all. His impious reputation, in-

From raw material to finished goods.

cluding the evidence of 325 sons in 10 years, perhaps spurred him to atone.

He set out to make a rival to the Kairouyine Mosque and the Medrassa did become one of the most important religious buildings in the city. He failed to achieve his greatest desire to have the Call to Prayer transferred here from the Kairouyine, but the Bou Inania was granted the status of Grand Mosque, unheard of for a *medrassa* in Morocco, and the Friday prayers are still heard here.

It follows the usual layout, but the quality and intricacy of the decoration is outstanding. The courtyard façade is decorated with carved stucco, above which the majestic cedarwood arches support a frieze and corbelled porch. The interior shows us some of the finest examples of cedarwood carving, stucco work, Kufic script writing and *zellige* work. It is the only building in religious use that can be entered by non-Muslims. Even then, they have access to only the courtyard, where you see the faithful carrying out their pre-prayer ablutions in the fountain watered by the Oued Fez.

Opposite the Bou Inania is a remarkable **water-clock**. Thirteen wooden blocks balancing 13 brass bowls (only seven original bowls remain) protrude beneath 13 windows. Sultan Abou Inan erected it opposite the Medrassa to ring out the hour of prayer, hoping its originality would bring further fame to the Medrassa.

There has been much speculation over the mechanics of it but the system was thought ingenious. Sadly, it no longer works. The legend goes that a curse was put on the clock after it had alarmed a pregnant Jewess passing beneath it to such an extent that she miscarried her child. It is one of many things on the Unesco repair list.

The **Talaa Kebira**—the upper of the two main arteries—leads eventually to the Kairouyine Mosque and Zaouia of Moulay Idriss. The impact of smells, sounds and numbers of people is enthralling. If you walked through blindfold, despite a lack of air and draughts, the pungent areas of mint, spices, wood

The corner grocer.

and leather would assault the nostrils but seldom merge—an exercise in identification.

There is a feeling of perpetual motion, even though the street stalls are manned by often motionless sellers sitting cross-legged behind their heaps of wares. Craftsmen, sometimes four to a tiny stall, work intently on their tasks, looking out occasionally. Tourists are tolerated here and only in the shops geared to the traditional trades is any attempt made to interest and sell. Everyone is occupied and engrossed in their purpose.

The younger generation show more interest and call out to passing groups, while the smaller children follow persistently just by the elbow, repeating "Madam, Monsieur....Madam, Monsieur...", to be swept aside by the guides or fade out of necessity in the path of an on-coming mule.

The overall impression of the medina is chaotic but its structure is quite rigid. Each quarter has its own mosque, *medrassa*, *foundouk*, Koran school, water fountain, *hammam*, and bakery. Everyone in the quarter brings their own dough to be baked in the central ovens (odd marks of identification are used to avoid rows). Daily prayers (four times a day) are taken in the mosque of the quarter, the Grand Mosques being used on Fridays, when people flock from all areas for this special prayer day.

Daily life continues. Screams of "*Batica! Batica!*" ("Watch out" or "Get out of the way") precede the long-suffering tread of the mule carrying some huge, often precariously balanced, burden, forcing the flowing crowd to pin themselves against the walls. If Westerners weren't so obvious by their dress, they would certainly be identified by their sudden movements interrupting the otherwise smooth flow of the Fez crowd.

The Fassis are so familiar with sounds that they duck and weave past obstructions, keeping on the move, but there is the occasional impossible load that brings even the Fassi to a standstill.

The contemplative life.

It perhaps isn't surprising that these tend to be mechanical trucks going about the restoration programme rather than the malleable beasts of burden.

The crowds continue down Talaa Kebira, whose roof, covered in rushes, lets in shafts of light. Uneven illumination creates some beautiful images. Brilliant colours of the spices become patterns in shade and sun. Bundles and bundles of mint smell fresh and strong. Heaps of dried grass by the side of stalls are sold to Berber women for cleaning teeth. A type of Moroccan floss?

Walking down the street, you come across large buildings now mainly used as warehouses for stalls in the souk; these are the *fondouks*, another integral part of the medina, created at about the same time as the *medersa*, as hotels for traders and doubling up as stables. They have the familiar structure of a courtyard with galleried sleeping area.

One of the most well-known is the **Fondouk Tsetaouyine**, near the Kairouyine; frequented by the reputedly dishonest traders from Tetouan, the *fondouk* became renowned as a centre for loose living (today it is used as one of the carpet co-operatives). There were over 200 *fondouks* in Fez el Bali; many survive and it is remarkable to see such highly decorated buildings now being used as warehouses.

Nearing the end of Talaa Kebira, you might get a whiff of the very strong smell from the **leatherworkers' fondouk**, which stores the drying skins from the slaughterhouse before they're sent to the dyers. Close by where the road becomes Rue ech Cherabliyin, the leatherworkers have their stalls.

Babouches, the famous leather slippers worn in various forms by most Moroccan men, are sold here. The most common colours are yellow and white, but in Fez you can also buy grey ones, considered unusual and to be envied.

The street bends down towards the Grand Kairouyine Mosque. This area is the commercial and formal centre of the medina. (Islam strongly approves of trade.) The **Souk Attarine** (the spice-sellers' souk) and the **Kissaria** comprise what is considered the most sophisticated part of the medina. The Kissaria is famous for its embroidery stalls, silks and brocades, as well as stalls for imported goods. The fire that wiped out the Kissaria in 1954 leaves it rather characterless in structure with modern roofing, but you are quickly distracted.

Just below the **Souk Attarine** you enter the *horm*, a sacred area around the **Shrine of Moulay Idriss II**, the effective founder of Fez. A wooden bar at donkey-neck height denotes the area. Until the French protectorate this barred not only mules and donkeys but also Jews and Christians. It also indicated a refuge for Muslims, who could not be arrested in this area.

Today it is a popular spot for beggars hoping to tap pilgrims on their way to devotions. Rows of stalls sell candles of all sizes and colours, incense, and many other religious and devotional materials, mainly bought by women to lay before the great Idriss tomb.

The tomb was built by the Idrissids in the ninth century but was allowed to fall

No way out but up.

192

into decay by ensuing dynasties until it was rebuilt in the 13th century by the Merinids. The Wattasids rediscovered the tomb and from this period it became the revered shrine it is now. A glimpse through the doorway reveals a colourful and mystical sight—the smell of incense and the flickering lights of candles surround prostrate figures.

The street follows the wall of the *zaouia*, and through another very richly decorated doorway you can see the room of prayer. This contains innumerable chandeliers and, around the tomb, a rather surprising collection of clocks, considered an upmarket offering in the 19th century. These, though, are not usually visible to the non-Muslim.

Follow your nose to the **Souk Nejjarine** (carpenters' souk) filled with the intoxicating smell of cedarwood. Here craftsmen crouch over finely carved tables, bedheads, chairs and every kind of wooden creation. Most Moroccan furniture seen in hotels and private houses is wooden and made with meticulous care in the medina.

Place Nejjarine, alongside the souk, is one of the oldest in Fez, and the *fondouk* at the corner of the square dates from the late 17th century. A huge doorway richly decorated is all that is left to see; the place is closed and the interior a crumbling ruin. The **Nejjarine Fountain**, the focal point of the square, is an outstanding example of *zellige* decoration and stands almost like a shrine to water.

From here you pass into the **henna souk,** where an inexhaustible supply of hand and face dyes are packed into the stalls. Women stand about testing the dyes and experimenting with elaborate patterns on their hands.

All roads in the medina lead to the **Kairouyine Mosque**, or so the saying goes. Rivalled in size only by King Hassan's new mosque in Casablanca, it can accommodate 20,000 people, only a fifth of the number that live and work in the medina. It was founded by a pious woman in 859 in memory of her father; each ruler added to it and changed it.

The Merinids' alterations in the 13th

A photographer displays his art.

century left it in its present form. Green tiled roofs cover 16 naves, and the tiled courtyards have two end pavilions and a beautiful 16th century fountain reminiscent of the Court of Lions of the Alhambra Palace in Granada. It is jealously guarded from the eyes of non-Muslims but you can snatch glimpses of the interior from the numerous doorways.

The sanctuary interior is austerely simple with horseshoe arches over plain columns. It was the first university in the Western world and its reputation brought in over 8,000 students in the 14th century. Considered one of the great seats of learning, it even boasts a pope as one of its past students.

The **Kairouyine Library,** opposite one of the entrances to the Mosque, is also thought to have been built in the ninth century. Closed to the public, it contains one of the most renowned collections of Islamic literature in the world.

Nearby the Kairouyine you come into **Place Seffarine** (the area of metalwork-

ers), an enchanting square shaded by trees. Huge cauldrons stacked in every available space, donkeys being loaded up, work in progress—all accompanied by a cacophany of hammering. Cauldrons and giant trays are specially made for feast days and weddings. Every kind of metal is used and the intricacy of patterns worked with tiny chisels is quite beautiful.

The same skills were used on the redecoration of the great doors to the King's palace, now difficult to get close enough to appreciate. (When the King is in Fez no one is allowed near). Place Seffarine is one of the prettiest squares in the medina, and if you can gain access to the **Seffarine Medrassa** close by, the roof offers a good view of the overall scene.

The **dyers' quarter** constitutes a narrow unevenly cobbled street close by the Place Seffarine. Cauldrons of dye stand at the doorways and all around skeins of freshly dipped silk drip their bright colours into the gutters. These join in streams hurtling towards the river. The men stand around with stained feet and hands, the narrowness of the street giving them little room to manoeuvre amid the constant pressure of people, and tourists dodge the coloured water determined to wage war on their espadrilles.

The **tanneries** near the river offer a yet more extreme experience. The area has hardly changed since medieval times. The position of stone vats, one against the other, make shifting the skins in and out of the different dyes an athletic achievement. Scantily-clad men crouch and balance over vats dipping the hides; roofs around are thick with drying skins. Natural colours are still used: yellow (saffron), red (poppy), blue (indigo) and black (antimony).

The tanneries are run as a co-operative, with each foreman responsible for his own workforce and tools. Jobs are practically hereditary. This primitive but skilled trade, carried out mostly in intense heat and restricted surroundings, is the most haunting in Fez. The strong smell of animal skins, dye mixed with cow urine (for preservation), and

Left and **right,** the tanneries: Moroccan leather has a worldwide reputation.

human sweat, is at times nauseating, but you get used to it.

Tourists are trooped through the narrow walkways and helped up small uneven steps to vantage points for photographs. Terrible bottlenecks of mint-sniffing visitors move hesitantly along the walls and roof tops, incongruous in their artificial colours and whirring video cameras.

From here you can cross the bridge to the **Andalous quarter**. The mosque was founded a little after the Kairouyine in the ninth century and embellished by the Almohads at beginning of the 13th century. It is the main sanctuary on the east bank and has some beautiful carved cedarwork, but viewing is difficult. Of the two *medersa* in this quarter, the **Es Sahrij**, early 14th century, is well worth seeing. *Zellige* decorations are some of the oldest in the country and there is plenty of fine wood carving. (Note: part of the *medrassa* is inaccessible because of restoration work).

This quarter is less intense, both in its structure and number of inhabitants.

Walking up the hill towards the **Bab Ftouh**, which marks the eastern limits of the medina, you pass the potters quarter. Fez pottery, with its distinctive blue design, is sold all over Morocco and its craftsmen are much admired.

Retracing your steps past the Kairouyine and up the hill westwards, you emerge beside the **Palais Jamai** hotel beside the Bab Guissa. It was built by Si Mohammed ben Arib el Jamai at end of the 19th century and is a finer example of the architect's work than the palace of the same name built in Méknès housing the Musuem of Morrocan Arts.

Now an extremely comfortable, expensive hotel, its position on the edge of the medina, enclosed in a walled garden of palm trees and roses lulled by the sound of water and birdsong, is probably the best. The sound of the 5 a.m. call to prayer—"*Allah Akbar*"—echoing across the medina from the Kairouyine Mosque, joined by a chorus of *muezzins*, is a good reason to stay within earshot of the medina—it is a voice of Morocco and should be heard at least once during your stay.

A short taxi ride from Bab Guissa and you're back at Bab Boujeloud.

Fez Jdid was planned by the Merinids in the 13th century to incorporate an impressive Royal Palace and Gardens (entry to both now, sadly, prohibited) and as the administrative centre of Fez. The role of this part of the city diminished when the governmental function was moved to Rabat by the French. At about this time it became known as the red-light district of Fez and now remains a slightly melancholy area with the almost deserted *mellah* tacked on to the south-eastern corner.

The Grand Mosque presides over the north end of Fez Jdid, with the Grand Rue de Fez Jdid the main artery linking this part of town with the *mellah* (Jewish quarter). The main street, lined with souks selling vegetables, textiles and household items, is not of any particular interest and offers none of the cohesion and mystery of Fez el Bali.

The **mellah** was originally sited by the Bab Guissa. When Fez Jdid was

Outside the Attarine Madressa.

built the Jews were ordered to move to their new quarter near the sultan's palace. Many Jews who had interests in the medina preferred to become Muslims and thus stay in Fez el Bali. Those who did move were promised protection in consideration of certain supplementary taxes.

This ghetto was given the name *mellah*, which means "salt" in Arabic, because it was the Jews task to drain and salt the heads of decapitated rebels before they were impaled on the gates of the town. The Jews' position has always been ambiguous and, although ostensibly under the sultan's protection, their lives before the protectorates were severely limited. No Jew was allowed to wear shoes or ride outside the *mellah* and further restrictions were placed on their travel elsewhere.

Very few Jewish families remain; most left for France, with a few setting up home in Casablanca. What remains are their tall, very un-Arab buildings retaining a certain dignity even in their fast-decaying form. There is a sad rather run-down souk mainly of clothes and household item, tapes, T-shirts and other cheap, generally low-quality Western goods.

One of the oddities of this area—and quite difficult to find among the twisting, abandoned streets—is the **Hebrew cemetery**. Rows of pristine white gravestones very close together cluster on the slope of the hill stretching down towards the river.

The area between Fez Jdid and Fez el Bali, joined in the late 19th century by Moulay el Hassan, contains the **Dar Batha Palace**. Formerly part of the link between the two, with gates at both ends, it now houses the **Museum of Moroccan Arts**. Definitely worth a visit (except on Tuesdays, when it is closed), it has a fascinating collection of artefacts, carpets, mosaics, pottery and jewellery. It also offers many interesting examples of stucco work and carving—useful to see (because they give a good idea of developments in techniques) before embarking on the tour of *medersa* and mosques.

The *mellah* in Fez el Jedid.

MÉKNÈS

As a celebratory gift to mark the beginning of his long rule in the mid-17th century, Moulay Ismail displayed 700 heads on the walls of Fez. This did the trick. His love of blood is legendary and he ruled Morocco from his capital Méknès for 55 years, more or less as an united country. It became a noteworthy country in Europe and he considered Louis XIV, his contemporary in France, a close friend.

Méknès has been called the "Versailles of Morocco". Moulay Ismail's large-scale palace, which enabled him to keep most of his subjects under his surveillance, is possibly where the comparision begins and ends.

Certainly there is evidence that he saw himself as a Moroccan Louis XIV, albeit superior to the French monarch, to whom he suggested the Muslim faith and offered to take one of his daughters as a wife. Both these suggestions were refused. The two grandfather clocks on display behind Moulay Ismail's tomb are reputed to be a pacifying gift from the French king after this effective snub.

Although surrounded by fertile land and a good choice in terms of trade connections, Méknès was not very easy to defend. Before Moulay Ismail took control Méknès had had a turbulent history. Founded in the 10th century by a Berber tribe known as Meknassass, it passed through the hands of the 11th-century Almoravids and the 12th-century Almohads to the Merinids and Saadis.

Infamous Ismail: Moulay Ismail was the governor of Méknès for his father, the Alaouite Sultan er Rashid, and succeeded him as sultan in 1672. His excesses were notorious. Statistics vary wildly but it was said that 500 women served him and of the many hundreds of children he fathered he had the girls strangled at birth and was not averse to slicing off the limbs of erring sons.

His vision of power, amounting to mania, has left Méknès a graveyard of huge palaces and buildings. The 16 miles (25 km) of walls built around the city were only part of his grand plan. He gathered together an army of 30,000 Sudanese soldiers—a "peace-keeping" force—who roamed the country ensuring the sultan's control was felt.

Back in Méknès, more than 25,000 unfortunate captives were among those brought in to execute his vision of palaces, walls and fortresses. They were penned at night in dark subterranean chambers dug for their habitation. Scott O'Connor, in his *Vision of Morocco*, describes Moulay Ismail's ferocious economy: "When the slaves died they were used as building material and immured in the rising walls, their blood mixed with the cement that still holds them together in its grip."

There are plenty more blood-curdling stories. Méknès has suffered from a history of such grim blood-letting. Its medina and imperial city now present rather a tragic sight, "Miles upon miles of cemented walls run their mournful course about the city" is how it was described early this century.

Preceding pages, Bab Mansour, Méknès. **Left**, the reign of Moulay Ismail heralded a decline in craftsmanship. **Right**, the wool market.

Within these walls lie the remains of a dream of some 30 royal palaces, 20 gates, mosques, barracks, and ornamental gardens. It is magnificent and lunatic in its scale of conception, and Moulay Ismail has to be admired for his perserverence. He built Méknès into one of the four great imperial cities and it remained so until his death in 1727 when his heir removed the capital to Marrakesh. The son destroyed a number of buildings as a parting shot and from then the city declined.

The New Town: The French built the **New Town** early this century on the other side of the **Oued Boufekrane**, which runs through the valley between the two parts of Méknès. It remains a prosperous provincial town. Local industry and excellent farming land provide its wealth.

There is little of interest in the new part—a few hotels offer uninspiring accommodation. One five-star hotel, the Hotel Transatlantique to the west of town, provides excellent views across the river to the medina. There are some good shops, a few restaurants, and the banks and administrative buildings are in this area. Fairly lively by day, Méknès, new and old, has died by about 10 p.m.

The main part of a visit should be dedicated to **old Méknès** and the **imperial city** on the east bank of the river. All roads lead to **Place el Hedim** (sinisterly named Place of Destruction). A huge open square, it used to be part of the medina but was razed to the ground by Moulay Ismail to create an approach to the main entrance of his palace via Bab Mansour.

It is almost too large to be lively. Stalls cling to the east side and benches line the west. A fairly constant stream of people cross from the medina to Bab Mansour and round towards the new town; buses forever disgorge their bulging loads into the square. Briefly it fills, then just as quickly it empties.

The area is dominated by the **Bab Mansour**, commissioned by Moulay Ismail himself but finished during his son's reign in 1732. Brilliantly deco-

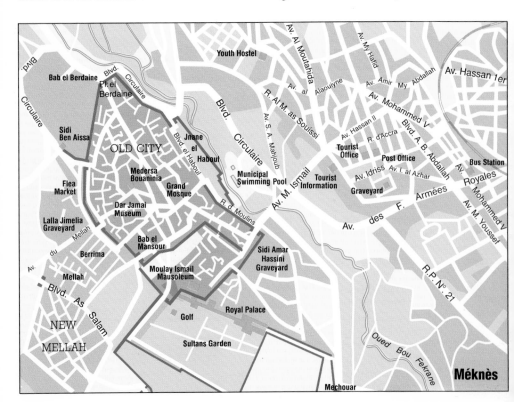

Méknès

rated in green and white ceramic tiling, it is flanked by two square bastions supported in part by marble columns taken from Volubilis. Remarkable for its size and symmetry, like much of Ismail's grand vision it proves overpowering and heavy.

A tour of the Imperial city may start from here. Although a guide can be useful in Méknès, one isn't essential. Versions of history differ radically. You will probably be approached either in Place el Hedim, the Bab Mansour or as you arrive at the traffic-lights close to the centre. The Tourist Office doesn't appear to operate the same system of official guides here as they do in Fez and Marrakesh, so it's a free-for-all. There's often fighting between guides vying for your dirhams. The attitude and atmosphere is different in Méknès; there's not the sense of pride and unity you feel from the people in Fez.

So, with or without a guide, you find youself in **Place Lalla Aouda**, just inside the Bab Mansour. The domed pavilion **Koubbet el Khiyatine** on one side used to be used to receive embassies. Inside, a stairway leads down into subterranean vaulted chambers said to have been used as a granary and to house the Christian slaves. The rest of the square lacks a sense of purpose. There are a few orange and nut sellers and small groups scratching idly in the dried earth waiting for something to happen. It is destined for improvement, with gardens and a public park.

The gardens stretching out behind the walls have been turned into a **royal golf course**, with access for the King and visiting dignitaries only. Through another gate, you come upon one of Méknès's main sights, the **Tomb of Moulay Ismail**. Restored by Mohammed V, it is the only shrine apart from the mausoleum of Mohammed V in Rabat that can be visited by any non-Muslims.

Only the courtyards are open, but you can see the tomb and into the sanctuary. The fine tile panels are in excellent condition; rigidly simple geometric patterns contribute to the splendour of the

Left, Ismail's granaries: ready for a siege. **Right**, the water seller, familiar in all imperial cities.

whole. The walls and courtyard are highly patterned and the stucco work is striking.

A very good example of the uniformity achieved in the conception of some of the great buildings can be seen from the number of carved doors continuing a pattern already established by the tile mosaics.

Moulay Ismail's reputation for great violence and cruelty does not seem to have diminished the reverence paid to him. It is perhaps odd that such a keen blood-letting ruler should have a shrine of such magnificence, and one that still attracts Muslims from all over Morocco. The people believe that his tomb has *baraka* (magical powers) which will be bestowed on the believer. A doorway opens from the mausoleum on to a cemetery for those wishing to be buried alongside this infamous ruler.

A walk along the corridor-like road between the walls offers the most impressive sense of their size. Most of the palaces behind them are crumbling ruins, although a few have been restored and are used for military or educational purposes.

The Dar el Kebira, Moulay Ismail's main palace complex, was destroyed by his son and remains a sad ruin. **The Dar el Makhzen**, one of the last palaces completed at the end of the 18th century, has been restored and is used by the present royal family as an occasional residence, emphasising by default the madness of Ismail's vision.

One of the most remarkable sights within the Imperial city is the **Heri as Souani**—a wall of high vaulted chambers now overgrown at their bases— which were used as huge store-rooms and granaries. The chambers are immense. Moulay Ismail was always ready for a siege.

The **Aguedal Basin** nearby covers 25 acres (10 hectares) of water but, as with all the sights within the Imperial city, its abandoned grandeur makes it a mournful and gloomy place. The vision was so mighty but the spaces were never filled—the scale was too huge.

The **Royal stables** are the best ex-

Sixteen miles of wall surround the city.

204

ample of this excess. They were built for more than 12,000 horses, each with its own groom and slave. Their grain was kept below in the granaries at a constant temperature assured by the thick walls. Ismail also constructed a canal providing fresh water for the horses without them having to move from their stalls. The horse was considered one of the noblest of animals.

The building stretches for almost three miles (five km) and the crumbling remains still show the extent of decoration that once existed; tiles and *zelliges* are visible on pieces of partially overgrown wall. The place now belongs to the goats.

The Medina: Returning to the Bab Mansour, you can park just inside the walls for a few dirhams and enter the **medina** at the west end of the Place el Hedim. **The Museum of Moroccan Arts** housed in the Dar Jamai is discreetly positioned at the corner of the square beside the entrance to the medina. It is worth a visit to see the fine examples of Berber rugs before visiting any of the carpet shops inside. It also has an interesting collection of local artefacts and pottery.

The building itself, built by the architect who designed the Palais Jamai hotel in Fez at the end of the 19th century, is on a less grand scale. Some of the upper rooms are decorated and furnished to give an idea of 19th-century domestic Moroccan life. If you've already been to the medina in Fez, this one will be a disappointment, so try and see it first.

The best view of the layout of the area can be seen from the roof of the **Medrassa Bou Inania**. You can see the green tiled minarets of the mosques of each quarter and the roof of the Grand Mosque from here.

The main street, covered by a corrugated iron roof, contains most of the usual stalls and is an animated, bustling thoroughfare. **The carpenters' souk** is permeated by the sweet smell of cedar wood. If you find yourself in the souk as darkness falls, the light can be deceptive and it's very easy to get hopelessly lost. You can be pursuing a shaft of light, thinking it will draw you to the outside, only to find yourself beside an illuminated stall and another street stretching in front of you.

If you continue through the carpenters' souk, you eventually emerge at the west end where the artisans' markets are in full swing. It is quite a scruffy area but has some interesting co-operative workshops—basket-makers, saddlers and others. Fruit and food stalls are found spasmodically placed both in this area and in the souk.

The Aissawa Brotherhood: Out of the medina, beside the **Bab el Berdain**, is a huge cemetery containing the shrine of **Sidi ben Aissa**. Built in the 18th century for this strange saint, it is not open to non-Muslims. The Aissawa cult spread all over North Africa. Ben Aissa was supposed to confer magical powers on his followers—they could eat anything, however grim, without the slightest ill-effects.

On the eve of Mouloud, the date of their annual *moussem*, over 50,000 devotees would gather and in an induced trance devour live animals and pierce their tongues and cheeks. It was similar in style and intensity to the Hammaacha of Moulay Idriss, whose *moussem* is so vividly described in Paul Bowles's *The Spider's House*. The government has now outlawed the most extreme practices of these cults, but their annual *moussems* still take place.

The new and old *mellahs* to the west of the medina and Place el Hedim have markets and souks of their own. It is a busy but very run-down area, with buildings built into the crumbling walls of the old houses. It is one of the poorest parts of town.

Whether because of the bloody actions of Moulay Ismail, reputed to have slaughtered over 36,000 with his own hands, or the combination of grandeur and decay, Méknès has a strange atmosphere. The emptiness of the vast crumbling edifices in contrast to the intensity of the slightly shabby medina reinforce this uneasy feeling. Méknès lacks the cohesive feel of Fez; its inhabitants have none of the proud confidence in their city that the Fassis show. Maybe Méknès lived with fear for too long.

MOULAY IDRISS

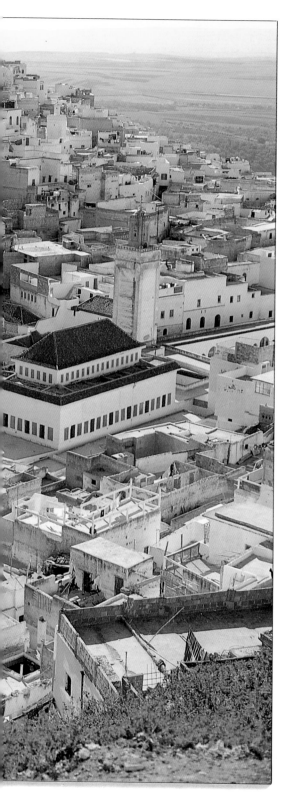

You are visiting a town; but it is essentially a shrine to Moulay Idriss I, whose tomb rests here.

It is hard to imagine when you first catch sight of the cluster of white houses on the hillside that this is where the sects of Hamaacha and Dghoughia, trance-induced, performed grim and violent rituals during the annual *moussem*. Slicing into their heads with hatchets and heading cannon balls were only two of their more popular antics. The more extreme activities of the sects have been outlawed by the government, but it is rumoured that they continue where unobserved.

The *moussem* is held after the harvest, usually beginning on the last Thursday in August. It lasts for several weeks and is considered the most important religious festival in Morocco. Pilgrims unable to make the journey to Mecca can settle for Moulay Idriss, rated as second in sacredness to Mecca in the Islamic world, though the revered courtesy title of "*el Hadj*" is bestowed only on those who reach Mecca.

Originally a purely religious festival, it has come to include fantasias, singing, dancing and markets. The hillsides are covered with tents, and prayer, feasting and general rejoicing continue throughout the festival. Tourists are tolerated but it is a purely Muslim festival and it's probably best to visit in the daytime.

Origins: At the end of the eighth century, Moulay Idriss el Akhbar (the elder) arrived in the village of Zerhoun. The great-grandson of the Prophet Mohammed, he fled to Morocco to escape persecution and death. He stopped first at Volubilis, later building his town nearby, and set about his task of converting the Berbers to the Islamic faith. He was well received by the mountain people, who recognised him as their leader. He became the founder of the first Arab dynasty in Morocco. A year later he began the founding of Fez—a labour completed by Idriss II.

News of his popularity and success reached his enemies and an emissary was sent to poison him in 791. His dynasty lived on through his son, born two months after his death.

The town: Moulay Idriss is set in the spurs of the hills just east of Volubilis. As you approach from Méknès, the town looks a compact, predominantly white whole, but it is really two villages. The Khiber and the Tasga quarters join together around the mosque and shrine.

Arriving by car, you can park either in a small area close to the main square, or to the north of the centre. It is not a tourist attraction and, although a peaceful and simple place, there is much poverty. The streets are clean, a few children play on ice-blue doorsteps, and veiled women move silently about their chores.

Moulay Idriss exists seemingly oblivious of the 20th century, although Méknès is only 16 miles (25 km) away. There are few concessions to Western visitors. The souks—insofar as they exist at all—sell basic wares and are in the Khiber quarter, spreading rather thinly back up the hill from the *zaouia*. The best views of the town are from the terrace **Sidi Abdallah el Hajjam**, above the Khiber quarter. The thin empty streets make up a complicated network and it's easy to climb into a dead end. There are, however, plenty of boys happy to lead you to the terrace for a few dirhams. A rather reticent biscuit and postcard seller sometimes appears on the mud terrace, but there is no pressure to buy.

From here the structure of the town is clear. White and grey cubes fall down below you to where the quarters merge beside the tomb and *zaouia* of Moulay Idriss. The green-tiled roofs and arched courtyards of the mosque and shrine are clearly visible.

The mausoleum was rebuilt by Moulay Ismail, who destroyed the first structure at the end of the 18th century in order to create a more beautiful one. This was later embellished by the Sultan Moulay Abderrahmen. The minaret, somewhat paradoxically in this almost

Preceding pages, Moulay Idriss. Below left, a Heath Robinson-type construction near the city gate. Below right, the annual **moussem**.

timeless town, was rebuilt in the 1930s. Its striking cylindrical shape is unique to Morocco.

You can get a good look at half of it from one of the streets close by. The green ceramic tiles are decorated with stylised printing from the Koran. Non-Muslims are forbidden entry to the tomb and shrine. The *horm* (sanctuary area) is clearly marked by the low wooden bar placed across the entry to repel Christians and beasts of burden bent on access.

The main square—more of a rectangle—opens out from the holy area. It is the busiest part of the town, especially around the beautiful tiled fountain. Opposite the entrance is a group of makeshift stalls selling nougat and nuts in abundance. Nougat, giant poles of it, like furled umbrellas in every imaginable colour, is a speciality of the town, as it is in any place of pilgrimage in the Arab world.

Quite a wide road with a smattering of stalls leads down to the city gate where people wait for lifts. Transport is either by bus, communal taxi or pick-up trucks, which stop and are filled in an instant by those bound for Méknès, Fez or Sidi Kacem.

Before you go: Worth looking out for on the left as you walk down to the main city gate is an extraordinary house. A Heath Robinson-type construction, a mish-mash of materials—TVs, motorbike parts, bits of cloth and metal—rising three storeys, it is almost the only building acknowledging the modern world in Moulay Idriss. It's remarkable in its incongruity.

Although hundreds of tourist buses visit Volubilis, only one kilometre away, there are none to be seen in Moulay Idriss. At one time Christians were forbidden in the town, and until recently not permitted to stay overnight. Nobody is unfriendly, but you may feel you are invading their privacy. Bear this possibility in mind if you can because it is an unique place and, with the proposed site of the five-star hotel above Volubilis, its days of peace may be numbered.

Ceremonial serving dishes are prepared for the *moussem*.

VOLUBILIS

Just above the ancient site of Volubilis in the foothills of the Zerhoun mountains is the proposed site of a five-star luxury hotel. It isn't hard to imagine how this introduction will alter what is now a beautiful and peaceful spot.

Three approaches offer agreeable variety to a round trip from Fez via Méknès, Volubilis, Moulay Idriss and back. This trip can easily be done in a day: 94 miles (150 km) in total.

Approaching from Méknès, you slowly climb the hillside until, rounding a corner, you can see **Volubilis** stretched out on the ledge of a triangular plateau 127 ft (390 metres) high. By-passing the turn to Moulay Idriss (clustered between two hillsides to the northeast), you take a left fork and soon the sand-coloured buildings around the entrance to Volubilis are visible just up to your right. A car-park and a couple of souvenir shacks welcome you. Just beside the entrance is a well-positioned shady café looking across to the site.

There is a small, moderately interesting **open-air museum** in the garden as you enter through the southeast gate. Many pieces of inscribed stone and other fragments lie haphazardly around. The archaeologically important finds have been removed to the archaeological museum in Rabat.

Following a well-worn path through olive groves and across the small **Fertassa river**, you clamber leftwards up the opposite hill to the beginnings of the site. The sense of peace is immediate, unless you're unlucky enough to arrive with a batch of coaches. Best times are early morning before they arrive, or evening when the buses have left.

Traces of a Neolithic settlement have been found here, and those of an important Berber village thought to have been the capital of the Berber kingdom of Mauritania. Caligula was responsible for taking over this kingdom and from A.D. 45 Volubilis was subject to direct Roman rule, making it the Empire's most remote base.

During this time, oil production and copper were the city's main assets. The profusion of oil presses found on the site confirms this—one or two to a house. Most of the buildings date from the beginning of the third century, when the number of inhabitants is estimated at 20,000. By the end of the third century the Romans had gone.

There was only very gradual changes; Volubilis maintained its Latinised structure and when the Arabs arrived in the seventh century the mixed population of Berbers, Jews and Syrians still spoke Latin. The culture and teachings of Islam took over and by 786, when Moulay Idriss I arrived, most of the inhabitants were already converted. He preferred to build his city (Moulay Idriss) nearby, and Volubilis began to decline. Moulay Ismail desecrated it by removing the marble to adorn his palaces in Méknès.

The earthquake in Lisbon in 1755

damaged the city and it fell into ruin. A story goes that it was rediscovered by two diplomats on a tour of the area at the end of the 19th century, but it is hard to believe that it could have been ignored for so long considering the splendid Triumphal Arch, the only edifice to remain standing, keeping sentinel over the site. Excavations were begun during the French protectorate in 1915 and continue, funded by the Moroccan government.

Volubilis is small and easy to cover. Some of the main buildings have been half restored or reconstructed. The most remarkable finds have been some bronze statues and the amazingly well-preserved **mosaics**. The statues are now in Rabat but the majority of the mosaics remain *in situ*. For purposes of identification, the houses are named after the subject of the mosaic within them.

All follow the same basic structure: every house had its public and private rooms. The mosaics usually decorated the public rooms and internal courtyards; the baths and kitchens being the private areas of the house. First is the **House of Orpheus**, the largest house in its quarter. It has three mosaics: a circular mosaic of Orpheus (God of music) charming the animals with his lyre, remarkable for its detail and colours; another of nine dolphins, believed by the Romans to bring good luck; and the third portraying an attractive scene of Amphitrite in a chariot drawn by a seahorse.

Wandering up the wide paved street, you pass the remains of the **public baths** restored by Gallienus in the third century. Bathing was given high priority by the Romans and public baths provided a meeting place to chat, gossip, do business, eat and drink, though grander houses had their own elaborate heating systems providing hot water and steam for baths and heat.

The street opens out into the **Forum** (public square) with the **Capitol** and **Basilica** to the east: an impressive collection of administrative buildings comprising the centre of the city.

The Triumphal Arch.

The **Capitol** is a small rectangular building of classic type; originally the central area would have been surrounded by porticoes and contained a temple fronted by four columns. The terrace and several Corinthian columns have been reconstructed. Inscription dates it 217 and dedicates the temple to the cult of Capitoline, Jove and Minerva.

The **Basilica** is a larger building beside the Capitol. It isn't easy to see its structure now but it would have been divided into five aisles with an apse at both ends, doubling up as the law courts and a place of commercial exchange.

The **Forum,** completing the administrative centre, is an open space used for public and political meetings (a glorified Speakers' Corner) of modest proportions. Nothing remains of the statues of dignitaries that would have adorned the surrounding buildings.

Between the Forum and the Triumphal Arch in the **Acrobat's House**, you can see two well preserved mosaics. The main one depicts an acrobat riding his mount back-to-front and holding his prize. Another, ruined, house nearby did contain the famous Bronze Dog, now in the museum in Rabat and well worth seeing.

The **Triumphal Arch** is the centrepoint of Volubilis and provides an impressive, if non-functional, ceremonial monument. Contemporary to the Capitol, it was built by Marcus Aurelius Sebastenus in honour of Caracalla and his mother Julia Domna. It is supported on marble columns and highly decorated only on the east side. Records and the inscription suggest it was surmounted by a huge bronze chariot and horses. It was a magnificient celebration of the power of the Emperor Caracalla and remains a remarkable edifice.

The main paved street, **Decumanus Maximus**, stretches northwest straight up to the **Tangier Gate** (the only one of eight remaining), lined with what must have been the finest houses in town. Their frontages were rented to shopkeepers, who sold their wares from

One of the well-preserved mosaics.

the shaded porticoes on either side. The layout is similar to parts of the Moroccan medina today.

Behind, in a number of ruined houses, are more mosaics. The **House of Ephebus** boasts the Bacchus mosaic, depicting the god of wine in a chariot pulled by panthers. A bronze head of Ephebus was found in this house but has been despatched to Rabat. The **House of Columns**, recognisable by the remains of columns guarding the entrance to the courtyard, has an ornamental basin surrounded by brilliant red geraniums.

The **Knight's House**, next to this, is in a poor state except for the mosaic of Dionysus discovering the sleeping Ariadne, one of the loveliest sights of Volubilis.

Most of the larger houses on this northwest side of Decumanus Maximus contain well-preserved mosaics; but don't miss the **House of Venus** and the **House of Nereids** a couple of streets in, to the west side. The former must have been the home of an important dignitary, for here the bronze heads of Cato and Juba II were found (now in Rabat). Beautiful mosaics depict mythological scenes, including the abduction of Hylas by Nymphs and Diana bathing surprised by Acteon.

The well-worn path curls round behind the Basilica and Forum, bringing you back to the entrance. The mint tea in the open but shady café looking across to the site is delicious.

The position, atmosphere and mosaics combine to make Volubilis an essential stop on any itinerary. The excavations and reconstructions are extensive enough to give you an idea of life in the third century and later. Geckos running up and down the crumbling walls, darting into invisible holes, occasional whiffs of highly-scented flowers, the clear air and the silence on the plateau all combine to make it an unforgettable visit.

Worth remembering if you're a keen photographer is to carry a large bottle of water. The Moroccan sun is fairly reliable and the colours of the mosaics are heightened when wet.

218

MARRAKESH

The name itself beckons—though less seductively, perhaps, than Isfahan and far Samarkand, for **Marrakesh** boasts no works of a Shah Jahan nor of a Tamerlane the Great. Compared with these dazzling centres of Islam, Marrakesh is to be appreciated more for what it does than what it is.

As the "Kingdom of Marrakesh", it is said to have given its name to the country, although the greater generalisation of "Mahgreb" also has its claims. In any event, Marrakesh has always been a place of some importance and it is well aware of the fact.

The location is perfect. Man settled here since before the dawn of history. The land is watered in abundance by the rivers and streams of the Atlas Mountains, which provide a spectacular backdrop as they rise to some 12,000 ft (3,800 metres) and stand at just the right distance from the city to fill out the most impressive perspective. In the summer months the heights are often lost behind a haze of heat and, it must be said, the polluting products of Marrakesh's burgeoning industry. The winter visitor has the best of it, for then the peaks are covered in snow and, to those from higher latitudes, snow in Africa is always a beguiling prospect.

As a winter haven Marrakesh lives up to its promise. The luminous sky indicates that the Atlantic Ocean is not far away; but it is the depth of blue, telling of the wider sand sea of the Sahara, that gives a clue to the true nature of Marrakesh: an oasis, a city of the desert.

Look for confirmation to the profusion of greenery, the gardens set there just to challenge the advance of aridity, and the pride with which they are shown off and tended. And note, too, the broad avenues lined with orange trees, their golden fruit a gesture of triumph that outdoes the sterile palm or strident cypress. Then, as a foil to level light on primary colours, every building of Marrakesh, new and old, comes in its particular shade of dusky pink. And that's just the beginning of its charm.

The city's founding: Like many another city, Marrakesh grew up around a fortified settlement. It developed enclosing walls within which outworkers and pastoralists with flocks could seek refuge when under threat. Markets were established, and the settled way of life was seen to have advantages that led to prosperity. More recently, in colonial times, new development tried to conserve what was there already. Marrakesh, in fact, is the paradigm for a city.

A date for the casting of Marrakesh in this mould lies somewhere in the later half of the 11th century. The original, stone-built *ksar*, or kasbah, was most likely set up at this point by the Almoravid, Abou Bakr, as an act of defiance towards the marauding tribes that populated the foothills of the Atlas, and which would unite him with the more sedentary peoples of the valleys and the plain.

As such, it was well located to take advantage of the sea ports on the Atlantic coast and the northerly trade routes of the Sahara. In the centuries to follow, nowhere else laid claim to be the Mahgreb's southern capital.

Marrakesh was the creation of Abou Bakr's successor, Ali ben Youssef. It was he who built the mosque that still bears his name and, significantly, it was he who constructed the system of elaborate underground water ways that channel the streams and rivers of the hills to irrigate the extensive palmeries and formal gardens.

It was this plentiful supply of good water that enabled the city to be built so rapidly and with such abandoned display of energy. The evidence is all around today, and at its most imposing in the massive walls and gates: where these are modern restorations they follow closely the line and dimensions of the original structures.

As elsewhere, the fortunes of Marrakesh were bound up with the fortunes of its rulers. In the middle of the 12th century, the Almohad dynasty ousted the failing Almoravids in three days of fire and pillage. Good works came after the destruction: Abd el Moumin built

Marrakesh

500 m

Av. el Jadida

to Fez Meknes

Route Principale N°. 24

Oued Issil

Route des Remparts

Sidi Bel Abbes Mosque

Derb Kaa el Mechra

Bab el Khemis

R. Assouel

R. de Bab Khemis

Zaouia Sidi Ben Slimane

R. de Bab Taâhzout

Antaki Hospital

R. el Gza

R. Boutfouil

Bab Doukkala

ed el Mellakh

R. el Adala

Kouba Almoravid

Bab Debbarh

R. de Bab Debbarh

Medrassa ben Youssef

Tanneries

Bab Doukkala Mosque

Rue de Bab Doukkala

R. Fatima Zohra

R. Issebtiyne

MEDINA

R. Azbezt

Bab Larissa

Echrob ou Chouf Fountain

Pl. R. Kedima

Bab Ailen

R. de Bab Ailen

Town Hall

R.S. el Yamani

SOUKS

Av. Mohammed V

Rue Mouassine

R.S. Smarine

R. Dabachi

R. A. el Abbes Sebti

Triq el Koutoubia

Djemma el Fna

R. Bab Ahmad

Yarmouk

rrachid

R. el Mouahidine

Bank of Morocco

Koutoubia

Medina Post Office

R. Riad Z. el Kedim

R. Riad Z. el Jdid

La Bahia

Av. H. el Fetouaki

R.S. Mimoun

R. Oqba Ben Nafaa

Av. H. el Fetouaki

Pl. des Ferblantiers

R. Berrima

Badi Palace

Bab er Rob

Saadian Tombs

Royal Palace

Bab Ahmar

R. de Bab Ahmar

Route N°. 501

Route N°. 513

R. de Bab Irhli

AGDAL GARDENS

to Ourzatate Le Golf

the Koutoubia mosque, in two distinct phases, it is now known; after him, Abou Yacoub Youssef extended the walls and his heir, Yacoub el Mansour (said to be a black man, like his father) built a new mosque, a new Kasbah, and founded a hospital.

To this hospital came the celebrated Abou Marwan Abd el Malik ibn Zoar (known to the scholars of the West as Avenzoar) and Mohammed ibn Rashid (or Averroes). These Arab philosopher-physicians, in observing that people suffering from an illness can transmit it to those they contact, propounded a germ theory of disease—and this at a time when European response to pestilence was to crowd into churches and pray.

After these great days, Marrakesh fell once more in disarray. It had its periods of glory under various occupiers, but it was not until well on in the 16th century that Abdullah el Ghalib set about restoring the old, ruinous buildings and constructing some of his own. He made a customs house for the Christian community and formalised the *mellah* so that the Jews could trade and worship apart from the Muslims. His death allowed disorder to break out. During the reign of Ahmed el Mansour Marrakesh prospered: he built El Badi Palace and the Saadi Tombs and his was a city of learning.

The 18th and 19th centuries saw Marrakesh undergo further depredations and refurbishment: Moulay Ismail has not had a good history on account of his stripping El Badi Palace, although it seems to have been in a sorry state even before he lifted a finger. In the early 1800s Moulay Sulieman rebuilt the Ben Youssef mosque, and laid out the Menara gardens. But it was not until the French arrived, resettled the medina, constructed the new town of Gueliz, and ordered things generally that Marrakesh assumed the happy condition in which the visitor now finds it.

Evening Assembly: If the heart of Marrakesh beats for the visitor, it beats most vitally in a clearing at the centre of the medina called the **"Djemma el**

Preceding pages, limited reconstruction at Volubilis; wandering through the souks; late afternoon, and events on the Djemma el Fna begin. **Below,** crowds soon gather.

222

Fna". The name has been well chewed-over to yield a meaning as to the prime function of this place. Does it mean "The Mosque that came to Nothing"? Hardly. It would be an overweening builder who sought to outdo the great Koutoubia so close at hand. Or is it "Assembly-place of the Nobodies"? *Djemma* means "assembly" as well as "mosque" and it is recorded that the spot was a place of execution. Most likely, it always was as now: a gathering ground for merchants, touts, beggars, fake water-sellers, acrobats, snake-charmers, medicine men, performers of each and every sort, and just about anyone with indeterminate business to conduct in public.

It is a great show. Activity commences as the sun begins to set. Groups of *djellabah*-clad figures give an authentic air: this is no mere tourist event. Well, yes and no. The crowds are for the most part out-of-towners, in from the surrounding countryside to gape and marvel. Townspeople come only to show the Djemma to their friends and visiting relatives.

A good vantage point is the upper level of the Café de France where, for the cost of a mint tea sweetened just the bearable side of drinkable, many scenes can be taken in at once.

They are desultory performers: groups form in a ring around one lot, they dissolve, and form again. Any apparent lack of purpose betrays a want of knowledge of the matter in hand. Two men are tied back to back while a third squirts water from a blue plastic bottle over them. Their heap of props gets soaked. Then one puts on a board as an apron and the others beat him loud and long. The crowd knows the story, reckons it badly brought off, and wanders away.

The snake-charmers and their bored reptiles have a thin time apart from a tourist camera. Water-sellers, bulled up like old sergeant-majors, pose too. And who, in the rank of blind beggars, has the half of an eye to prompt the wailing? Single-headed drums rattled with a bent stick, and double-reed pipes obeying a scale all their own keep up their tattoo

for all-comers. To join the throng is inviting, the promise of an encounter worth the telling.

Down in the Djemma the show appears self-perpetuating, and there are appetising smells as the food stalls light up for business. Passing the quiet, knowing old men seated among their pots and jars and apothecary scales ready to dispense a cure for impotence, the pox, and anything else known to respond to a spell and a specific, the visitor can make his choice of meal. The thick soups, strings of little sausages, and sizzling stuffed aubergines must be measured against the temperature of blue-smoking fat: do the numbers on a pole mean hygiene regulation?

Move on to the fuss around the tooth-puller; he is hamming it for a tourist. The photographers frame the heap of teeth, but avoid the rows of old, well-worn dentures. They tell a pathetic tale of hardship and pose the worrying question: How many poor does it take in Marrakesh to make one rich man?

The Souks: North of the Djemma lie

The apothecary stall: herbs, cosmetics and dead animals.

the tempting souks of Marrakesh. This area, by no means as extensive as the maze and ramifications of its alleyways may suggest, is best visited of a morning and, even if you set out with all the good intentions of keeping to a route and not getting lost, you will find the chief fascination is to wander.

Textiles in the **Souk Semmarin** soon give on to the carpets of the Berber dealers, with the coppersmiths over to the left and the jewellers to the right; the **kissarias**, covered shops devoted to Western-influenced goods, lead to the leather-workers of the Souk **Cherratin** and then, if a northerly direction has been maintained, out into the open space in front of the **Ben Youssef** Mosque and its attendant *medrassa*.

The bewildering cries and the press of the throng can be off-putting to the unaccustomed visitor, but he can be sure of a ready welcome at any of the quaint, narrow little shops, open-fronted and packed with goods for sale, especially if he has money to spend. Most of the stuff is of poor quality and the readiness of the tourist to pay for shoddy work no incentive to do better.

Here is the point to remember the local Arabs' attitude to travel; having no experience of travel themselves, save for the pilgrimage to Mecca, they regard Westerners as pitiable fools sent into their hands by a benificent God. With tourists compounding the folly by unquestioning payment of an asking price, it is little wonder that the souks are so generously provided with mosques and that thankful Muslims flock to them five times a day.

The visitor may choose to take a "guide" into the souks, or call on one to find his way out; but he should be aware these importuning individuals are out to do themselves a greater service than that of their charges. At best, engaging one keeps the others at bay. As with the useful *petit taxi* and the *calèche*, it is advisable to fix a price at the outset and stick firmly to it. The inhabitants of Marrakesh carry a lot of Berber blood in their veins and they can be assertive to the level of aggression (the hill people

Left, inside a carpet factory. **Right**, a theatre poster.

of Syria, and the Afghans, come to mind in this respect) and it ought to be recognised that a rebuff is not going to be accepted graciously.

While a driver will settle for a dirham a head from locals, he demands more from the visitor and the four-mile (six-km) drive from Marrakesh airport to the medina must surely be the world's most costly journey (always excepting a camel ride round the pyramids of Egypt). For this reason, it is no bad idea to stay near the medina and investigate Marrakesh on foot; the distances are not great and the going pretty smooth.

From the area north of the souks (which peter out into dwellings) it is possible to visit either the stately Ben Youssef complex or to strike out west towards the **Bab Debbagh** and the **tanneries**, located on the outskirts of the medina for reasons all too obvious. Looking down on the colourful and animated scene with its effortful energy, its flood of oaths and imprecations, there is indeed an impressive sight for those whose sense of the picturesque is not diminished by the all-pervading stench and the manifest evidence of slaughter and flaying. Nonetheless, it is perhaps as well to be reminded such civilised pleasures as a fine morocco binding have their origins in a shambles. Regrettable, too, that the days when entire European libraries were sent to Morocco for rich binding and exquisite tooling are long gone; now a treasured volume is likely to come back bound upside down, back to front, or both.

In Islam's name: Dating from the first quarter of the 12th century the **Ali ben Youssef Mosque** is the oldest in Marrakesh; it is not only heavily restored but was virtually rebuilt by Moulay Sulieman in the early 19th century. Apart from the magnificent ceilings, it is a plain building, and the minaret by no means impressive.

Subsidiary to the mosque is the annex for ablutions, the **Koubba el Baroudiyin**, only recently discovered (1947) and remarkable as the sole surviving Almoravid structure in Mar-

Peddling religion.

rakesh. It consists of a two-storey kiosk with a grey dome; it exhibits a good deal of intricate work inside and out, and is a building of supreme importance in the development of Islamic architecture in the Maghreb.

Significant too is the **Ali ben Youssef Medrassa**, located to the east of its mosque and set at an angle to it. The *medersa*, or teaching establishments, were unknown when the mosque was built and consequently it is of a later date, being founded by Abdullah el Ghalib in 1565, when it was the largest of the Maghrebi *medersa*. The entrance is almost concealed and, once found, leads indirectly by means of a vestibule to the inner court: as such it prepares for the air of quiet contemplation within.

Features of the court are the colonnades running along two sides, the prayer hall, and the area devoted to ablutions. Stairs lead up to the students' cells on the upper storey; although there are possibly no more than 100 of these, some 400 teachers and pupils are said to have studied here at one time.

Worthy of note is the rectangular marble basin now standing in the prayer hall: covered with carvings of animals and plants, it shows a fine disdain for Islamic proscription on representing living forms. It can be dated to the 10th century, traced to Cordoba, and is known to have been brought by Ali ben Youssef to stand in his mosque, where it stayed until it was moved to its present site during the Saadi's reconstruction.

Dominating the city of Marrakesh is the minaret of the **Koutoubia** mosque, a building of great age lying in unprepossessing surroundings a little to the south of the Djemma el Fna and itself the focal point of the southern half of the medina. The name "Koutoubia" is a corruption of *kutub*, the Arabic root of words meaning "to write" and hence "books". It is applied to the mosque because early descriptions spoke of it being at the centre of the shops and stalls of more than 100 booksellers.

Even allowing for exaggeration, and that "hundred" is often synonymous with "many", this suggests a quite in-

City of cyclists and charmers.

credible degree of literacy in medieval Marrakesh. More likely, there was a large number of scribes plying their trade here as well (their descendants can be seen in the barest of the souk's booths: a couple of chairs, a table and an ancient typewriter are the give-away).

The Koutoubia mosque was built in two stages, the first was begun in 1147 and the second, on the present irregular ground plan (an attempt to re-align the *quibla* or prayer niche while respecting the former one), in 1158. This mosque, and what excavation has revealed of its predecessor, offer much to the specialist in Islamic architecture, particularly when parallels with contemporary structures as far away as Damascus, and those of Cordoba and Kairouan can be so readily drawn. The visitor must accept this as further evidence of the extent of the glorious flowering of Islamic culture throughout a period when northern Europe was enveloped in a Dark Age of its own making, and turn his attention to the unsurpassed minaret.

Seen from a distance the **Koutoubia minaret** proclaims its ancestry: as with the desert lighthouse and the ancient ziggurat, it is a landmark. (Within the city it can be a deceptive one: at a casual glance many a minaret of Marrakesh looks like the Koutoubia.) The tower is almost 230 ft (70 metres) high and 42 ft (12 metres) square, a pleasing proportion of five-to-one. No other building in Marrakesh, not even among the hotels and apartment blocks, is higher; only a telecommunications mast outdoes it.

Started around 1150, it took some 40 years to complete and, unlike other towers of a similar age in Seville and Rabat, the Koutoubia, has not thus far been restored. Whether it should be subjected to restoration, to produce something akin to the minaret of the Kasbah Mosque, is the subject of heated debate.

The tower has inner and outer walls with a ramp running up in between. This is characteristic of towers in Europe, which were thus built to allow pieces of ordnance to be hauled up to a height so that an increase in elevation would be matched by an increase in range. That the Kasbah Mosque was damaged in 1569, when the magazine it contained blew up, does suggest Marrakesh's minarets might have had some military function in their past.

The Koutoubia minaret contains six vaulted chambers, one above the other. The outer wall is perforated by richly-carved window arches at differing levels on each face, and the detail of the ornamented stonework opens out in perspective as it rises. The upper stonework is less fine than that of the lower levels and, for purely practical reasons, the individual blocks are smaller nearer the top; the somewhat shoddy appearance this gives does indicate, however, that the surface was rendered and painted. Little now remains of the faïence band that once ran round the upper level.

The lantern sitting atop the tower is sizeable; it has two chambers but is rather concealed by the high parapet of machiolation that surmounts the body of the tower. Above it the two gold balls and pear-shaped drop of diminishing

The Koutoubia minaret.

size are a feature found on nearly all of Marrakesh's minarets. Legend has it that Yacoub el Mansour's wife relinquished her jewels to provide them as a penance for breaking the fast of Ramadan. Legend says the same about the Kasbah Mosque. The curious gibbet-like structure to one side is, in fact, a flagpole of venerable age.

In the last decade of the 12th century, when Yacoub el Mansour built the present Kasbah to replace the Almoravid one, he also established the **Kasbah Mosque**. Although greatly altered over the centuries, it retains its original square plan; it is a complex of subsidiary chambers and courts; of the seven doors installed by Yacoub, four now remain to open on to the public square.

The minaret, to the northwest corner, rivals that of the Koutoubia in grandeur. Its gleaming, pristine tiles are the outcome of skilled and dedicated restoration and, to some eyes, it makes an eloquent case for similar treatment of the Koutoubia. Lying in a secluded enclave to the rear of the Kasbah Mosque are the **Tombs of the Saadis**, a singular necropolis that was lost to the world between the death of the demented Moulay el Yazid (who was the last ruler to be buried here in 1792) and its re-discovery during a survey by the French in 1917.

So as not to intrude on worshippers at the mosque a new route to the tombs was driven in a narrow defile to the right of the mosque and following the enclosure wall erected by the Saadis. He is a lucky visitor who has the place to himself and the chip, chip, chip of the restorers' chisels, the fluttering of the doves, and the attention of a friendly cat (of all the animals of Marrakesh, cats seem to have the best of it); all that is wanting is the tinkling of a fountain.

There are 100 or so graves scattered about, each with its tiled slab, and two principal mausoleums having 66 burials within them. The first mausoleum, on the left by the entrance, was built by Ahmed el Mansour for himself, and the further one for Lalla Masuda, his mother.

A morning shave.

The work here is of the finest, a tribute to the ancient hand that fashioned it no less than the modern one that put it back into order. Note the dignified form of the vaulting competing with the exuberance of the decoration; observe the cleverly-calculated effect of the filtered light; and then give an eye to the crowding of the burials into this favoured place, and the elaborate Koranic inscriptions.

There are two important *zaouia* in Marrakesh; a *zaouia* is a religious foundation, part monastery, part cult centre, and strictly forbidden to non-Muslims. The **Zaouia of Sidi bela Abbes** lies at the northernmost corner of the medina; it is dedicated to a 12th-century miracle-worker and the present buildings were erected by Moulay Ismail, less out of piety than political expediency. The smaller, yet equally active, **Zaouia of Sidi ben Slimann** is to the southwest. These *zaouia* maintain their educational function alongside charitable activities; food is distributed to the blind of an evening.

The **mellah**, or Jewish Quarter of Marrakesh, lies off the Place des Ferblantiers (formerly the Place du Mellah); it is much reduced in size now, the Jews having emigrated during the 1950s and 1960s, and what is left are typically narrow houses, densely packed and enclosed, and exuding an air of poverty. Just why the *mellah* was established (in 1558) is not clear; there may have been a pogrom, it may have been advantageous to have the Jews in one small area for purposes of taxation (they controlled the Saadi sugar trade), it may have also been useful to have scapegoats strategically placed between people and palace, or perhaps it was simply in order to allow Jews and Muslims to work and worship without each offending the other.

For the few elderly Jews who remain, there are some synagogues, mainly in private houses; one is attached to a hostel kept up by American Jews. The Jewish cemetery is to the east of the enclave.

The palaces of the successive rulers of Marrakesh are, by and large, poor reflections of former glory. The most celebrated, **El Badi Palace** of Ahmed el Mansour, is now a ruin. It is reached from the **Place des Formentiers** by way of the **Bab Berrina**, a roundabout route that should not disorientate the visitor: El Badi is hard by the Saadi Tombs and Kasbah Mosque. Built between 1578 and 1602 El Badi was a sumptuous affair funded by trade in slaves and sugar, and gold from the capture of Timbuctoo and the plunder of Saharan caravans. El Badi is currently the site of a folk festival, usually held in June: a nice irony.

What remains of El Badi is mostly the ceremonial parts of the Palace. Now laid out as gardens with lofty trees, it presents a strange appearance, as if everything was planted in holes (as, indeed, are the trees along Marrakesh's modern avenues). This is because of the underground system of irrigation tanks and channels and raised walkways. The central court, 425 ft (130 metres) long and very nearly as wide, was once surrounded by stately pavilions, the most

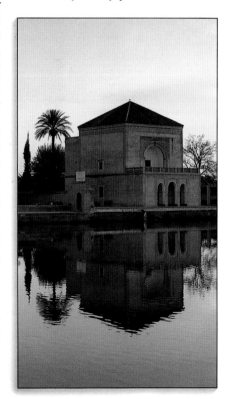

THE HARD SELL

There is a character in Tangier whom every tourist is likely to meet. If it's car hire that is wanted, or a hotel reservation, or a good restaurant, he materialises as though by magic. He has a broad smile and handsome face; his manner is persistent but unfailingly courteous and humorous. At some point in the conversation he usually boasts of being included in the book *The Rogue's Guide to Tangier*, an irreverent excursion round the town's *demi-monde*.

Instead of fleeing in haste at this information as any sensible tourist should, the tendency is to ask him to elaborate. He must do good "business", one remarks, noticing his fit, sharply-dressed physique. "Good at the moment," an eavesdropper replies. "He is the greatest hustler in Tangier. When he has no business, he is like a dried and withered plant." Later it materialises that the speaker is the contender to the title, the town's second biggest hustler.

Hustlers are endemic in Morocco, particularly in Fez, Marrakesh and Tangier, though increasingly in the previously relaxed south. Even visitors spending a holiday touring the Atlas by bicycle experience the menace; shepherd boys cease to seem straight out of an Arcadian idyll when they fail to extract the desired cigarette or dirham from the passing cyclist. They are usually armed with stones, and are practised shots.

The main aim of the worst kind of hustler is to entice the gullible tourist into the carpet and brassware shops, invariably owned by an "uncle" or "brother" who can offer "special price", and collect their commission on goods bought. Usually they pose as guides offering to provide a tour of the souks for a reasonable enough sum or in return for the chance to practise their English, German or Spanish—whichever is the language of their prey. The number of ageing, pot-bellied characters claiming to be "students" strikes even the greenest tourist as suspicious.

In cities such as Fez and Marrakesh, certain hustlers work particular hotels. The younger, apprentice hustlers hang around the entrances to the souks—the Bab el Ftouh in Fez and the Djemma el Fna in Marrakesh. Past these points it is perfectly possible to proceed unharassed and to consult normal Marrakshis or Fassis (who are not even aware of the problem) for advice.

The amount of commission earned from a purchase is usually 30 percent. It is never claimed there and then. The hustler, or "guide" to give him the euphemistic title he prefers, keeps quiet during the bargaining and departs with the tourist as though he has no interest in proceedings. He returns to claim his cut later.

Pressures to buy are enormous. There are few browsers to divert enough attention for one to bolt. Sometimes, lured into a shop for a cursory glance round, the visitor is uncomfortable to find a succession of lights switched on for his exclusive benefit, the tea already brewing and carpets unfurled on which he is supposed to sit. The sales patter is often laughably theatrical.

The Moroccan government is just beginning to recognise that unofficial guides, who to begin with were considered colourful and amusing (as well as not adding to the unemployment problem), have become troublesome. When the less sophisticated hustlers turn nasty, as they often do in Fez and Marrakesh when failure to respond to persistent pressure can result in a tirade of abusive language and accusations of "racism", it starts to become a deterrent to visiting the country. (Incidentally, one should remember that Morocco has a rich tradition of curses, which shouldn't be taken too personally.)

The best ways of dealing with hustlers is either to feign total deafness and blindness, though this requires nerves of steel and then one may as well be a package-tourist sealed up in air-conditioned coach and hotel apartment, or to judge each situation separately and employ varying measures of good-humour and firmness, a preferable option but requiring experience.

It can be worth hiring an official guide—well-trained and knowledgeable—at the tourist office. This costs around l00 dirhams for a morning, and this may be cheaper in the long run in view of all the leather pouffes that might be avoided. Even these guides, though, are sometimes keen to make a little extra profit.

splendid of which, a *liwan* of 50 columns, was used to receive important visitors.

Contemporary accounts tell of the glories of El Badi, not least the festivities marking its completion. When El Mansour asked his jester what he thought of his magnificent creation, back came a prescient reply: "It will make a beautiful ruin."

To the northwest of El Badi Palace is **La Bahia** (more properly, "El Bahiya" which means "the brilliant"), a late 19th-century construction, the work of one Si' Moussa, Grand Vizier to Sidi Mohammed II, and a building almost totally lacking in style, elegance or taste, compared with what Marrakesh had seen earlier.

Of the same period but far more restrained is the **Dar Si' Palace** to the northwest. This, too, was built by a Grand Vizier (to Moulay Hassan) whose brother was responsible for extending La Bahia. It serves to house the **Museum of Morrocan Arts**, a thought-provoking collection, often at variance with its surroundings, but which must be seen to appreciate fully the achievements of Maghrebi craftsmen through the ages.

Due south of El Badi is the **Dar el Makhzen** or Royal Palace where the King of Morocco reigns for three months of the year; it is heavily guarded and visitors are not allowed in.

A place for sybarites: A colourful figure of modern times was Thami el Glaoui, last Pasha of Marrakesh and an exotic remnant of a great southern tribe which commanded the Telouet pass in the Atlas south of Marrakesh. His palace, the **Dar el Glaoui**, lies at the northwest corner of the medina, by the Bab Doukkala. It is said to be what 1920s Hollywood might think of as Moroccan: kitsch amongst the traditional.

Thami, who died in 1956, was a shrewd and calculating supporter of the colonising forces; the parties he gave for them are legendary for their lavish dissolution. Among the gifts pressed on guests were everything from opium and diamonds to girls and boys fresh from

Carrying the vegetables.

the High Atlas. Winston Churchill, who was never particular about the company he kept provided it indulged him sufficiently, was a close friend of Thami, and a regular visitor to Marrakesh.

It still seems slightly shocking that Churchill should take off for his favoured Marrakesh at the height of World War II, albeit to get over a stroke. He used to stay at the **Hotel La Mamounia**, conveniently located in the **Mamounia Gardens**, just inside the **Bab Djid**: previously a palace of sorts, it was converted into an hotel in 1926 and underwent extensive renovation in 1986.

It claims to have carried this out in a 1920s style, and gives its Gallery the name of Rennie Mackintosh, but *art nouveau* was rarely as garish as this. The Winston Churchill Suite (No. 300) is a Moroccan idea of a gentlemen's club; pictures of (and by) the Grand Old Man abound; the valet's ante-room is fitted out for a bodyguard. Jalousies operate by a bedside button—and the tariff is impressive, too.

Marrakesh has remained a popular watering-hole for the rich and famous. The Shah of Iran used La Mamounia as a bolthole in 1979. Most recently, Marrakesh has attracted the biggest names in *haute couture*: Yves St Laurent, Pierre Cardin and Pierre Balmain.

The modern suburb: Gueliz, home to many of the city's 400,000 inhabitants, lies to the west of the medina; it can be reached by bus (No. 1) from the Koutoubia. Gueliz is laid out in familiar French provincial (and colonial) style, its broad avenues lined with orange and jacaranda trees and radiating from a central Place. Houses and blocks of flats, all in the dusty pink of Marrakesh, are neat and well-kept.

Gueliz accommodates the railway station, municipal buildings, a youth hostel and camping site; otherwise, like a sleepy French town, it is rather dull.

A stroll from the **Place de la Liberté** down, say, the shady **Avenue de France** (its name is not given in Arabic) shows where the quality of Marrakesh lives; here high walls conceal tempting gardens and substantial villas within.

The **public gardens** of Marrakesh are that city's abiding delight; and rightly so, for the garden has a place of affection in Islamic culture, a fact well recognised by ruler after ruler. There was Ali ben Youssef and his palmerie as early as the 12th century; but the present-day gardens of Marrakesh hardly go back as far as the 18th century, although some are replantings of older plots.

Most convenient to visit are the **Menara Gardens** to the south of the medina; the vast reservoir which is so notable a feature of the Menara may date from the time of the Almohads, who laid out the area as an olive grove. The pavilion is as recent as 1870 and replaces a Saadi building. This tranquil scene is the one that occurs so frequently on posters inviting travel to Marrakesh. It is no bad choice.

The **Agdal Gardens**, to the south of the Royal Palace, are more extensive; some two miles (three km) of irrigated land are given over to the cultivation of olives and oranges, figs, lemons, and pomegranates. Apart from the vast reservoir (possibly of Almohad date but certainly restored in the middle of the 19th century) which is filled by a series of subterranean waterways from the foot of the Atlas in the Ourika Valley, there are several lesser pools. A good overall view of the Agdal can be had from the **Dar el Hana**, a waterside pavilion built by the last pre-colonial rulers of Marrakesh.

There can be no better way of ending a visit to Marrakesh—or, for that matter, beginning one—than taking a tour of the medina walls by *calèche*. The afternoon is perhaps the best time of day for this excursion; when agreeing a price do not forget the circuit is quite a distance, and you should also allow time to descend and have a look at the more imposing of the gates, inside as well as out.

The walls are most impressive on the eastern side; the **Bab Doukkala, Bab er Rob**, and **Bab Ahmar** the most spectacular of the gates, but the beautiful **Bab Agenau**, and the recently-restored **Bab Larissa** should by no means be overlooked.

The annual folk festival in El Badi.

232

THE SOUTHWEST COAST

In l949 Orson Welles decided that **Essaouira** was an excellent place to film his *Othello*. It lies beneath low Mediterranean-type hills carved by small stony fields containing olive and thorny argan trees. After the wide lemon and pink plain west of Marrakesh, or the flat Atlantic coastlands to the town's north, the scales suddenly seem small and human. Houses are painted white and blue; there are hanging flower-baskets; there is a thriving harbour.

Yet the Alantic belts against Essaouira with vigour, and the town's fortified walls, rooted in a ragged outbreak of rocks above a sandy bay, and a crop of rocky islands opposite endow romantic drama. It has long been associated with artists (in l988 the Galerie d'Art Frederic Damgaard, showing works by new and established artists, opened in Avenue Oqba ibn Nafi), and in the l960s the most idealistic of youth cultures congregated here; Essaouira was a hippie heaven.

Pirate enclave: Until quite recently the town was known by its Spanish or Portuguese name, Mogador. It was founded in the l8th century by Sultan Mohammed ben Abdullah as a free port for those Europeans and their Jewish agents engaged in trans-Saharan gold, ivory and slave trading. Before this, it was a pirate enclave. It rapidly became a thriving town and many of Morocco's Jews migrated here. The writer Cunningham Graham, commenting on the number of Jews in Essaouira, remarked with a touch of anti-Semitism: "They sit in shops, lean out of windows, lounge on the beach, walk about slowly as if they stepped on eggs."

But Europeans, too, succeeded in incurring the dislike of the native race. The law of "protection", under which natives working for European merchants were exempted from Sultanic laws and taxation, was blatantly abused. The merchants (and diplomats) sold "protection" for exorbitant sums of money or goods in kind and the practice became a racket. The Jewish moneylenders reaped a fat rate of interest on the sums they loaned.

Designed by a European engineer (a captive of the Sultan Mohammed ben Abdullah), Essaouira has wider, more regularly shaped streets than is usual in Moroccan medinas. It also has, on Avenue Oqba ibn Nafi, a clock-tower (a most incongruous feature for Morocco), which houses in its base a late-night cigarette and postcard kiosk.

Place Moulay Hassan, just back from the harbour and the tourist office, is the town's social centre; men congregate outside the **Café de France** or play pool in its once elegant interior, the young gather at Café Sam's Macdonalds (not a burger bar, just borrowing the name) and women—without exception veiled—come to sit on the low walls in the late afternoon.

An area before the harbour, heavy with the whiff of smoking charcoal, is occupied by tables and benches. Here, from late morning, fishermen grill and

Preceding pages, back from market. Left, the battlements of Essaouira. Right, climbing a palm tree is possible.

serve sardines. At midnight the evening's catch from the larger trawlers is loaded on to lorries for transit inland.

Essaouira's main shopping thoroughfares lie behind Place Moulay el Hassan in **Avenue de l'Istiqual** and **Rue Mohammed Zerktouni**. To the right, between **Avenue Oqba ibn Nafi** and **Place Moulay el Hassan**, is an enclave of tourist shops and cafés. Toufik's House, with its cushioned low divans, brass tables and candlelight, and windows plastered with sun-blanched recommendations, is reminiscent of California at its most "ethnic" in the l960s. Self-consciously "Moroccan" it may be, but there is usually a musician to accompany the drinking of only a slightly pricey glass of tea.

The **ramparts**, though, are Essaouira's spectacular attraction. European cannons, several of British manufacture, gifts from the merchants to the Sultan Mohammed ben Abdullah, face the nearby islands, **Isles Purpuraires**, where Juba II established a factory for the manufacture of a purple dye (de-rived from a shellfish) much in demand in first-century Rome. At the end of the l9th century, the islands were used as a quarantine station for pilgrims returning from Mecca who might be importing plague. It is possible to visit the islands by fishing-boat but permission must be gained from Le Grand Gouverneur in the Province, a formality easily arranged through the tourist office.

In the potently-scented carpenters' souk beneath the ramparts, craftsmen carve everything from small boxes to tables out of cedar and thuya wood. One of the finest woodworkers' souks, it supplies shops all over the country.

Essaouira has long attracted European tourists, but it remains unspoilt. Some, those who have been let out of Agadir on coach trips, disappear at 5 p.m. Others tend to be independent holidaymakers, looking for peace and quiet. There is one upmarket hotel, the rather dour-looking **Hotel des Isles** on Boulevard Mohammed V, but for badly dilapidated grandeur and Atlantic vistas, there is **Hotel des Ramparts** built

Essaouira's harbour: one of Morocco's busiest.

into the fortified medina walls, whose entrance is on Zankat Ibn Rochd.

Essaouira attracts a veritable tide of French surfers travelling in jeeps and camper vans. Understandably, in the evening they are especially evident in **Sam's**, the fish restaurant within the harbour enclosure, and **Châlet de la Plage**. Both provide surfer-portions and are worth travelling for. Châlet de la Plage, incidentally, has a terrace-bar (popular with locals) and the bar prefacing the restaurant serves *tappas*.

Best beaches: An arc of sand lies to the south of town, but further along the coast, off the P8 rolling its way over the foothills of the snow-capped High Atlas to Agadir, minor roads and tracks lead to what the Moroccans call "*plages sauvages*", long stretches of white sand-duned beaches thickly fringed by prickly gorse and argan trees and disappearing into thin mists in the distance. Surfers—by all accounts more welcomed and much richer than their predecessors, the hippies—frequent **Cap Sim** and **Diabat**.

Sidi Kaouki, a beach dominated at its northern end by a spectacularly sited *koubba* is an excellent and more accessible alternative. A closer inspection of **Cap Tafourney**, on the other hand, a white sandy bay enclosed by hills and sheltering a small community of picturesque fishing huts (some of which sell a frugal selection of stale and sea-damp provisions), reveals washed-up detritus and animal droppings.

Less disappointing, inland north of Agadir and high in the mountains, **Imouzzer des Ida Outanane**, with its cascades and flourishing almond orchards, is worth discovering—especially as it contains one of Morocco's untouted gems, the inexpensive hotel **Auberge des Cascades**.

The villages south of **Tamri**, set in vast banana plantations, and **Cap Ghir**, the most westerly point of the High Atlas, are quiet, undeveloped places still retaining much of the appeal they had to the hippies in the 1960s—in contrast to their utterly modern neighbour, **Agadir**.

ishermen's
ea break.

THE ATLAS MOUNTAINS

Any mountain range 450 miles (700 km) long and with summits over 13,100 ft (4,000 metres) must be counted as a major topographical incident on planet earth. Since the first attempts by Europeans in the early 19th century to follow Arab trade routes across this great barrier, the number of foreign travellers penetrating the Atlas for pleasurable exploratory purposes until World War II probably never exceeded 1,000. The slogan "Death to the infidel" applied to all unaccompanied strangers in this "China of the West".

The suggestion of violence goes right back to the fanciful name bestowed by Europeans on these ranges. After the Titan Atlas was turned to stone by the cowardly Perseus (who possessed Medusa's head), his burden became a mountain allegedly supporting the heavens. The story goes that Atlas, under the weight, genuflected towards the setting sun in the northwest part of Africa.

The Atlas mystique lasted even after a prominent pass (**Tagharat**) and a distinct summit **Gourza**: 10,700 ft (3,280 metres) had been reached by outsiders in 1871. The Hooker-Ball-Maw expedition observed, "The climate is admirable, the natural obstacles of no account, but the traditional policy of the ruling race has passed into the very fibre of the inhabitants, and affords an obstacle all but impassable to ordinary travellers."

Motoring: These days the Atlas is more accessible and its inhabitants, having developed keen entrepreneurial instincts, more hospitable towards visitors. Three main roads penetrate the High Atlas from Marrakesh: the Tizi n-Test pass; the S511 through the Western Atlas to Agadir; and the Tichka Pass to Ouarzazate. From the direction of Fez, the P21 quickly climbs into the Middle Atlas, an altogether wider, more expansive mountain range than the Rif to the city's north.

Along all these routes, the contrasts in landscape are spectacular. Descending from the Middle Atlas from the rather bourgeois, almost alpine, environs of Ifrane and Azrou to the desert plain on the way to Midelt and the start of the South, motorists are struck by a pink, blue and gold infinity which looks more like a distant ocean than terra firma. Travelling in the other direction on the road from Ouarzazate to Marrakesh, it is possible to witness startling yellow desert oases, dotted with date palms and *ksour*, crowned by snow-covered peaks.

At first sight the Atlas appears to be remote. In fact, one quarter of Morocco's population lives on ground over 3,300 ft (1,000 metres) above sea-level; innumerable tiny villages populate the area, inaccessible to the hired Renault or Peugeot.

On the major roads, motoring conditions are good but, as the number of luxury coaches bearing ugly dents parked beside the Djemaa el Fna in Marrakesh testifies, vehicles whose owners are familiar with the routes are

driven with perilous speed.

Seven waterfalls: If you are staying in Marrakesh but not planning to travel in Morocco, it would be a shame not to venture into the Atlas for a day or two. The easiest excursion—still recommended, despite now being a tourist draw with its fair share of attendant entrepreneurial Berbers—is to the **Ourika Valley**, about an hour's drive south along the S513, or a one and a half hour bus journey from the Bab er Rob in Marrakesh.

The road, following the river and flanked by a string of luxury mountain villas and humble Berber homes, leads to **Setti Fatma**, high in the cleft of the valley. A busy mule track cuts deeper south, but the main attraction is the series of seven waterfalls on the far side of the river, the first of which is reached after an easy climb through the rocks and trees. In the summer, this is a popular spot for young tourists and Marakshis. There is a small café and swimming in a deep, icy rock pool. Above, wild monkeys stalk the craggy heights and shower walnuts.

In the village there are a couple of hotels, and the number of cafés, offering mainly *tajines* and omelettes, is proliferating. Typically, the owner of the Café Cascades, at the foot of the path to the waterfalls, having done well selling his exorbitantly-priced *tajines*, is planning to expand his premises into a hotel. That said, tourism is still low-key and indigenous; even in high summer the valley is an escape from Marrakesh's heat and hassle.

High hiking: In the Marrakesh district mountain climbing has expanded fivefold since 1975. Shimmering in haze beyond the pink walls of the old imperial city, long flecks of snow barely 38 miles (60 km) away brush the rugged profile of the southern horizon. Roads, teeming with peasants and animals and scooters and lorries belching diesel fumes, cross the hot Haouz plain to Asni village, where olive-covered foothills rise. Somewhere in the distance, beyond the terraced crops of maize in the Mizane valley, reigns Toubkal, the

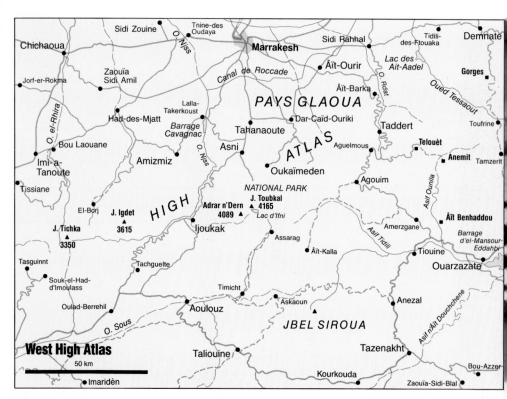

highest mountain in North Africa. Asni marks the end of French cuisine and comfortable quarters. Hereabouts the map is captioned Toubkal National Park, but such a claim is a myth seeking the reality of funding and infrastructure.

A starting point: As nothing is done by the clock in country districts, a bus comes and goes according to whim along the 11 miles (17 km) between Asni and the Mizane roadhead at **Imlil**, a good base from which to explore the Toubkal area. There are two basic inns, refreshment and food purchase, but life revolves around a snug mountain hut, with a self-catering kitchen or meals to order from the warden's family. From here, for those shod in boots, a recommended hike aims for the **Tamatert Pass** (7,475 ft/2,279 metres, 90 minutes, alternative four-wheel drive piste), then up adjoining scrub ridge to **Tanamrout** (8,650 ft/2,636 metres, 75 minutes) with its superb panorama of the Toubkal massif.

The pastoral mosque at the collection of hovels called **Sidi Chamharouch**

lies two hours along the mule trail in the upper Mizane. Like a beacon, its white roof draws many on a day outing; walk or ride a local beast. Mule hire can be expensive, even after haggling, as you pay for the animal's handler as well (£6/$10 for the round trip is about right). Among this huddle of little houses squeezed into a niche at the foot of a rockslope all Berber life is exposed to public view.

Several hundred people come to Imlil in spring and early summer to climb **Toubkal** (13,670 ft/4,167 metres). For a mountain of this height and accessibility to have had its first recorded ascent by a French party under the Marquis de Segonzac not earlier than 1923 testifies to the tribal fortress mentality maintained by the natives well into the 20th century. Visitors also go hiking round the district—there are various five to 10-day circular tours, staying overnight in remote huts, Berbers outposts and sometimes open air bivouacs.

Trekking companies predominate in these activities and supervised touring

Among the aspen trees in winter.

parties are thus spared the hassle of dealing with astute Berbers over porterage, provisions and sundry tactical and logistical matters. Hyper-friendly and super-indulgent to tourists, the natives are expert in taking advantage of unprepared travellers, but impecunious private parties can always backpack and dispense with "professional services".

Allow four to five hours for walking up the Mizane valley to the Toubkal (Neltner) hut. One-way mule hire costs £6 ($10), local guides for this and the climb on the following day £10 ($17) per day. In the vernacular these men are called *accompagnateurs*; they are registered by the local authority and twelve are resident in the Imlil district. They speak French, but rarely any other European language. If you fail to understand anything else, note that mules are not supposed to be ridden, especially up the steep, dreary stretches after Sidi Chamharouch; one mule carries the baggage of three trekkers equipped for three to four days. With snow cover on the trail before May, mules stop short of the hut and packs are carried by their handlers.

At the Toubkal hut there are spartan facilities: rain water is collected from the roof (boil first), and gully water in the stream below flushes the "toilet" outflow. Refreshments (at a price) and simple meals can be ordered from the warden. Generally, the hut is overcrowded and resulting bad tempers are common.

It is sensible to book from Imlil, preferably one day before going up to the hut, either by radio telephone, via the Imlil hut warden, or a message carried by the in-season shuttle of mules and porters. For all this and a night on a communal paillasse you pay about £2.50 ($4.25). Watch out for extras, such as use of stoves, consumables bought, tips expected (though illegal) and the application of new taxes—an attempt by the government to profit from the expanding hiking activities in the Atlas.

If you climb Toubkal before mid-May (and you should leave the hut by

Tattooed girl near Setti Fatma.

6.30 a.m.), apart from stout boots and proper clothing, you may need crampons and ice-axe for complete comfort, though experienced alpinists won't bother. Knowing the prevailing conditions, a guide will advise exactly.

As a climb, the ascent is perfectly straightforward, merely a gradual walk up a stony slope, until one reaches the notorious upper scree, where care must be taken as one false move might be dangerous. Moreover, the path is ruined by careless footwork performed by thousands of tired limbs.

The route is graded by Atlas mountaineer Peyron at "type boulevard" and, indeed, about four hours later, the summit appears like a big open corral where you half expect to see horses galloping round. In fact, you'll find people stamping feet and trotting round to keep warm, usually the T-Shirt and flip-flop brigade.

Mule riding: A popular excursion for gentle exercise and, if you wish, mule riding, goes from Imlil over the Tamatert pass to **Tacheddirt** in a relaxing

three and a half hours. It is a charming Berber settlement epitomising self-sufficiency (though when a new lorry road is completed much of this simplicity will be lost). There is accommodation in a typical mountain hut with the usual appointments.

Next day, a big climb to the Ouadi pass (9,600 ft/2,900 metres) is rewarded by views of ravined peaks zebra-striped with long streaks of snow. Riding a mule will be allowed only on the easy downslope to the broad pastures of **Oukaimeden** below. A ski resort during the winter, in spring this site is quiet and almost deserted and its hut is like a hotel, with all mod cons. Equally welcoming is a small but comfortable hotel called Chez Ju-Ju.

A local viewpoint, with orientation table, behind the condominiums commands a wide prospect towards Marrakesh, and there are prehistoric rock engravings along the north side of the pasture plateau. Huge flocks of sheep and goats graze here, as well as mouflon, best described as a cross between-

Aït Benhaddou, setting for many a Biblical epic.

the two. The Berbers are justly proud of these animals whose numbers rival sheep in the Australian outback.

The massive hulk of **Angour** dominates the scene. While an asphalt road goes back to the city, the proper completion winds westwards down paths through stunted walnut forest and evergreen oak back to the terraced fields of the Mizane and Asni—a five-hour hike.

The Toubkal area is bordered on the west by the S501 **Tizi n-Test** road. Beyond rises the Western High Atlas, remote to most tourists but surprisingly densely populated and supporting a thriving agricultural economy. The **Seksawa** valley, its boxy dwellings planted on mountainsides prickling with television aerials, is the principal inroad by transit lorry from Marrakesh. Adventurous tourers bent on exploration away from the crowds will find many diverting sights in this region.

Historic sites: After Asni, further south on the Tizi n-Test road, the route is tarred to **Ouirgane** (luxury hotel called La Roseraie) and **Ijoukak** (inn). Close by stands the ancient kasbah of **Talat n-Yaaqoub**, surrounded by olive groves, and the foaming Nfis river lapping at the foot of its ramparts. Dominating an adjacent knoll, with the snows of the western monarch **Igdet** as a backdrop, is the **Agadir n-Gouj**, a former stronghold of the Goundafi tribe, notorious in the 19th century for its dungeons. The entire location is now regarded as one of the outstanding beauty spots of the Great Atlas chain.

Higher up on the other side of the stream is the ancient mosque of **Tin Mal**—birthplace of the Almohad movement that eventually gave rise to the famous Berber dynasty of the Middle Ages. For a small *pourboire* the guardian will open up the ruins for inspection.

The mountain behind the mosque is **Gourza**, climbed by the initial Hooker botanical expedition in 1871. The Test road becomes hardcore towards the top of the pass, where it narrows, but has a good surface again all the way to Taroudant. Scenes of bad deforestation in a desolate landscape unfold on the Sahara

side of the range. Animals, winding along in Indian file, and sentinels watching over groups of dromedaries are some of the images for travellers, but the scene is actually an environmental disaster: vast forests have gone for building materials and firewood.

Here, and similarly along the eastern boundary of the Toubkal massif plainly marked by the **Tichka pass** commercial road, the watershed divides the lush from the barren. A quilt of green fields stitched round a few oases occasionally brightens the monotony.

Aït Benhaddou, which regularly functions as a set for Western film epics, is a sort of tumbledown sculpture in rusty brown mud, full of corridors, rooms, storage compartments, walkways and turrets dating from antiquity, in which some Berbers still choose to live. Their lifestyle, governed by relentless wheeling and dealing and dodging authority, is poised on a see-saw of choices and temptations.

The Glaoui, the ruling tribe across the Tichka pass area, was formerly one of

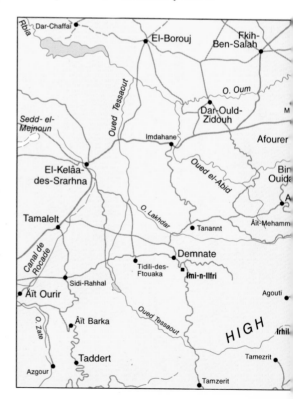

the most powerful and belligerent Berber families. They controlled trade from the Sahara to the Mediterranean over the historic **Telouet** caravan pass—the old salt road—from their kasbahs here. This route is a sporting access route for trekkers into the Central High Atlas. Beyond the Anemitèr roadhead the terrain demands toughness and stoicism.

Central High Atlas: Base centre on the north side of this sector is the **Bou Guemez** (Wgmmaz) valley, a broad expanse of greensward sprinkled with small villages, with an administrative post at **Tabant**. Once a Shangri-La, it can be entered by sturdy vehicles along a lorry track from Azilal and Aït Mehammed, normally without problems after early May but difficult in winter and spring. A new all-weather road is under construction (in 1988) due south of Azilal following the Bernat and upper Lakhdar valleys, where the highest point is the Oughbar pass.

Anticipating rapid expansion of interest in mountain activities, the authorities have singled out the Bou Guemez for absolute control by resident officials, who administer a tariff for "services" rendered; this means, for example, no choice when beds are allocated in one of the registered local Berber bunkhouses. Removing the freedom of choice in this and other matters is bound to create problems.

An outdoors centre has been opened at Tabant by the CFAMM (*Centre de Formation aux Métiers de la Montagne*). This organisation has wide powers over the supervision of tourists—accommodation, meals, provisions, mule hire, guides, search and rescue services, and co-ordination with outlying destinations. One of the ulterior motives is to curb private treaties between Berbers and tour operators.

CFAMM also dispenses grant aid to foster local agriculture and economic developments and introduce the latest technology to craftsmen working in the district. Two modern mountain huts are projected—at Azurki and Izourar—for spring skiing and summer ascents. Izourar is a seasonal lake with doubtful

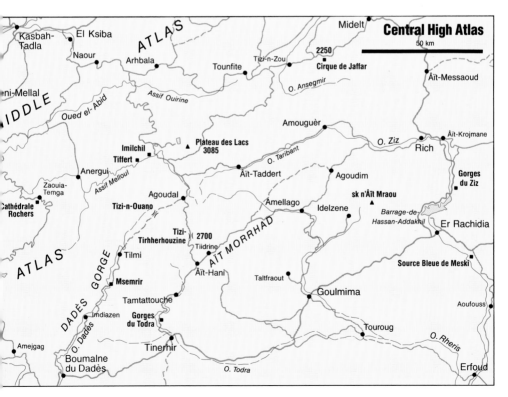

watersports and fishing potential.

The tremendous barrier ridge of **Irhil Mgoun**, 12 miles (20 km) long, dominates the area; it remains a formidable target of endurance until sleeping quarters are established. Comparatively easy to reach are the mammoth whalebacks of **Azurki** 12,100 ft (3,677 metres) and **Ouaoulzat**, or Wawgoulzat, 12,340 ft (3,763 metres), about four or five hours apiece.

Requiring stoicism: Mules and porter assistance are *de rigueur* in the Central High Atlas: it is virtually impossible to cover the ground and distances without them. Thus supported, there are fine expeditions to be made to big marble synclines like **Tignousti** and **Rat**, and cross country and valley riverbed journeys of several days to attractive villages such as **Magdaz**, where the famous poetess Mririda n-Ayt Attik was born under the tutelary pyramid of Lalla Tazerzamt. The Wandras and Arous gorges invite wetsuit wanderers and rock climbers. These grandiose features are concealed in branches of the Tassout (Tassawt) valley system draining west and northwest from Mgoun.

Another way into the area can be made from **Demnate** (62 miles/100 km from Marrakesh) along the lorry *pistes* of Tifni, the Outfi pass and Aït Tamlil. Tour operators work most of these valleys (but rarely ascend their great mountains).

Coming from the south, the valleys off the P32 Dadès road from Ouarzazate to Skoura, El Kelâa and Boumalne (the so-called Route des Kasbahs), are harder still and the preserve of seasoned expeditioners accustomed to treeless and waterless wastes. Guiding services are found at El Kelâa.

River gorges: The Sahara side of the Central High Atlas is cut by several gorges of some repute. Two have become well known as scenic routes following recent improvement to their piste tracks. **The Dadès**, emerging at Boumalne, and the **Todra** at Tinerhir, both on the P32 road, can be traversed throughout their great length (though in days rather than hours) over the arid

Middle Atlas in winter.

roof of Morocco to **Imilchil** and eventually **Beni-Mellal**.

After quitting the gorges, desolate passes are crossed in wilderness tracts before the two trails unite at **Agoudal** 7,753 ft (2,363 metres). One of the highest inhabited villages in Morocco, its sheik is a good friend to long distance trail-bums, and its kasbah is illustrated on the five-dirham banknote. Here the infant Melloul stream trickles north to Imilchil. Centuries of scavaging for firewood have uprooted all the scrub willow that bonded the earth in these parts, so that scenes of irreparable damage are the lasting impressions of this journey. In reality few visitors come this far. The options are hiring a well-equipped, self-drive 4WD vehicle (very expensive), or rolling among drums and boxes in a lorry delivering to the numerous villages in these gaunt uplands.

Tourist hikers are taken on a two-gorge circuit in groups of four to nine for a trip of five to six hours, including halts and meal breaks. Protect your backside with an inflatable cushion and dress in safari kit or old togs. Proceeding up the Dadès from village to village (whose names are all preceded by the Berber word *Aït,* meaning "of the people"), the verdant narrow valley meanders.

The road, looping west to avoid obstacles, rejoins the river at Aït-Arbi, with its characteristic watch-towers set among gardens shaded by venerable walnut trees. Dazzlingly bright, the white limestone spurs jut into the valley. The vertiginous incision of the gorge commences outside Aït-Oudinar.

After a ford-bridge to the east bank the *piste* has been blasted from sheer cliffs. The avuncular native chauffeur who comes with the Boumalne tour rental vehicle takes the hazardous driving ahead with confidence. Crazy sights of primitive hoeing and ploughing practices ensue as the gorge relents. Near the last ford a glimpse west into the broad Oussikis hollow reveals the density of villages crammed round a jigsaw of simple green patches. The Berbers

milchil: the ■rides' ■estival.

spend their lives trying to recover and develop arable land.

So to **Msemrir** (40 miles, 65 km) with its colourful Saturday market and the historic meeting place between three major transhumant tribes—the Atta, Haddidou and Merghad—enemies among themselves to a man until they came together under the Yafelmane federation.

Grand canyons: The dirt road ahead begins a long crawl to the Ouerz pass. In just over a mile a prominent fork right is reached at point 1996, where there is a survey pillar, signpost and drinking fountain. The *piste* curves east between stark escarpments to attain the Ouguerd-Zegzaoune pass in an empty quarter of the "badlands". Even at this height you can be caressed by dust clouds in burning heat and a mirage lurks round every hairpin.

A longer descent and another fork south deposits the vehicle in **Tamtetoucht** on the seasonal Temda stream—the chief feeder to the gorge lower down—and site of several mara-

bout (*koubba*), burial chambers of local saintly persons. The road winds south and in three miles (five km) enters the upper Todra gorge. The variable water level at times of flood closes the canyon to vehicles. Parts of the new *piste* have been raised above the riverbed, first on the west side and latterly in the main gorge on the east side, which starts at a ford just after the tight bend at point 1599.

One extraordinary sight is palm trees sprouting from the stony bed. When the river vanishes in the dry season, it is used as a highway by pedestrians and animals. Though less forbidding than the Dadès, the rock walls soar 1,300 ft (400 metres) and the defile at its narrowest point is impressive. A restaurant at the exit precedes a series of pretty Todra villages along the west bank. Gardens, small fields, date palms and fig trees presage the magnificent oasis of **Tinerhir**—noted for its gold and jewellery workshops, proud castellated buildings and decayed palace (19 miles /30 km from Tamtetoucht).

On the P21 between Er Rachidia and Midelt—the boundary of the Eastern High Atlas—the **Ziz gorge** seems to belong to a standard of upkeep that would bring a nod of approval from a landscape architect. One must expect this along a classified asphalt road with USA style "turn-outs" for viewing a miniature edition of the Grand Canyon.

Pot-holing and caving: South of Anargi (Anergui) and spreading east towards **Agoudal** over the vast undulating tableland called **Kousser**, the terrain is cracked by several precipitous watercourses. Discovered by Europeans after 1950, these "secret" canyons have been investigated by a few enterprising explorers. The spectacular Tiflout is the master canyon, fed by snaking tributaries of some complexity. This system of ravines introduces another dimension to Atlas exploration. Pot-holing, caving and rock-climbing techniques, sometimes calling for bold swims in squeezes (tunnelled rocks), require equipment and experience.

Astonishingly, these gorges and their mysterious branches have been used for

Left, the Todra Gorge **Right**, powderplay in the Middle Atlas.

centuries by the Haddidou Berbers as shortcuts during their migrations. Tarzan-like jungle tracks among creepers, waterfalls bulging over sheer drops into deep pools, or raging torrents can all be experienced. Rope bridges (*passerelles*) must be treated with caution.

One of the main arteries is the fairly simple Melloul—a stretch of 12 miles (20 km) between Anargi and Imilchil populated by cliff-dwellers. The others are the Tiflout (22 miles 35 km), Wensa (9 miles/15 km) and Sloul (9 miles/15 km). Approaches and exits add to these distances and represent the serious work.

The most frequented canyon trek in the region is the **Mgoun** (**Achabou**). It winds south from the Central massif to the Dadès valley at El Kelâa (Qalaa't Mgouna) on the P32 road. In one place it forces a passage between overhanging rocks for five miles (8 km), while the total river distance from El Mrabtin to the Issoumar/Bou Taghrar dirt road is 30 miles (50 km) (two days). Supported by mules and porters, supervised parties go from Tabant-Bou Guemez over the Aït Imi pass to El Mrabtin, an arduous leg even without the burden of a rucksack. The best season to tackle it is late May to late July when assorted plunges and wading shallows are appropriate for bathing-suits and gym shoes. But there are no technical difficulties; pack animals unable to follow through the narrower sections are obliged to detour along a dizzy man-made staircase clinging to the canyon wall.

Berbers use the river bottom as a conventional thoroughfare, and you'll stumble upon family groups crouching among the boulders, brewing mint tea. The trek is subject to the level of spate and weather conditions (dangerous in thunderstorms), and a guided tour is possible from El Kelâa in a three or four-day outing. To quote Peyron once more: "Not all of it is hard work—there are moments when the magic of the canyon plays on the mind—inducing serenity and reverie."

Eastern High Atlas: The extremities of this great massif, culminating in the **Ayyachi** (12,300ft/3,750 metres),

whose backbone is double the length of Irhil Mgoun, receive the attention of tourists while the maze of interlocking parallel ridges and valleys comprising the parched interior is almost unknown to foreigners.

Brides and bikers: An elbow of the upper Melloul river at **Imilchil** skirts the basin the French called **Plateau des Lacs.** The lakes establish a natural boundary between the Central and Eastern massifs. This magnificent high grazing area translates as the Celestial Fields of Berber legend.

According to the tale, the lakes of Isli (the man) and Tislit (the woman) were formed by the tears of two young people whose wedding was cancelled because their respective families belonged to opposing sides in a feud. Today the *moussem* at Imilchil (an autumn gathering of the clans, like a county show or state fair) is dominated by a brides' festival held to celebrate the legend. Young men and women dressed in their traditional finery go courting from tent to tent while families barter about the

Young woman of the Aït Haddidou tribe.

chattels a marriage might produce.

This unique aspect of the Imilchil gathering—otherwise unremarkable as a religious-cum-rural fête with strong sporting (games) and commercial (fierce trading) overtones—leaked out in the 1960s, since when it has attracted hordes of "undesirables", as the intelligentsia of Rabat puts it. Some believe that this anachronistic ritual cannot survive its exposure.

Consequently a backwater has been transformed into an important crossroads and stopover for 4WD-borne safari mountain tours. The great and the good of Western society and the Hollywood set have been here but have hurried away after inspecting the amenities. Nothing so titillating happens at the other end of the massif, where sightseeing parties based in Midelt invariably take the mandatory jeep excursion to the Jaffar cirque.

Beni-Mellal, the logical centre for exploring the Eastern zone, offers the shortest route to Imilchil. Along the secondary 1901 road (hotel at El Ksiba)

towards Aghbala, a fork south at Azaghar Fal proceeds to the Abid bridge over the Ouirine river, where the tarmac runs out. In dry weather the continuation *piste* can be managed by ordinary cars given good ground clearance; tour firms use a variety of 4WD. Drive through sundry villages among oak forests, over several rivers, up to Tassent and along its ravine with tricky zigzags and broken edges, past the old French Army memorial to a moderate descent round Tislit and into Imilchil, 69 miles (110 km) from El-Ksiba, 106 miles (170 km) from Beni-Mellal. The journey takes five hours.

Caterpillars of Suzuki-borne trippers, roused at dawn, may cause holdups reminiscent of the Costa del Sol hinterland. Bikers have discovered a paradise up here and add their discordant note to the rowdy scene.

Accommodation in Imilchil is available in two small unclassified hotels anxious to emulate French standards, plus Berber inns and cafés. The village also runs to a weekly market and stores

A bride of Imilchil.

and a local authority headquarters. There are gentle river walks beside fine turreted buildings with many recent edifices, or longer strolls across miles of pasture between the lakes (piste tracks) among shepherds' huts galore and livestock by the thousands. Bathing and windsurfing have been introduced, though it can snow at this altitude until mid-May.

Local vantage points are Amalou n-Tiffirt (8,100 ft/2,470 metres), one hour; and Bab n-Ouayyad (9,200 ft/2,804 metres), three hours, reminiscent of Striding Edge, on the Lake District's Helvellyn. True summits in the area are merely long hikes. **Msedrit** (10,100 ft/3,077 metres) is probably the most frequented and takes two days without 4WD assisted approach.

Tourers on wheels can leave Imilchil by the pulverising trail south to Agoudal (Central High Atlas), push on over the Tirhizit pass into the Todra gorge and reach Tinerhir. A similar lorry-pounding piste twists east over the Tioura col to Ou Tarbat and down the remorseless Haut Ziz watercourse to the improved stretch after Amouquer and emerges at Rich, something of a misnomer, near the P21 road to Midelt.

The Jaffar Cirque: Named after a local saint, this inlet with parking places marks the best departure point for an ascent of the mighty **Jbel Ayyachi** (12,300 ft/3,747 metres). A rutted and often crumbling *piste* of 15 miles (24 km), known as the axle-breaker, extends from Midelt, and there is a similar but longer unmade track from Tounfite. Picturesque rock cataracts, the ravined Ijimi valley and clumps of dwarf conifers combine to make the area a popular picnic spot (though take water). Hotels run vehicles here as demands arises.

Snow cover on the mountain is normal until June; on this north side it lies in long trailing ribbons sometimes for weeks later. Most attempts to reach the summit start at dawn from a cosy bivouac at 7,200 ft (2,200 metres), about 30 minutes above the road, and a fit party can attain the summit in five and a half hours. Seen from the north in full winter

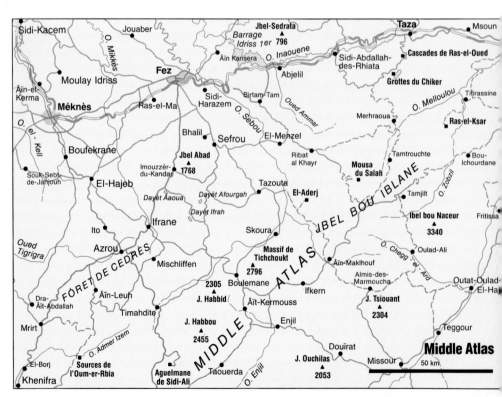

256

robe, 25 miles (40 km) long and with a dozen named summits, the mountain is one of the most arresting spectacles in Morocco. A disguised marquis de Segonzac made the first known ascent in July 1901 by the Ijimi route.

Middle Atlas: Once regarded as a wasteland these far-flung, slatted highlands attach themselves piggyback to the Great Atlas across the wide open spaces of the Moulouya headwaters. The **Zad pass**, between Midelt and Azrou, is a more precise point of reference. The size of the region can be judged by the perimeter roads, joined at three corners of a triangle formed by Fez, Midelt and Guercif, amounting roughly to 500 miles (800 km).

French administrators of the 1930s were endeared to a number of attractive features on this perimeter, which can be observed for great distances as a limestone escarpment, paralleled internally by successive corrugations or slats. The best of these natural objects have been designated areas for preservation. Almost without exception they may be conveniently visited in comfort from reasonable roads.

In the north, near Taza, the **Tazzeka** touring circuit is a one-day educational course in Moroccan landscape. It covers varied colourful ground of forests and gorges, passes waterfalls, caves and subterranean caverns, skirts sink-holes and sunken lakes, and crosses little cols between quaint hamlets along narrow, winding corniche roads. Dominating the centre, a television mast on Jbel Tazzeka (6,500 ft/1,980 metres) commands extensive views in all directions. The similar but more contrived **Kandar-Sefrou-Sebou** circuit is the most popular country district trip outside Fez.

Fit for a king: Where the roads from Fez and Méknès converge at **Azrou** we reach a district created by the French as a summer retreat alongside the most famous cedar forests in Morocco. The purpose-built resort of **Ifrane** (very bourgeois and, some say, the King's favourite residence) epitomises the idyll of the original scheme.

Extending in patches above and below the Middle Atlas escarpment at 5,200-6,900 ft (1,600-2,100 metres) over a distance of 62 miles (100 km), a concentration of these splendid giant trees, 200 ft (61 metres) high and mingled with oak, spruce and cork, contain many charming walks between **Ain-Leuh** and the **Vallée des Roches**. Lanes and *pistes* zigzag through the district, near the P24 Azrou Ifrane road.

Next to a coniferous forest standing in a volcanic depression among beds of limestone, the **Mischliffen** skiing grounds, deserted out of season, emerge as meadows covered with sheep and goats. There are signs of severe overgrazing and cedar-stand cemeteries are dotted round the district. Excessive tree felling has been curbed and a programme of replantation has operated for over half a century.

Nomadic Berber tribes called the Beni Mguild inhabit the forest in spring and summer. As well as tending their animals, they engage in woodland occupations such as making simple furniture and carving trinkets, carried on in large tented encampments.

Giant cedar tree, 200ft high.

THE SOUTH

To brochure browsers, Morocco's south—the vast area on the map separated from the industrialised and cultivated western plains by the great chain of the High Atlas—conjures images of a grandiose but inhospitable land relieved only by picturesque oases farmed by peasants. Deserts, the brochure browser would say, are barren, they produce mirages, they are where people get lost, where people fry to death and provoke tabloid headlines. Desert-inspired pondering on the power of landscape and the insignificance of man is the response only of existentialist poets. What good could possibly come out of a desert?

It is true, of course, that the cooler, damper western plains and northern tip of Morocco are indeed the most economically developed parts of the country, partly because of their geographic amenability and partly because, when Morocco was first colonised, the settlers were driven back from more widespread penetration by the efforts of the indigenous Berbers.

But, with only the Idrissids as an exception, all Morocco's ruling dynasties have originated from the South, either from the Western Sahara, the Souss or the Tafilalt. The Alaouite dynasty, to which the present king belongs, hailed from the Tafilalt, the palm-rich oasis in Morocco's southeastern corner.

The Tafilalt also has a history of some prosperity. It was on the trading routes to Timbuctoo, and, in the past, it was to the Tafilalt that ruling Alaouite sultans sent troublesome relatives. Moulay Ismail, infamous builder of palaces and lover of women, used to send any concubine or wife who had reached the age of 30 to the Tafilalt to retire.

Even today, despite appearances it is a well-populated area. Although traditionally its inhabitants have been great wanderers (hence the dynasties), emigration to Europe from this region is far lower than elsewhere in Morocco.

Southerners are deeply conservative. Women, often tattooed on the chin and forehead, are almost all severely dressed in black *haik*—though a less enveloping garment, with fluorescently bright trimmings, seems to be *à la mode* in the western regions.

Also, the population is staunchly royalist. Any driver will notice writings picked out in stones on hillsides—all messages thanking and complimenting the King. In the 1980s Hassan's visits to the region, which had suffered severe drought, were considered great successes, arousing rapturous welcomes in every town and village. The Alaouite sultans have always made pilgrimages to their founder's tomb near Rissani.

The South is where the government has most recently and heavily invested in the tourist industry. Luxury hotels and "club" complexes abound; the French hotel chain PLM is particularly evident. Roads, much newer than those in the north, are fast and relatively empty, and in contrast to the Hollywood image of "desert", the kasbah route

from **Er Rachidia** to **Ouarzazate** makes perfect territory for a very bourgeois motoring holiday. The only disadvantage to the area is soaring summer temperatures of over 38 C (l00 F). Out of season, from October to May, temperatures are a comfortable 21 C (70 F).

Stunning—and, if the light is right, surreal—views stretch south from the High Atlas. A heat haze can produce layers of colour ranging from lemon to crimson to deep indigo, surmounted by purple-coloured mountains, and crowning the green of palm fronds and pink castellated *ksour*.

The sandcastle look: The *ksar* (*ksour* is the plural), an imposing square construction of mud mixed with fibrous palm trunk (*pisé*), often with a watchtower in each corner, resembling nothing so much as a child's sandcastle, characterises architecture in the south. The region's history of tribal warfare determined the defensive form—though it didn't take into account an obvious enemy tactic: that of diverting a stream so that it undermined the mud foundations.

Generally *ksour* are found south of the Ouarzarzate to Er Rachidia road in the trans-Atlas, but travelling south from Fez, you find the first example just outside **Midelt**, an exciting preview of what is to come.

A *ksar* might be the single residence of a family, or house within its tall walls, sometimes decorated with patterned perforations, a village or small town. In Risanni in the Tafilalt, for example, the streets form tunnels. The design of the *ksar* includes stables on the ground floor and family quarters, barely furnished, above. From the outside its windows appear tiny, usually covered by wrought-iron grilles; but they are numerous and, with the inside shutters thrown open, admit light in surprisingly bright pools.

Their blank exteriors look discouraging to the tourist and an approach to a village *ksar* usually draws hordes of running children, who bang on the car and hang on the door-handles—an exaggeratedly terrifying experience. In most cases, there is little reward for the casual visitor to the smaller *ksour* and it is a brave tourist who is bare-faced enough to intrude (the gates are often actually closed at night); but for an invited guest it's a different matter, likely to develop into a social occasion for the neighbourhood. Milk and dates, Moroccan symbols of hospitality, are customarily preferred.

More than any other buildings, the *ksour* demonstrate the Islamic disinterest in preserving architecture. The Prophet apparently thought building the least profitable cause for expenditure. The *ksour*, victims of rare but occasionally heavy rainfall, rise and fall with inconsequence. Many are ruined and abandoned, few are older than a hundred years old, others are brand-new; in any case, there are few signs of evolvement in design.

Even new urban architecture reflects the *pisé* tradition, though banks, shopping arcades, modern hotels are more likely be made of concrete with a thin *pisé* façade. Still the only exterior decoration will be bold geometric carvings

on doors, a definite African/Saharan trait; and the only relief to the pervasive red and sand coloured towns will be the white-painted domes of *koubbas*.

Military manoeuvres: Many of the towns (only recently developed from villages) have a military character. At one time they hosted the French Foreign Legion, the foreign mercenaries who formed the most romantic of French army divisions; and since independence, a concentration of Moroccan military forces. The heads of the Draa and Tafilalt valley roads are practically within firing range of Algeria, Morocco's uneasy neighbour. When Algeria became independent in 1962, a series of border skirmishes at **Tindouf** developed into a localised war. King Hassan eventually withdrew and Tindouf became part of Algeria. And since the Spanish vacated the Western Sahara (an area rich in phosphates and rumoured to have petroleum) in 1975, leaving it to Morocco, Algeria has been accused of supporting, even creating, the Polisario Front, a rebel force in the area, whose victory could grant Algeria convenient access to the Atlantic.

Relations are currently amiable between Morocco and Algeria but still liable to change. In 1988 diplomatic relations were renewed and borders were reopened after 13 years. During this time only tourists, with some difficulty, and people who had relatives across the border were allowed through.

Despite a troubled relationship, the countries—both of which have an indigenous Berber race and are former French colonies—have everything in common. Language is only slightly different and in the south of Morocco specifically Algerian words are included in speech; for example, you will notice the common place name *Hassi*, the Algerian word for "well". Algerian radio dominates the airwaves.

On the road: The P23, the longest stretch of road in Morocco, runs from Agadir on the Atlantic to **Figuig** on the Algerian border. It connects with the two most stunningly beautiful passes of the Atlas—the Tizi n-Test and the Tizi

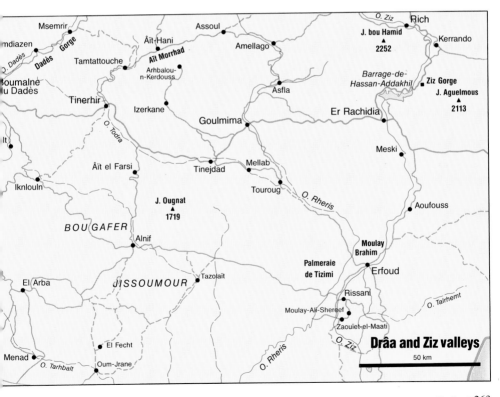

Drâa and Ziz valleys

50 km

n-Tichka—both to the southern capital of Marrakesh; it connects with Morocco's most spectacular gorges, the Todra and the Dadès; and marks the head of the lush desert valleys of the Ziz and the Draa.

Figuig, in the very east of the region, is set amid an utterly barren landscape of stripated mountains, dramatically lit. A remote, alien landscape, it can seem sobering or liberating, depending upon your mood. In any event, you could defy the most prosaic visitor not to feel moved by something. The town itself is a date-palm oasis (Morocco's best dates come from here), watered by hot springs, containing seven village *ksour* with gardens.

Historically, such was Figuig's isolation, that its villages feuded with one another over crops and water rights rather than with any outside invaders. But in 1900 when the French installed a garrison at Beni Ounif, a few miles south in Algeria, the inhabitants united in harassing Legionnaires. This was all the more galling to the French forces

because Paris, who had definite designs on Morocco but was determined to annex it by peaceful negotiations with the sultan, had forbidden its Legionnaires to retaliate. The "troublesome oasis" added to French fears that Algeria would not be secure until Morocco had also been subordinated.

Tourists who now pass through Figuig won't receive the same treatment (for one thing, there is a hotel) but, even so, few visit. The railway line is for industrial purposes only and the road north to Oujda, though excellent, is probably more attractive to the lonesome aesthete than the motorists in their hired Renaults tootling along the Dadès valley, who almost all turn off at Er Rachidia at the head of the Tafilalt.

A royal region: The first glimpse of the Tafilalt, whose fame the London *Times* correspondent Walter B. Harris attributed to the fact that its dates were enjoyed in the drawing-rooms of Edwardian London, is caught just beyond Rich on the P21 through the Atlas. The Oued Ziz has carved a fertile gorge supporting flocks of goats and the first palms—heralding the date-oases south. The gash of green is sudden.

Er Rachidia itself, just over the mountain, is a French-created administrative centre (i.e. new wide roads, banks, hotels, tourist office), with a large concentration of military. But south of here, just off a signposted road 14 miles (22 km) out of town, is a desert oasis corresponding to the perceived stereotype: **Meski** on the **Source Bleu**. Palm-groves and cultivated strips of land flank the stream where Berbers come to wash clothes and aluminium household pans; on the other side of the bank, protruding through the palms, there is an ancient ruined *ksar*.

Inevitably there have sprung up a café, overlooking a man-made pool fed by the spring (in which you can bathe), a camping site providing tents, and numerous stalls selling rugs and leather goods. But if you don't mind a laid-back, indeed largely horizontal, 1960s atmosphere—guitar-playing, communal-living, and, it should be added, litter—Meski holds a modicum of charm.

The Source Bleu at Meski.

Before Erfoud the lush palmeries, which flank the road for most of the valley's length after the fork to Figuig, suddenly subside and the desert proper encroaches. Small sand-dunes thrill the newcomer; a dusty film may obscure the view; vehicles fling up gusts of sand in their wake; and men, as well as women, waiting by the roadside are veiled against the elements.

Erfoud, another recently developed town—no medina, streets laid out in a grid—but pleasant nonetheless, is well prepared to meet the needs of tourists. A base for those exploring the Tafilalt, it has several hotels and a worrying (or reassuring if your vehicle is already suffering) number of mechanical repair garages. It holds a date festival in late October. Further south accommodation is limited, but Rissani does now contain banks and petrol stations.

Rissani is an appropriate place to witness the southern way of life. Though a destination where tourists head, it cares little about pleasing them. The large, central 17th-century *ksar*,

crumbling untidily, is the venue for a vast market held three times a week. At one time it was a centre for slave and gold trading but now it is more likely to be dates and donkeys that are auctioned.

Areas are carefully partitioned into categories—vegetables, dates, mechanical parts, meat, offal, livestock, jewellery, rugs—the piles often tended by women, who are more heavily veiled than anywhere else in Morocco but no less vocal. Everything is basic, sometimes shocking, totally Third World. The parties of tourists paraded through its maze seem almost ridiculous, strung as they usually are with cameras and attired in pastels.

But, apart from the market, they are drawn to three specific attractions near Rissani: **Sigilmassa**, named after the Roman general who founded a camp here; the **tomb of Moulay Ali Shereef**, founder of the Alaouite dynasty; and, two hours away, **Merzouga**—aim of dawn expeditions through the desert sands. Sigilmassa, to the west of the P21 as you approach Rissani is a meagre

Crossing the Draa near Zagora in winter.

collection of ruins marking a medieval town established in 707 by Musa ben Nasser and later restored by Moulay Ismail which for centuries was the capital of the region.

The tomb can be approached from the small road that loops back around Rissani (be warned, it later peters out into a track) marked *Circuit Touristique*. The road, whose bad state defeats, and potholes full of dust obscure the "touristic" nature of the detour, passes through a palmerie shading various ruined and inhabited *ksour* which belonged to the Alaouites. The *zaouia* of Moulay Ali Shereef is near its end, behind Rissani—unmissable because of the crowds of children who will mob you and drag you towards it.

Merzouga, within 12 miles (20 km) of the Algerian border, with its Erg Chebbi (literally "small desert"), is as close as easily accessible Morocco gets—with the exception perhaps of M'Hamid in the Draa valley—to Beau Geste country. It can be approached by car from Erfoud or Rissani, but for a more comfortable desert approach it is possible to join one of the Land-Rover tours (or hire your own four-wheel drive vehicle) from either town.

The Dadès Valley: The settlements on the road from Er Rachidia to Ouarzazate form the string of pearls among the Tourist Office's most vaunted gems. But the landscape between, particularly the eastern stretches, though not unimpressive, is *hamada*, stony scrub, with the Atlas and the Anti Atlas rising gloomily across the plains on either side. Strange craters mark the sites where undergound irrigation channels have been repaired; a few nomadic settlements, occasional camels, and the oases of **Goulmina** and **Tinejad** break the lunar scene. (Coming from the Tafilalt, you can cut across country from Erfoud to Tinejdad along a perfectly sound and attractive route via what in the past was the horse-breeding centre of the Ait Atta tribe, Touroug.)

As the road travels west, the *ksour*, usually set back from the road, become

An evening sky near Erg Chebbi, Merzouga.

less irregular in shape and more like four-square sandcastles. The lushly cultivated surrounds of **Tinerhir** at the foot of the **Todra Gorge**—olive-groves, palmeries, small fields of crops, almond orchards—are dominated by a *ksar* which belonged to the Glaoui.

This powerful tribe, whose base was the Telouet pass from Ouarzarzate through the Atlas, controlled the area well into this century. **Boulmane du Dadès** is similarly dwarfed by a former Glaoui structure. Thami el Glaoui became the Pasha of Marrakesh, a notorious opportunist in pre-Independence politics who connived with the French to discredit Mohammed V. Following independence and the widespread disgrace and dispersion of the Glaoui family (and the death soon after of Thami el Glaoui), their possessions were seized by the government and the *ksour* were abandoned as huge white elephants. They are now often inhabited by former slave families.

The gorges that cut into the Atlas at these points make spectacular walking detours (*see chapter on The Atlas*). They are abundantly verdant, as are the oases of **Skoura** and **El Kelâa des M'gouna**, both notable rose-growing areas further along the Dadès valley. The latter contains a factory where attar, rose essence, is distilled and holds a rose festival in late May or early June that is worth catching. Such is the beauty of Skoura, albeit a rather pampered, cultivated sort (witness the expensive villas), that it has attracted a Club Méditerranée, not an organisation which will choose any old site to settle. It contains several former Glaoui residences that can be visited.

Ouarzazate is the most obviously tourist-orientated town of the South after Agadir. It was an impoverished backwater before the government and private businessmen realised its potential, poised as it is between the Draa Valley and the Tizi n-Tichka pass to Marrakesh. In autumn and winter **Toubkal** forms a dazzling white backdrop to the north. Though small and strung mainly along one wide Moham-

In the grain market at Taroudant.

med V Boulevard, it contains many hotels (several luxurious), tourist shops and petrol stations.

Chez Dimitri, a distinctly superior looking café in the centre opposite a small supermarket (also belonging to the enigmatic Dimitri, who is rumoured to have been a friend of Thami el Glaoui and at one time to have had the monopoly on alcohol in the south) is an excellent inexpensive restaurant, with a huge old-fashioned bar, running to French-style casseroles and *crêpes suzette*.

The road to **Zagora** from Ouarzazate, following the course of the Draa (note that in the winter access to the P31 from the south of town may be closed due to flooding), passes through a landscape resembling the Scottish Highlands to Tolkienesque peaks eroded into fantastic shapes upon which every layer of rock is delineated. Vegetation is confined to tiny pockets of green and the occasional stray palm-tree, which, when the skies are as dark as the mountains (yes, quite possible late in the year), seem wildly incongruous.

The other side of the great **Tizi n-Tiniffift** the astonishing oasis of **Tamnougalt**, once the capital of the region, stretches south. This is arguably Morocco's most stunning view. *Ksour* of varying sizes and designs guard the valley all the way to **Askjour** south of Zagora.

Zagora is reputedly the hottest town in Morocco. A mock sign featuring a string of camels and claiming "*Timbuctou 52 jours*" marks the end of town. It is a desultory place whose shops, garages and uninviting cafés line one street. There are usually a few buses depositing valley dwellers visiting its market, or picking up traders wishing to travel to a neighbouring village souk. Markets govern the frequency and times of public transport throughout the Draa.

Visitors staying overnight experience Zagora at its most memorable: still, quiet and illuminated by brilliant desert skies. Night is the most dramatic time to climb the 11th-century Almoravid *ksar* on the other side of the

Below, a *Maison Berbère*. **Opposite**, *Lawrence of Arabia* was partly filmed in Morocco.

ON LOCATION

If there is one complaint more consistently bellowed at location managers during foreign filming expeditions, it is that there are no hot showers and the food is awful—which, come to think of it, is what constitute most people's idea of a bad holiday. Morocco, however, for all its Islamic customs and African attachment, has satisfied Western expectations of service. For the first half of this century Tangier's international city status opened its doors to a curious assortment of Western influences, including well-known writers and Hollywood stars.

Cary Grant shared nuptial bliss with Hollywood-style Woolworth heiress Barbara Hutton in the Kasbah overlooking Tangier's port, while Marlene Dietrich marked her US debut in l930 in a film called simply *Morocco*, in which director Von Sternberg shocked many with Dietrich's lingering screen kiss to another woman before she strode off into the desert dressed in full tuxedo and high heels.

It was after the making of such films as *Our Man in Marrakesh* and *Tangier* that the French set up the Centre Cinématographique Marocain to encourage film-making in Morocco. After all, even the most famous films associated with the country, Bogart's *Casablanca* and the Bob Hope and Bing Crosby comedy *The Road to Morocco* had had to be content with Hollywood versions of desert backdrops and Arabian palaces. The CCMF still functions to facilitate permission for foreign films to be made, recruit extras, advise on locations, arrange accommodation and props.

But it was David Lean's Oscar-winning *Lawrence of Arabia*, the film that launched the international careers of both Peter O'Toole and Omar Sharif, which really put Morocco on the location managers' maps. It showed that a director could marshall a whole company through many months of arduous conditions on the edge of a desert, with all the paraphernalia and supplies necessary for such a military-style campaign.

Film companies, like tourists, often leave legacies of their encampment, and in the wake of Lean's expeditionary force there emerged a Moroccan legion of extras, assistants, translators, controllers and location gurus who had cut their teeth on *Lawrence*. Lean's film showed off the "real" Morocco in all its Technicolor beauty.

Huge expanses of wide-screen blue sky and rugged splendour, plentiful supplies of Semitic-looking extras and medieval cities, whose trades and traditional ways of life still functioned, tempted an influx of foreign producers. One director, Alberto Negrin, in the film *The Secret of the Sahara*, even used 500 northern Moroccans, with blue eyes, to play French Legionnaires.

It is Ouarzazate, once a functional garrison town which has unwittingly found itself at the centre of film-making; its proximity to both the desert and the imposing Atlas making it a suitable, if remote, choice.

Today Ouarzazate can boast two primitive "studios" (originally built so that film-makers could operate in peace, without getting mobbed), but foreign productions tend to use them only as production base-camps, taking advantage of the more sophisticated filmic infrastructure left by predecessors. The nearby village of Aït-Benhaddou, with its exquisite kasbah, can claim several major screen credits. It was the focus of the TV epic *Jesus of Nazareth* and more recently Martin Scorsese's controversial *Last Temptation of Christ*.

The Moroccan government is vigilant in its scrutiny of foreign productions (even though it neglects to support the home-grown cinema industry, which is entirely private-funded in both distribution and production). Had Scorsese's film been the *Last Temptation of Mohammed*—who by all accounts was a far more worldly character than Christ—the film crews would never have been admitted. As in any Islamic country, censorship is governed by strict moral considerations; it is no accident that Moroccan films rely so heavily on symbolism.

Censorship, of course, takes no account of merit. *Ishtar*, a particularly feeble desert romp, managed to attract the talents of Dustin Hoffman and Warren Beatty, but the only fame the actors found in the Moroccan desert was for appearing in one of the most expensive cinematic flops of all time—a $45 million loss of face for the two stars.

Draa and to the south of the town.

After the backwater, one-donkey town (no, not even a camel) of Zagora, **Tamgrout** 14 miles (22 km) further on surprises by the fact that it has claims to high culture. It houses a *zaouia*—which is the base of the ancient Nassiria brotherhood, still active in the country—and a library containing 13th-century illuminated Korans, scientific works, and volumes of poetry, prose and mathematics, a couple of which are written on gazelle skin. A guide greets every tourist car that comes in search of this pocket of intellectual striving. The *zaouia* contains the tomb of the founder of the Nassiria brotherhood, Sidi M'Hamid ben Nassir, who, according to the old man who is the guide, was on his way back from Mecca when he settled in Tamgrout with his books. There were once 20,000 volumes but many have now been lost to libraries in Fez and Rabat and only a few thousand remain. Outside the shrine, there is an outer sanctuary where the sick visiting the tomb may stay. Admission to the library is gained by walking up the lane to the right as you leave the shrine and knocking on a large heavy door. A guide usually shows the way.

At **M'Hamid**, 56 miles (90 km) further south, the Oued Draa peters out, though it re-emerges west of here to flow to the Atlantic, a course carved during the European Ice Age. This small town is on the verge of the Sahara. You can encounter wind-sculpted dunes, desert nomads, some of whom camp in huge black tents on the outskirts, even Blue Men (or at least people wearing the charateristic blue cloth of the desert), and camels.

Monday is market day. It was in the marketplace here, in February 1958, that Mohammed V controversially laid claim to the Western Sahara. It has suffered guerilla attacks by the Polisario Front and has at times been out of bounds to tourists.

West to Taroudant: From Ouarzazate, those not travelling east usually turn north through the High Atlas to Marrakesh. The road to Agadir via Tarou-

Left, drawing water in Taroudant. Right, Testing marrows in the market.

dant is a stretch more commonly covered by tourists using the airport at Agadir. Much of the road beyond **Talioul-ine** passes through scrubland. After skirting the Jbel Siroua and intersecting with the other great Atlas pass, the **Tizi n-Test**, it follows the course of the Oued Souss. There are few villages along the way. **Tiliouine**, dominated by another enormous and ruined Glaoui kasbah, is one of the more interesting.

Taroudant is the major town and, unlike Ouarzazate and Er Rachidia, it has some of the character associated with ancient origins: it is enclosed by fortified walls and contains the traditional craft souks (including tanneries) found in Marrakesh and Fez—albeit on a much smaller scale.

After a determinedly independent history, with only intermittent rule imposed by forces beyond the Souss, it became the capital of the Saadian dynasty in the 16th century, before the honour fell to Marrakesh. Originally, the Saadis were invited there to bless the date crop with their *baraka* but they liked it so much that they stayed. Under their rule it prospered and cotton and sugar were produced for Europe.

Unfortunately, the bulk of this trade later shifted to the West Indies and the town declined. It became the focus of a series of revolts against successive sultans and later the French. El Hiba, the main resistance leader against the French in the south, made Taroudant his stronghold. Only after his defeat in 1913 did Taroudant return to the *bled es makhzen*, the part of Morocco governed by the sultancy.

Desert places: Taroudant contains two of Morocco's most impressive hotels. **Hôtel la Gazelle'Or**, once the home of a French baron, with its own extensive gardens and renowned French restaurant, lies just outside the town, and **Hôtel Palais Salam** occupies a former palace built into the kasbah quarter of the walls. It is to these that the well-heeled arrivals at the international airport of Agadir are more than likely heading—leaving **Agadir** to the modern fans of beaches and bathing.

Silver, best bought in the south.

AGADIR

The Moroccans shrug, or sneer. Yes, Agadir's okay—for tourists. But it's not *vrai Marocain*; it's a European city. So said a souk trader, and he's partly right. Others—friends, guidebooks—say wisely that you haven't seen Morocco if you stay in Agadir: and that's also true. It lacks the frantic concentration of life and energy that is typically Moroccan. It has no medina. But it's easy to get to, and an ideal base from which to venture into some of Morocco's most spectacular scenery.

A good beach, even the critics have to agree; unmistakably a seaside town: straggling bunting hanging over palm-lined boulevards; roadside trees trimmed into neat cubes; white concrete and stucco architecture; a couple of 10-storey tower blocks; and even gaunt steel cranes near the beach—all are signs of a town anxious to be seen as an international resort. But there are a lot of resorts in the world with more pretensions—and far worse beaches.

This sounds like damning by faint praise, but there comes a time in many Moroccan itineraries when culture shock has given way to culture fatigue. In that mood, it's possible to find in Agadir a respite from the whirl of typical Moroccan-ness; from colours, sounds and smells, from insistent offers of help and constant pressure to buy. Of course, that's not a feeling that one boasts about. But it means that it's easy to start feeling more affectionate towards the place, as long as you're not stranded there for too long.

A new town: During the night of 29 February 1960, an earthquake destroyed the town of Agadir. The quake wasn't strong, but its epicentre hit the old town right in the kasbah. Agadir had for centuries been a fishing port and a market centre for the valley of the **Oued Souss**, which runs out to sea to the south. But on the morning of 1 March, most of the town was rubble: 3,650 buildings were destroyed, 15,000 people died and 20,000 were homeless.

Morocco, about to celebrate the fourth anniversary of independence, needed a new centre here. It couldn't be anything but modern, of course. It was bound to be a showpiece for the new state; at the same time it had to serve as port, market place, and industrial and administrative centre.

And so modern Agadir was conceived and built almost in segments. There are the port areas: the fishing port visible from the beach and heavier industrial docks invisible round a headland to the north. There are the poorer residential and industrial quarters to the southwest of the town. Immediately behind the beach, and seaward of the broad dual-carriageway of Boulevard Mohammed V, is the wedge-shaped tourist quarter. Inland of the boulevard is the town's commercial centre—shops, banks and travel agencies.

A beach resort: Six miles (10 km) of broad sandy beach and a claimed 300 days of sunshine every year are a potent combination. The beach—Agadir's chief boast—is huge. Souvenir sellers'

camels lope along the waterline. A *gendarme* on horseback rides the other way. Hundreds of sun-bathers are laid out, either on loungers or on the powder-fine sand, the colour of a murky *café au lait*.

Bathing flags tell you how safe the Atlantic is, but nothing warns you about how cold it is. The beach is between 200 and 400 metres deep and, apart from hired beach umbrellas, without shade (the walk to the trees behind the beach is too far for swimmers).

At the centre of the beach is a ridge of rocks connected to the shore by a spit of sand, like a squat T, uncovered at low tide. This shelters a small area from breakers. It's here that most beach life goes on, with the support of a handful of "beach clubs" in the middle.

Hotels are some distance from the beach: those that aren't guard their own sand jealously, so most visitors, if they want shade or the right to use a toilet, hire a lounger at a beach club (15 dirhams a day in 1989, reductions for season ticket holders).

The scene behind the beach—cranes and half-built hotels—is almost Spanish, and most of Agadir's hotels are indistinguishable from those of Europe: standard bedrooms with bathrooms and balconies; "continental" set menus for dinner; chips with everything at a poolside bar. But striking Moroccan decor, Moroccan speciality restaurants and friendly service reflecting old traditions of hospitality attempt to assert at least some character.

It makes financial sense for them to carry on building: it makes even better sense to build more hotels with direct access to the beach. And, as elsewhere in the country, the top-of-the-range hotels are very stylish indeed.

The climate, Agadir's other great advantage, is remarkable. Winter is only slightly cooler and wetter than summer (although it can be much duller). On average, in the whole of the five months from May to September there are between four and five rainy days. During the same months, and even into November, daytime tempera-

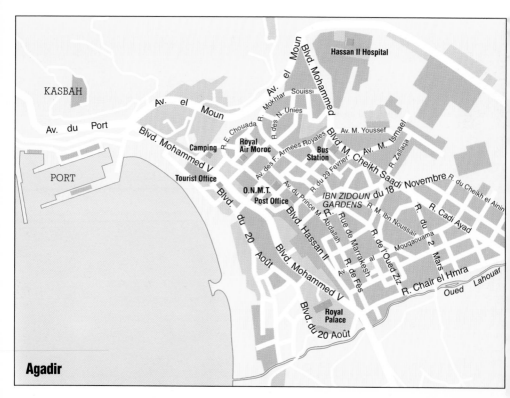

Agadir

tures routinely reach the mid-20s centigrade—cooler than the Greek islands, southern Spain and indeed the rest of Morocco in high summer, but with an advantage over them in the late autumn and spring. This is the best time to go, while the inland towns are relatively cool.

Agadir after dark: So the resort has the right qualifications—but it doesn't create quite enough excitement. Most hotels sit between the **Boulevard Mohammed V** and the narrower but livelier **Boulevard du 20 Août**. It's on the 20 Août that the evening happens. The street is peppered with open-air bar-restaurants displaying illuminated boxes on which are painted menus in French, German, English and Italian. Omelettes, pasta and pizza are much easier to find than anything Moroccan.

The atmosphere is animated: people forge friendships over a drink or over a bargain struck in the nearby shops, which are open well into the evenings. But there are long walks between the jolly bits and, apart from hotel discos

Agadir bay from the hill. **Overpage**, mending nets in the harbour.

and folklore evenings, there's not much else to do. If discos are what you want, the Byblos at the Hôtel Dunes d'Or is the best (but also the most expensive) choice.

Shopping scene: There is a *souk* in the industrial quarter, surrounded by a pink battlemented wall, but it's only for those who really know what they want (and know the right price). Otherwise, it's less hassle to buy souvenirs from the **Centre de l'Artisanat**, or from **Uniprix**, a cheap fixed-price shop on **Avenue Hassan II**.

There are plenty of other shops in the centre which advertise fixed prices, their bags and trinkets spilling out on to pavements and along trellis-like frameworks, turning shopping walkways into a concrete *souk*, with the same traditions of attention-grabbing and prices high enough to come down if necessary. There are also several upmarket shops selling designer sportswear, leather luggage, smart clothes and shoes, again at fixed prices. And there's an **English language bookshop** on the big concrete

square of Place Hassan II.

What else to see: You can visit the regional **Centre de l'Artisanat**, west of the town centre, where children are taught handicrafts, and where carpets, woodwork, jewellery and pottery are on sale in a fixed-price shop, or direct from craftsmen working in workshop units.

The only sight with any history behind it is the ruined **Kasbah**, reached by a winding road above the port. There's no need for a guide here (although you'll get one if you're not careful), since so little has survived; but the view of the town and beach is splendid. The old gateway still has an 18th-century Dutch inscription: they were colonists before the French.

The best view of the new **Royal Palace** is from a plane; hope for a clear day as you fly into or out of Agadir. The buildings are reminiscent of Olympic rings in plan; the whole like a fantasy ranch, with green pantiled roofs glinting in the sun. Emerald lawns surround the palace between the southern end of town (which also looks handsome from here) and the Souss estuary. You can't get more than a vague idea of it from the ground.

Excursions: Most travel agencies will arrange for coach tours to pick up from any hotel. For more independence—and rather more money—you can easily hire a car from one of the many offices along Mohammed V and Avenue Hassan II. Excursions by Land-Rover or minibus can also be arranged.

Cascading spring waterfalls and lush palm-lined gorges in the **Pays des Ida-Outanane** are reached by a turning eight miles (12 km) north of Agadir; it's signposted **Immouzer des Ida-Outanane**, the main village with a prettily sited hotel between it and the cascades. Seabird watching is possible in the mouth of the **Oued Souss** estuary; but the range of species is better at the lagoon of **Sidi Rabat**.

Longer-range excursions can be made south to **Tafraoute** and north to **Essaouira**, both through superb landscapes; south to **Tiznit**; southeast to **Taroudant**; and a very long day—or, better, two days—to **Marrakesh**.

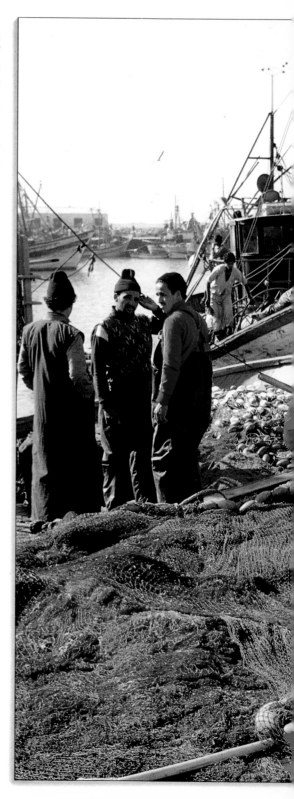

THE DEEP SOUTH

As you leave Agadir to the south, the real Morocco crowds back around the roadside. For the first few miles, you're still in the estuary plains of the Oued Souss: flat fertile land where trees line the road and villages are rows of small, cell-like shops—arcades where metal-workers are next door to butchers.

From time to time you'll pass big white farmhouses with multi-coloured metal doors in their outer walls. The road skirts the town of **Inezgane**, almost a suburb of Agadir, and splits into three in the centre of **Aït Melloul**. One road leads up the Souss river, westwards to Taroudant and the High Atlas; a second road runs south to Tiznit, and a third via the mountains to Tafraoute.

A trip to Tafraoute: A triangle of roads connects Aït Melloul and Tiznit to Tafraoute, and the fastest way to reach the valleys around Tafraoute is to keep to the wider, straighter road via Tiznit. This is what the coach excursions have to do. But if you have a car and a certain amount of nerve (and/or mountain driving experience), it's worth travelling on the narrower road.

Both routes pass through mountains, but you'll get to them more quickly by a northern route. The way is full of surprises, such as the curious sight of the town of **Aït Bahia**, a jumbled cluster of low, white, mostly modern buildings, invisible until you top a mountain ridge.

Older villages cling to hillsides, crowd in on top of cols and hillocks: most have *pisé* walls the colour of the mountainside. The slopes are corrugated with terraces ploughed by donkeys driven by black-clad women. Craggy red ochre outcrops at the peaks look like a continuation of the terraces' reinforcing walls: such is the harmony between the unchanging habits of the mountain people and the sombre majesty of the mountains.

The landscape around Tafraoute is startling. From crumbly sandstone looms a jutting ridge of pink granite, purple in shadow, the **Djebel Lekst**.

Below it, a lush series of palmiers: thousands of date palms spread in the **Vallé des Ameln**, and above them villages in earth colours: umber, pink, red and yellow ochre. The granite behind them looks like a series of cascades, geysers solidifying as they fall. This remote area is prosperous: partly due to its fertility, and partly because many *épiciers* move here when they tire of shopkeeping and have built large villas with mint green balconies and bright shutters.

Dozens of villages cluster about Tafraoute; they're more fun to explore than the town, whose main square has several souvenir shops, all overlooked by the imitation kasbah which is the Hôtel les Amandiers. Also signposted from the square is the town's best restaurant, L'Etoile du Sud. The first villages to see are **Oumesnat**, to the northeast of Tafraoute, **Agard Oudad** to the south, and **Adai** to the southwest.

Along the road to Tiznit, on the outskirts of town, are huge weathered boulders of granite, weird contorted shapes in striking contrast to the rigid outlines

of the date palms. The grandeur of the mountains and the thousand-year-old lifestyle are as impressive here as along the northern route. In early spring the hillsides are full of almond blossom; but once out of the mountains, there's a long stretch of pre-Sahara to cover before reaching **Tiznit**.

Walled city: Tiznit's four miles (six km) of four-square ramparts look more solid than most: and so they ought, since they're only just over 100 years old. Wide roads skirt round them, and moped riders will track you down if you arrive on your own. But there's only one must inside the walls: the *souk des bijoutiers* (jewellers' market). A short walk from the *mechouar* (main square), grouped around a courtyard, the jewellers work delicate silver filigree into swords and daggers as well as heavy bracelets and necklaces.

Tiznit's walls are *pisé*, built of impacted earth the colour of ginger biscuits. So are most walls as you continue south into the pre-Sahara and the mountains of the Anti Atlas, which rear abruptly from the plain.

Bleaker terrain: Sharp contoured valleys divide mountainsides covered with green stubble that look smooth from a distance. They turn out, on closer inspection, to be a mass of knobbly boulders and ground-hugging cactus. Barbary figs (prickly pears) and low, bushy argan trees grow in deeper soil. Argans, native to Morocco, produce a fruit like an olive, which is pressed for oil. The goats like these trees, too; it's not unusual to see them in the spreading branches, nibbling the vivid green leaves.

Below the tortuous mountain road, which descends as abruptly as it climbs, the landscape becomes more deserted. This is where the pre-Sahara begins emotionally. In vast open spaces stand swirled mountains like frozen sand dunes: others, with dark patterns, look as if a dry brush laden with dark green paint has been drawn over a light brown background. The sheer extent of these landscapes can be unnerving: there is no human reference point. The abrupt ap-

Oumesnat Village, near Tafraoute.

pearance of a marching line of pylons can turn the landscape into what seems like a post-industrial wasteland. But it isn't—it's just a desert.

The Blue Men: The town of **Goulimine** (some signposts say Guelmim) might not seem like somewhere to write home about. Although the town is an administrative centre, its chief claim to fame is as the venue of a camel and livestock market every Saturday morning, where the *hommes bleus*, or blue men, come from the outlying mountains to trade.

The town is also close to a group of oases, and you'll have no trouble finding somebody to take you out to one or all of these. They'll probably offer to introduce you to a blue man, or to a nomad, as well: if you're really "lucky", he might just have some carpets and jewellery with him. Of course, what you believe, who you meet, what you buy, is up to you. Even if you feel pressured, there's a friendly feeling in Goulimine, particularly if you stay there.

The only classified hotel is the Salam, a 2*B with showers in some rooms. It's a little fly-blown in the dining-room; bedrooms open off an upstairs courtyard with lurid murals, but because there's so little else to do, you can find yourself making friends and spending hours just talking there.

On the road south, the occasional convoy of monstrous tank transporters forces oncoming vehicles half off the road. Table-top mountains surrounding Tan Tan look no more substantial than sandcastles. Camels graze amid the roadside scrub, apparently wild.

Tan Tan is made up of custard yellow buildings (the sort of colour that paint manufacturers might call Sahara). The turquoise dome of a mosque stands out, visible from the edges of the vast basin in which the town stands. There is a very military feel: lots of flags, men in uniforms and garrison compounds. There are some hotels, but none of any special note.

The sea is 16 miles (25 km) away at **Tan Tan Plage**: a dusty half-way house, divided into a sardine port (a guarded private complex) and genteel

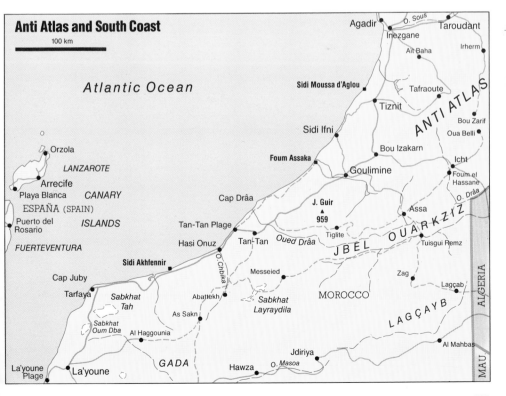

Anti Atlas and South Coast

100 km

Atlantic Ocean

resort. Small, elaborate seaside bunga-lows in a *nouvelle*-Moorish style would be better placed next to the Mediterra-nean. But the wind whips creamy spray from resolutely Atlantic breakers be-fore they hit a crescent beach of sand, layered rock and the odd boulder.

During the week at least, nothing much stirs apart from boys mussel-hunting in rock pools. A 100-bedroom 4*A hotel, the Ayoub, is under con-struction, due for completion in 1989 or 1990, but don't hold your breath.

Police and Polisario: The reason for the military lorries and surfeit of troops from Tan Tan southwards is political. It was from Tan Tan that troops, followed by King Hassan II and 350,000 un-armed Moroccans, marched to claim sovereignty of the then Spanish Sahara in 1975. The anniversary of the *Marche Verte* (Green March) is celebrated as a public holiday every 6 November; post-ers, postcards and even the crockery of Layounne's Hotel Massira commemo-rate it in bold green and red.

Consequences for travellers are,

nowadays, few and not really irksome. You are likely to be stopped by the Gendarmerie Royale on either side of Tan Tan, where the white roadside checkpoint buildings are as bare as cells, and the Moroccan flag flapping on its pole is the only sound as a *gendarme* writes down your name, address, car registration, marital status, and the first names of both parents. This rigmarole is much more likely if you're heading south; going north, you're unlikely to be given more than a cursory once-over.

On to Layounne: This is an exhilarating route where the desert meets the sea and where a tarmac road wanders in and out from the coast, occasionally dusted over with blown sand. Between Tan Tan and Tarfaya, crumbling tableland comes to an end, and at once gives way to unstable cliffs. Butterflies play along the edge of the red earth, while pound-ing Atlantic surf blackens the grey rocks below.

Flocks of seagulls congregate on certain stretches of road: off it are Land-Rovers, swathed in nets and wearing

Heading south.

fishing rods like huge antennae, and fishermen casting from the cliffs. At times, the road swoops down into a valley of brackish water—a sea inlet, a river outlet, or a salt lake (it's never quite clear which). There are gulls here, the occasional heron, and—with luck—flamingoes. Harsh, semi-arid plains alternate with shifting sand dunes, looking (deceptively) as cosy as any seaside version.

Here and there are desert cafés: green or white or yellow painted, one-storey concrete cabins whose cheery colours seem to underline their isolation. A whole village of cafés has grown up 63 miles (100 km) north of Tarfaya, at the base of a headland pitted with gaping caves. This is a useful petrol stop: you can rely on petrol every 100 km from Tan Tan to Layounne. But you can't rely on French or English being spoken: you may need the Arabic for "water" as well as "please" and "thank you".

One potential hazard: in 1987, and again in the late autumn of 1988, huge clouds of locusts descended on southern Morocco (as they did on much of northern Africa). Like pink smoke clouds when they're in motion, and like a rose-coloured carpet as they bask on the road, flying up at approaching vehicles they are extremely unpleasant for drivers. They are also potentially dangerous: you can skid on them, they block up the radiator grille and spatter across the windscreen. If you hit some, drive slowly through, and clear them from the engine and the grille with a stick as soon as the swarm has gone.

Locusts aside, the journey south is eerily quiet. Other vehicles become quite an event; the occasional well-hidden pothole in an otherwise reliable surface is less welcome. North of the little, Spanish-influenced port of **Tarfaya**, the spooky mood is enhanced (or aggravated) by the hulks of abandoned ships and large fishing boats leaning half grounded just offshore. They're too recent to look like wrecks, and some seem as if they're only resting: but they're definitely dead. Nobody will tell, but they're quite probably victims

Dates are harvested in October.

of the Polisario's guerrilla attacks before the desert walls were built.

Denuded bleakness: The animation, size and modernity of **Layounne** are a jolt to the senses after the denuded bleakness of the desert. Passing through two police checkpoints and a huge ornate gateway, and crossing the Green March bridge, the paradox hits you: Layounne has been designed as a city of the desert.

Since the Green March and King Hassan's return visit 10 years later, a lot of money and energy have gone into making the city an emblem of the benefits that Morocco can give to the people of the Sahara. A new hospital and airport have been built, and public housing and civic buildings are in vernacular style: dome-topped houses, a courthouse like a desert fort.

There is no medina, and the huge modern square—the **Place de l'Allegeance**—is not the focus it sets out to be. The real animation of Layounne is in street after street of shops and daily produce and livestock markets.

For visitors, Layounne puts on its best face in the Hotel Parador: a mock castle enclosing a series of lush courtyards and shallow pools (and one swimming pool); there's Arab decor and green trellises throughout. The alternative is the Hotel Massira—mostly booked out by groups.

Big plans are afoot for the development of tourism in the Sahara, but they still have a way to go. Trips to the "sand sea", an area of shifting dunes, are easy to organise, and are occasionally laid on (together with folklore displays, camel rides and dromedary kebabs) for the cruise passengers from the *MV Orient Express*.

Other regular visitors are the expatriate community in the nearby Canary Islands, who use regular flights to Layounne as an easy way of complying with Spanish immigration laws. **Layounne Plage**, 13 miles (20 km) west, is charming chiefly because it's so empty. A trip to Layouune can be fascinating—but come for the pleasure of the trip rather than the town.

A camel market.

286

REAL BLUE MEN AND FAKE BLUE MEN

Any trip south of Agadir is likely to involve an encounter with *les hommes bleus*, the blue men of the Sahara—those romantic desert wanderers depicted in Hollywood epics as blue-turbaned aristocrats mounted on pure white camels. Or, at least, you might *think* that you're meeting them.

Southern Morocco only brushes the Sahara, a desert that in part spans the width of Africa, but it is typical that Moroccans should make the most of it—especially when there are tourists to satisfy. In the town of Goulimine, one of the places where from out of the desert the blue men traditionally came to sell camels, the promise of nomads draws Saturday coach-tours from Agadir, the day when the weekly camel market is held.

So most of the traders are not real blue men at all, but common or desert townspeople intent on profiting from this source of revenue.

Desert nomads still operating as such are found further south and east, and it should be remembered that all the Soussi tribes have a preference for the colour blue. Real blue men, though fallen upon hard times, are not particularly interested in entertaining tourists, and their pride is legendary. Wyndham Lewis, who visited the region and recorded his adventures in his book *Filibusters in Barbary*, published in 1932, said: "At their feet you may look. A downcast eye, fixed upon the exceedingly filthy blue feet belonging to these lords, will not attract a bullet."

The genuine article belongs to the Taureg tribes, whose roots are spread through Mauritania, the Western Sahara (now part of Morocco), southern Algeria and southwest Libya. Physically, they are unusually tall, handsome, and altogether more African-looking than the average Moroccan. Their regal demeanour is emphasised by long flowing robes. And it is the Taureg men who wear the veil—designed to wrap over the nose and chin, in true desert fashion, to keep out the sand-laden wind.

Traditionally it was the dye in their robes that endowed the skin with an indigo hue, and it is

claimed that the origin of these nomads' relationship with the colour lies a long way from the Sahara—Scotland, in fact. In the 15th century an enterprising Scottish cloth merchant is supposed to have travelled to Agadir and introduced a blue-coloured calico—no doubt one which he couldn't offload at home. The fact that its dye permeated the skin was its main attraction, and a customer would test the cloth between wet thumb and forefinger to ensure the dye came off well.

The Taureg tribes are known for their nobility and historically their social hierarchy was strictly divided into nobles, vassals, serfs and slaves. The Harratin people, still found in the Draa Valley and at similar latitudes across the Maghreb, were once their slaves. It is ironic that many of the Taureg now do the agricultural work they have always looked down upon. Sedentary lifestyles and manual labour were always despised.

The Taureg are associated with a rich intellectual heritage, and literature and poetry in particular are valued. The women are known for *guedra*, an erotic dance which they perform on their knees (one theory is that the low tents in which it was staged dictated this position; but it might be that it more readily suggests sexual submission). The shows performed for Westerners' benefit are likely to be fairly sedate affairs, but at one time the *guedra* was the speciality of prostitutes, and might include varying degrees of striptease.

Such vestiges of their culture apart, the nomads' traditional way of life has eroded fast. Causes include the decline of the Saharan salt trade and improved methods of transport in the Sahara, the breakdown of the traditional status quo, and severe droughts which have effected the areas of grazing for their goats. At one time the caravans of the Sahara might include tens of thousands of camels. These days you are lucky if you see a thin trickle of camels trekking through the northern Sahara.

Many nomads have congregated in the towns, picking up odd jobs here and there, abandoning their culture and reluctantly leading a sedentary life. The Maghrebi governments have more pressing problems than the protection of endangered minorities. The blue men of the Sahara have had to be pragmatic to survive.

TRAVEL TIPS

GETTING THERE
290 By Air
290 By Sea
290 By Rail
290 By Road

TRAVEL ESSENTIALS
291 Visas & Passports
291 Money Matters
291 Health
292 What to Wear
292 What to Bring
292 On Arrival
292 Customs Formalities
293 Reservations
293 Extension of Stay
293 On Departure

GETTING ACQUAINTED
293 Government
294 Geography
295 Language
295 Time Zone & Climate
296 Weights & Measures
296 Business Hours
297 Holidays
297 Festivals
297 Islam & Ramadan

COMMUNICATIONS
299 Newspapers
299 Post &
    Telecommunications

EMERGENCIES
300 Security & Crime
300 Loss
300 Medical Services

GETTING AROUND
301 Orientation
301 Maps
301 Airport/City Links
302 City Transport
302 Local Transport
302 Private Transport
303 Internal Flights
303 On Foot &
    By Thumb
304 Complaints

WHERE TO STAY
304 Hotels

FOOD DIGEST
306 What to Eat
306 Where to Eat
308 Drinking Notes

THINGS TO DO
309 City
310 Country

NIGHTLIFE
312 Folklore/Fantasias

SHOPPING
314 What to Buy
314 Export Procedures
314 Complaints

SPORTS
315 Participant

SPECIAL INFORMATION
316 Doing Business
316 Gays
317 Disabled
317 Students

LANGUAGE
317 Useful Words

FURTHER READING
319 Films

USEFUL ADDRESSES
319 Tourist Ofices
319 Embassies & Consulates

GETTING THERE

BY AIR

The national airline, Royal Air Maroc, has Casablanca airport as its hub. There are flights from London Heathrow and from New York JFK to Tangier, Casablanca, Marrakesh and Agadir: many flights involve intermediate stops (often at Tangier) and sometimes a change of plane. Book a month in advance for an APEX fare. British Airways also fly from London Gatwick to Casablanca, Tangier and Marrakesh. There are several charter flights a week from London to Agadir, Marrakesh and Tangier (more in the winter season, November to March): these are theoretically meant for package tours but some travel agents will be able to quote a seat-only fare. If travelling to Tangier, it is worth investigating flights to Gibraltar or Southern Spain, only a short sea-crossing away.

BY SEA

The most logical point of entry by sea is from **Algeciras** in southern Spain across the Strait of Gibraltar to **Tangier** (around $2/¿^{TM}$ hours) or the Spanish duty-free territory of **Ceuta** (around 90 minutes). Tangier is better connected to public transport in Morocco; the Ceuta crossings are up to four times more frequent, and convenient for drivers who aren't daunted by arriving in *kif*-touting Tetouan as their first stop in Morocco. These short hops are the best bet for those in cars, since there are several sailings a day: on all the longer routes you will probably need a reservation—otherwise you run the risk of being blocked out by group bookings.

There are also hydrofoil services to Tangier from **Algeciras**, **Gibraltar**, and **Tarifa** (Spain's southernmost town). Hydrofoils don't run if the sea's too rough; nor do they run on Sundays. Spanish car ferries run from Almeria and Malaga to the Spanish duty-free port of Melilla ($6/¿^{TM}$ and 7 hours respectively). Finally, there are car ferries run by the Compagnie Marocaine de Navigation from Sète, in southern France, to Tangier or via the Balearic islands to Nador; the Tangier crossing takes 38 hours, so it's not for bad sailors or anyone in a hurry.

BY RAIL

Trains leave London Victoria and connect via the Algeciras ferry with Tangier, Rabat and Casablanca, by way of Paris, Bordeaux and Madrid. The total journey time, London to Casablanca, is around 60 hours. Travellers aged 26 and under can save by buying youth or student fares.

BY ROAD

Two options: drive through France to catch the ferry at Sète, or through France and Spain to take one of the Algeciras ferries. Coach tickets as far as **Algeciras** will be the least comfortable way to make the trip (around 48 hours from London).

TRAVEL ESSENTIALS

VISAS & PASSPORTS

Holders of full British passports (but *not* a British Visitor's Passport), and holders of valid United States, Canadian, Irish, Australian, New Zealand or Scandinavian passports need no visa for a stay of up to three months. Children under 16 without their own passports must be included in the passport of one of their parents.

MONEY MATTERS

The Moroccan *dirham* (DH) is nominally divided into 100 *centimes*—but these are sometimes called *francs*. Recent official rates have fluctuated between £1=14DH and £1=14.60DH; or US$1=7.83DH to US$1=8.12DH. Check newspapers for current rates.

There is one simple rule: Moroccan currency may not be imported or exported. Visitors can import as much foreign currency (in cash or travellers' cheques) as they wish: if the value of currency imported is more than 15,000DH, they must fill out a *déclaration des devises*, which should be kept throughout the trip.

It's useful, especially if entering Morocco outside banking hours (e.g. on an evening flight) to have some cash—it will be easier to change at airport exchange kiosks (mostly run by banks), who may refuse travellers' cheques or credit cards.

While in Morocco, travellers' cheques in either pounds or dollars are the safest and most efficient way of carrying money: exchange rates are fixed, whether in banks or

hotels. Most major banks do not charge commission. At the end of the trip, a certain amount of Moroccan currency can be changed back, but only if exchange receipts are produced (up to half the value of the receipts). It's simplest to exchange limited amounts at any one time, and to try to end up with as little Moroccan cash as possible when leaving the country. If you run out of money, it is possible to use major credit cards to obtain money in main banks (e.g. Crédit du Maroc, Banque Populaire or Société Générale Marocaine de Banques). Alternatively, you can telex your bank abroad and arrange for money to be transferred to a Moroccan bank. This takes about 24 hours.

HEALTH

No vaccinations are required by the Moroccan government for entry, unless you have come from a recognised infected area (e.g. a yellow fever, cholera or smallpox zone). For your own safety, however, inoculations against typhoid, polio, cholera, and tetanus are advised. A course of malaria tablets may also be advisable: these are normally taken for a week before, during, and for four to six weeks after travelling. The risk of malaria is highest in the summer: insect repellent gels or creams are sensible additional precautions.

Some protection against hepatitis may be useful if travelling in country areas. Injections of immuno-globulin give protection for about four weeks: they are no use for long trips, therefore, and should be discussed with a medical advisor. Contact with standing fresh water (swimming or paddling in oases, river valleys and lagoons) may carry the risk of bilharziasis. Rabies is present: take medical advice immediately if you are bitten.

Aids: Although figures aren't easy to come by in Morocco, AIDS is now considered to be prevalent in many areas of Africa, in both the male and female population. The disease can be transmitted either through sexual contact, or through medical treatment using infected needles, blood or blood transfusion equipment. Most Moroccan pharmacies now stock disposable needles, and clinics and hospitals are usually reliable: check with a consulate or embassy if in doubt over treatment. It is possible to buy medical "kits" containing sterile hypodermic needles and plasma which can be carried in case of emergency.

Humbler ailments are common. British government advice warns that the climate on the Atlantic coast is not good for sufferers from asthma, rheumatism, sinus and liver trouble—though this advice is primarily for those planning long stays. In a 1987 survey, the consumer magazine *Holiday Which?* found that 29 percent of its readers visiting Morocco had been ill on holiday. This compared with 56 percent in Egypt, 16 percent for Greece and Spain, nine percent in France and three percent in the Netherlands. **Stomach upsets** are top of the list, accounting for 60 percent of holiday illness: diarrhoea remedies or relief will come in handy.

Cutting the risks: use bottled water for drinking, brushing teeth etc; avoid standing food that has been re-heated, shellfish, ice-cream, and ice in drinks; be wary of salads or fruit that isn't peeled, unless it has been thoroughly washed.

The next most common cause of illness is usually too much heat or sun; light cotton clothing, moderate exposure and protective lotions all reduce the risk of sunstroke. (Also see Emergencies).

WHAT TO WEAR

Dress for comfort. Light-coloured, light-weight cottons are advisable (see above), and in the south, a sun hat in summer. Hotels are rarely dressy, although some four and many five-star hotels have formal restaurants where men will feel more comfortable in a jacket and tie, and women in a dress. When touring or sightseeing, let tact be a guide: jewellery and fine clothes mark the wealthy tourist in a poor country; expensive bags or cameras may also attract more attention than you would wish for.

WHAT TO BRING

Although cash tips are common, certain goods go down well too, with children who have posed for photographs or anyone who has helped you. European or American cigarettes (light tobacco) are worth carrying; so (for children) are coloured ball-point pens or crayons, small notebooks or wrapped sweets. Aspirin tablets will be useful as gifts in kind in country areas. Clothes (e.g. picture T-shirts) can be useful currency when bartering for larger items (such as rugs or killims) in the souks.

ON ARRIVAL

When you arrive you will be given an official form to fill in stating profession, addresses in Morocco and length of stay. Each time you register at a hotel you are required to fill in a similar form which is submitted to the police.

An international health and inoculation certificate is needed to bring pets into the country.

CUSTOMS FORMALITIES

Clothes, jewellery and personal effects including cameras and up to 10 rolls of film can be brought into the country temporarily, without formality. Foodstuffs and medicaments in reasonable quantities for personal use during the visitor's stay may also be imported. Duty-free allowances for alcohol, tobacco and perfumes are 400 grammes of tobacco *or* 200 cigarettes *or* 50 cigars; one litre of wine; one litre of spirits; a quarter-litre of eau de cologne. To import firearms, a licence is needed from the *Direction de la Sûreté Nationale* in Rabat.

Customs procedure on entry will vary according to point of arrival; baggage is often searched, and will need to be cleared by a customs official before entering the country.

RESERVATIONS

It's possible to book ahead from one hotel to the next: telephone charges will normally be added to your bill. But since communications, particularly with remote districts, are apt to be a little haphazard, it is often better to book hotel accommodation before your trip, especially in summer and midwinter. Flights should be reconfirmed at least 72 hours in advance; while this isn't vital, it will help if there have been any changes to schedules; contact an airport desk or Royal Air Maroc office, or let a travel agent or hotel member of staff do it.

EXTENSION OF STAY

Contact the local police department well in advance if your stay is likely to exceed 90 days. Extensions may be difficult: proof of funds is often required, and the purpose of an extended visit will be requested. It will be easier, at least in the north, simply to leave Morocco inside the 90 day period, and re-enter.

ON DEPARTURE

Apart from exchange regulations (in theory, a declaration of Moroccan and/or foreign currency is necessary, though this is often waived), the only formality on departure is a customs inspection.

GETTING ACQUAINTED

GOVERNMENT & ECONOMY

Morocco is a Muslim kingdom governed since 1961 by King Hassan II, son of the late king Mohammed V. It was Mohammed who changed his own title from sultan to king, and reigned when Morocco secured independence from France and Spain in 1956. In 1962, King Hassan put forward a new constitution which described Morocco as a Muslim sovereign state and a social democratic and constitutional monarchy, and which led to parliamentary elections. There have been periods of emergency rule, attempted coups and government by decree. The political structure remains parliamentary, with King Hassan firmly established in power (and much pictured in public places).

Agriculture: Exports include cereals, dates, figs, olives and almonds, sugar-cane, and most notably early fruits: oranges and tomatoes are the best known, but the Souss area has been experimenting with banana growing (and the cultivation of roses).

Minerals are dominated by rich reserves of phosphates; some three-quarters of the world's stock. The export of phosphates and its derivatives has historically accounted for something over 40 percent of export earnings. But energy has to be bought: there are some reserves of anthracite, and oil shales are beginning to be exploited, but most oil is imported. Hydro-electric power has contributed less to national needs as northern Africa has become gradually drier. A large lump of the country's foreign exchange comes from wages sent back home by Moroccans living in France, of whom there are over half a million.

Northern Morocco is a natural amphitheatre, with the Rif mountains (to the north) and the Atlas mountains (to the south and east) enclosing the basin of the river Sebou and the *meseta* or table land, which reaches south to Essaouira. The Sebou basin and the meseta are the country's richest and most fertile areas; the Atlantic plains and the lower valley of the Sebou support cereals and vines; higher plateaux around the edge of the meseta are covered by forest and pasture. The river basins and low coastal plains have been the natural settings for Morocco's northern cities: the ports of Casablanca and Rabat; Marrakesh between the meseta and the Atlas mountains; Fez and Méknès on the rich soils south of the Sebou.

The Rif mountains, falling abruptly to the Mediterranean on their northern side, slope more gently towards the Sebou to the west and south. Fields and olive groves surround tiny stone villages: the only towns of any size are industrial and touristic centres on the Mediterranean coast (Tangier, Tetouan, Al Hoceima), or in the foothills (such as the market town of Chaouen). Along the spine of the Rif, hashish is grown: the (illegal) hashish trade centres on Ketama, inland of Al Hoceima.

The Atlas mountains run in parallel ridges across Morocco from southwest to northeast. The Middle Atlas (up to 10,000 ft/3,000 metres) is part flat-topped, part corrugated, damp and green with forests of oak and huge cedars. The western plateaux are interrupted by volcanic scenery. Some of the predominantly Berber population are still nomadic, others raise goats and sheep.

The grand chain of the High Atlas (13,670 ft/4,167 metres at its highest point, the Toubkal) runs for 473 miles (700 km), across virtually the whole width of Morocco. Sandstone and granite peaks, snow-covered even in summer, contrast with the *pisé* built villages, narrow field-terraces, and the bright green valleys to the west of the Tizi n-Tichka pass. Further east, the mountainsides are largely devoted to goats.

A fault line runs from Agadir to Figuig, splitting the Anti Atlas and High Atlas ranges. At first it follows the valley of the river Souss, whose basin is desolate scrub, except in the lower valley between Taroudant and Agadir, where early fruits are grown. To the south is the pre Cambrian bulge of the Anti Atlas. Argan trees and small holdings flourish on the slopes facing west towards the sea. South and east again, the country is no more than desert, scored by oases-dotted river valleys. The pre-Sahara, made up of vast bare rocky plateaux, is swept by dusty winds, occasionally punctuated by flat-topped hillocks, or shifting dunes. The Sahara proper is less hospitable still, except at the chains of oases, where date palms interrupt the skyline. What were once watercourses are dry for most of the year, except after the occasional desert storm. Trickles of water are more common towards the hazy coast of sands and crumbling cliffs.

The northeastern extreme of the country comprises chiefly plateaux of 1,000 metres or more. In the main they are too dry to cultivate: even the valley of the river Moulouya, running out of the Atlas and east of the Rif, provides only a narrow corridor of cultivated soil. The wealth of the region, dominated by the town of Oujda, comes from the Mediterranean coast, irrigated and dammed, where the climate allows pockets of agriculture and market gardening.

POPULATION

The original people of Morocco—from the beginning of recorded history—were (and are) the Berbers: predominantly nomadic tribes and famously fierce. But the name Berber itself is thought to be derived from an Arab word for non-Arabs; and from the late seventh century A.D., Arabs and Berbers have shared the country and alternately held power—until colonial domination by Europeans. In troubled times, the Berbers retreated to strongholds in the Rif and High Atlas—where they have always been their own masters, and which still remain predominantly Berber today. The Arab population is today concentrated in the north and in the cities: in mountain and country areas three Berber languages are still spoken. But centuries of intermarriage have blurred a distinct Arab/Berber divide.

The population of Morocco is now estimated at a little over 24 million people, 90 percent of them living north of a line drawn between Tiznit and Oujda. Growth in recent decades has been remarkable: from 6.5 million in 1935, to 12.5 million in 1964, to nearly double that today. And it is a young population; four out of 10 Moroccans are said to be under the age of 15.

LANGUAGE

Moroccan Arabic is the official first language of the kingdom, although many people speak dialects of the **Berber** language, especially in and south of the High Atlas. Moroccan Arabic is unlike other forms of Arabic, so Arabic phrase books are not a good investment (although standard Arabic speakers will be understood). The easiest way to communicate for most Westerners is to use **French**, the second language, commonly used alongside Arabic on signposts, menus and in shops. The average Moroccan puts the average visitor to shame in his command of second, third and fourth languages. English, German or Spanish will be understood in many hotels or markets— or wherever tourists are found.

It's very useful to have a few words of Arabic as a matter of courtesy, and to establish friendly relations. A few useful words are listed below; an accent shows the stressed syllable.

Hello: *Saláam oualeïkum* (literally, peace be with you; formal greeting) or *Labás*.
Yes, no, okay: *Eéyeh, La, Wáha*
Thank you: *Shókran* or *Barakalléhfik* (literally the blessing of God with you)
Good, bad: *Miziéhn, Méshi Miziéhn*
God willing: *Insh'Allah* (used to qualify future events, e.g. we'll be coming back, Insh'Allah)
Goodbye: *Bsléhma*.

DAYS OF THE WEEK

Often used to identify towns and villages, which are named after the day of their weekly *souk*: thus Souk-Tnine is the town which has a market on Monday. On many road signs, the day is mentioned where the map or guidebook omits to mention it. The days are numbered from Sunday, with the exception of Friday, the day of Muslim worship, which has no number.

El had: the first day: Sunday
Et tnine: the second day: Monday
Et tleta: the third day: Tuesday
El arba: the fourth day: Wednesday
El khemis: the fifth day: Thursday
Ej djeema: day of mosque or assembly, Friday
Es sebt: the sixth day: Saturday

TIME ZONE & CLIMATE

Moroccan time is the same as Greenwich Mean Time; when it is noon in Morocco, it is noon in London, 7 a.m. in New York and 8 p.m. in Perth. This does not take into account local seasonal time changes; there are none in Morocco.

Climate: Three types of climate hold sway in three distinct regions: coastal regions have warm dry summers, are wet for the rest of the year and mild in winter: the coast is drier south of Agadir, where it is free of Atlantic depressions in winter. Agadir, sheltered by mountains, has a very well-protected climate, with a narrow range of temperatures; but in common with the rest of the Atlantic coast, cold offshore water can cause cloud and fog. The mountains get hot, dry summers and very harsh winters; parts of the High Atlas are under snow well into the summer. The remainder of the country has a continental climate, getting hotter and drier in summer to the south, but moderated by the sea to the west. In the inland Sahara very dry, hot summers give way to warm sunny days and cold (sometimes frosty) nights in winter. (See chart on following page).

MONTH		J	F	M	A	M	J	J	A	S	O	N	D
Agadir	Temp	20	21	23	23	24	25	27	27	27	26	24	21
	Rain	55	33	22	17	7	<1	<1	1	8	14	35	47
	Sun	7.7	8.2	9.3	9.9	10.0	9.6	9.4	8.7	8.6	7.9	7.6	7.2
Casablanca	Temp	17	18	20	21	22	24	26	26	26	24	21	18
	Rain	78	61	54	37	20	3	<1	1	6	28	58	94
	Sun	5.2	6.3	7.3	9.0	9.4	9.7	10.2	9.7	9.1	7.4	5.7	5.3
Fez	Temp	15	18	20	22	26	31	36	36	32	26	20	16
	Rain	80	72	71	64	37	12	1	3	15	36	61	85
	Sun	5.0	6.6	7.1	8.1	8.5	10.0	11.3	10.5	8.6	7.4	5.6	4.3
Marrakesh	Temp	18	20	23	25	29	33	38	37	33	28	23	19
	Rain	29	31	31	33	20	8	2	3	10	17	27	34
	Sun	7.0	7.3	8.2	9.1	9.3	10.7	11.5	10.6	9.7	8.0	7.1	6.7
Melilla	Temp	17	18	19	21	23	26	29	29	27	24	20	18
	Rain	52	30	28	28	38	8	1	1	11	27	33	66
	Sun	5.1	5.5	6.0	6.8	7.9	8.7	9.1	9.4	6.2	5.9	5.0	4.9
Ouarzazate	Temp	17	19	23	26	30	35	39	40	35	27	21	17
	Rain	8	5	15	7	6	5	2	10	21	20	17	19
	Sun	7.4	8.6	9.5	10.2	10.9	11.6	10.0	8.9	8.9	8.4	7.7	7.1
Tarfaya	Temp	20	20	21	21	22	22	23	23	24	23	23	21
	Rain	9	5	3	1	<1	<1	<1	<1	6	1	15	10
	Sun	6.6	6.9	7.7	8.5	7.9	7.8	6.5	7.0	7.2	7.1	5.9	6.6

Key:

Temperature: Average daily maximum (° C)

Rain: Average monthly rainful (mm)

Bright sunshine: Average daily hours

Source: Met. Office Statistics

WEIGHTS & MEASURES

Metric measures are used throughout Morocco: distances are in kilometres, quantities in litres and weights in grammes or kilogrammes.

Electricity: Most of the country's supply is rated 220 volts, but some places have a 110 volt supply; sockets and plugs are of the continental European type, with two round pins.

BUSINESS HOURS

Hours vary slightly, but the timetable is based around a two-hour rest in the middle of the day. Standard hours for **banks**: Monday to Friday, 8.30 a.m. to 11.30 a.m. and 2.30 p.m. to 4.30 p.m. For **offices:** Monday to Friday, 8.30 a.m. to noon, 2.30 p.m. to 6 p.m. For **post offices**: Monday to Saturday 8.30 a.m. to 2 p.m. (at least: the bigger the town, the longer they open). Telephone services, at the same offices, often open in the evenings (the biggest are open 24 hours). For **shops**: Monday to Saturday, 8.30 a.m. to noon and 2 p.m. to 6 p.m. Many shops stay open much later than this; some close on Friday (the Muslim equivalent of the sabbath) and some open on Sunday.

HOLIDAYS

There are two sets of holidays, religious and secular: the one based on the Muslim (lunar) year, and the other on the Western (Gregorian) calendar. Religious holidays are as follows; the exact dates according to the Western calendar get earlier each year, by 10 or 11 days. 1989 dates are shown: tourist offices will be able to supply exact dates.

Muslim holidays
Ramadan—(from 8 April)
Aid es Seghir—(end of Ramadan, 6/7 May)
Aid el Kebir—(feast of Abraham's sacrifice, 16/17 July)
Muslim New Year—(10 August)
Mouloud—(the Prophet's birthday, 14/15 October).
These are usually observed by shops and businesses, though these days some shopkeepers are sacrificing piety for prosperity.
State holidays
New Year's Day—1 January
Feast of the Throne—3 March
Labour Day—1 May
Green March—6 November
Independence Day—18 November.

FESTIVALS

Every religious holiday is marked by festivity in Morocco. The other staple of festival life is the *moussem:* a local festival (or pilgrimage) in honour of a saint or holy man. In the country you may occasionally stumble across one of these, a flash of colour and excitement in the daily round of subsistence; men and unmarried girls in costume, a courtyard laid with carpets and rugs, frenzied bands of musicians. But there are several *moussems* which are on a larger scale altogether and worth going out of your way for. Ceremonial dancing and fantasias (displays of horsemanship) may accompany them. There are also folklore and harvest festivals. Most of these are movable feasts and exact dates should be checked either before you leave or when you arrive.

Tafraoute: an almond blossom festival: February
El Kelâa des Mgouna (Ouarzazate region): festival of roses: May
Goulimine: *moussem*: June/July
Marrakesh: national folklore festival: early June
Sefrou (Fez region): cherry harvest: June
Setti Fatma (Marrakesh region): *moussem*: August
Imilchil (High Atlas): marriage *moussem* of the Aït Haddidou tribe, a sort of costumed mass pledge: September
Moulay Idriss (Méknès region): the country's grandest *moussem* commemorating the founder of Morocco's first Arab dynasty, and effectively the father of Moroccan Islam: throughout September
Fez: *moussem* of Moulay Idriss II, the founder's son: September
Asilah: an international music festival, including classical, folk and popular: October
Agadir: art and folklore festival: October/November
Erfoud: date (the fruit!) festival: October

In the fortnight before and after Mouloud, the Prophet's birthday (see above), there are processions and *moussems* in **Méknès**, **Salé** and **Asni** (Marrakesh region).

ISLAM & RAMADAN

Islam in Morocco is in a strange position: popular unorthodoxy is followed (rather than led) by the state; at the same time, many European habits of government remain. Unlike some Gulf Arab states, there is not much evidence of hard line Islam. Alcohol is not restricted by law. Sunday is the closing day for offices and shops. It is in souks (mainly those in the country) that *djemma*— the word means simply mosque—is observed on Fridays: on that day, country markets will often be closed after noon.

Morocco remains a Muslim country, for all its compromises with Western calendars and customs (a holiday on New Year's Day), and never more obviously than during the holy month of Ramadan (see below). But Islam in the country is a peculiarly Moroccan hybrid—the faith of the Arabs adapted by the tribes of Berbers. There is more emphasis on individuals and saints than rigid Islamic codes would sanction: and that is a direct result of a split between the population in the cities and the country.

Islam in the city is easy to govern. The minarets of the mosques are a constant visible reminder to the populace, and the faithful are loudly called to prayer five times a day. The mosque—and the wisdom and learning traditionally associated with it—are (often literally) central to town and city life. Koranic schools and conclaves of Islamic scholars reinforce orthodoxy, the most important tenet being that there is no God but God and Mohammed is his prophet. There are no vicars, no intermediaries: in praying five times a day, the Muslim is talking directly to God. At the same time, even without priests, the centres of religious devotion have immense influence—and power. And it is away from this urban structure of influence that part of Moroccan Islam has moved.

The first and most visible element of country Islam in Morocco is the popularity of the *marabout* or local saint—visible, because the countryside of remote areas is dotted with small whitewashed buildings with domed roofs. Each is the tomb of a saint; the tomb itself sometimes known as a *marabout* (otherwise called a *koubba*). Around these local saints, cults of devotion have grown up over centuries—over 1,000 years in the case of Moulay Idriss.

Rich cults have *zaouia*—educational colleges set up next to the marabout in the same way as a mosque set up a *medrassa*—but as an alternative to the city-based orthodox Muslim faith taught at the mosque. And every cult has its *moussem*—the annual festival in honour of the saint (see *Festivals*)—the scale of the festival reflecting the importance of the particular saint.

Ramadan: The ninth month of the Muslim calendar was the one in which God revealed to Mohammed the truths which were written as the Koran. In remembrance of this and in obedience to one of Islam's "five pillars", Muslims must observe a holy fast during the hours of daylight. This means total abstinence from food, drink, tobacco and sex between sunrise and sunset. Thereafter, Moroccans traditionally end the fast with a bowl of *harira* (stew: see section on *Food digest*) as soon as the mosque lamps signal nightfall. That's followed by an atmosphere of restrained nocturnal festivity, in the hours when a black thread cannot be distinguished from a white one—or at least in most of them.

For travellers: The unique atmosphere of Ramadan can be weighed against slight material inconveniences for the traveller. Non-Muslims are not required to observe the fast, but abstinence from smoking or eating in public is tactful.

COMMUNICATIONS

NEWSPAPERS

The main newspapers in Morocco are: *L'Opinion* (in French, circulation 60,000); *Le Matin* (in French, circulation 55,000); *Maroc Soir* (in French, circulation 35,000); *Al Alam* (in Arabic, circulation 30,000). The principal business magazine is *La Vie Economique*, a French language financial and economic weekly with a circulation varying between 2,500 and 5,000.

Enjeux, a current affairs, pro-government magazine, is a monthly put out by the publishers of *Le Matin*, and *Lamalif* is an arts magazine with left/centre viewpoint.

English newspapers are available in cities and resort hotels, as are most European papers, the *International Herald Tribune* and many magazines.

The **television** service of *Radiodiffusion Télévision Marocain* is government-run, along with the associated **radio** channel. There is another radio station based in Tangier, *Radio Méditerranée-Internationale*, that broadcasts to Algeria, Tunisia, Spain and the South of France as well. All carry advertising. The British World Service from the BBC broadcasts between 6 a.m. and midnight (try 16.94 m, 17.70 MHz). Details of BBC times and wavelengths are available from the British Council in Rabat. Satellite television is available in Rabat, Marrakesh and Casablanca. Sky Channel is to be introduced soon.

POST & TELECOMMUNICATIONS

Post offices (PTT) deal with postage, poste restante, telephone and telegraph services. But all of these are occasionally haphazard. For telephone connections, Rabat and Casablanca are best equipped, with international direct dialling from telephone booths in the telephone office. Theoretically, international calls are possible from any office, but you may have to wait—and wait. Calls from a hotel mean that waiting is more comfortable, but make sure that you are clear about the rate being charged before you go ahead. It's also becoming increasingly easy to dial direct from phone boxes in the street. Dial 00 for an international call, followed by the country code. Codes and costs (in 1989) are as follows:

Canada: (00 1); 26.90DH per minute
Great Britain: (00 44); 13.45DH per minute
USA: (00 1); 31.35DH per minute

Calls to most of western Europe and Scandinavia cost the same as calls to Britain.

Local calls can sometimes be made from cafés and small grocers. Cafés will add a nominal charge to the bill.

Postage stamps can often be bought at the place you buy postcards. A postcard to the UK costs 1.70DH, a letter costs 3.60 DH. Air mail letters normally take at least five days to reach Britain—sometimes a lot longer.

Telegraph rates to Britain are 2.40DH per word (ordinary rate); 4.80DH per word (urgent rate).

Telex facilities are usually available in large hotels for their own clients. Telex calls to Britain cost 6.45DH per minute.

EMERGENCIES

SECURITY & CRIME

Crime against tourists is not common, but neither is it unknown. In a survey published by the British consumer magazine *Holiday Which?*, it was found that 4.3 percent of visitors to Morocco had been victims of theft: smaller than 1 in 24. But any guide in the packed souks of Fez and Marrakesh will advise you to hold tightly to your bag. Violent attacks or muggings were still less common—less than one percent were affected. Nevertheless, both types of crime were found to be more common in African countries—including Morocco—than in Europe or America.

Emergency telephone numbers
Police: 19.
Fire services/ambulance: 15.

Elementary precautions: Avoid wearing jewellery, or carrying too much money in the streets: use hotel safe deposit boxes. If you're on the move, prefer a secure pocket or money belt to a shoulder bag for valuables; if you wear a bag, sling the strap over the head, not just the shoulder.

If you are threatened or attacked, don't put up a fight: better to lose money than risk being hurt. If driving, don't leave bags visible in the car, always lock it up and leave it empty overnight.

LOSS

If belongings have been stolen, a police report should be made. Do not be put off by hotel staff; insurance companies almost invariably require a local police report be-fore they will entertain a claim for theft. If tour company representatives are on hand, they may be able to help, and should certainly be informed. If your belongings do not arrive at the airport, it is the responsibility of the airline: ask for a Property Irregularity Form to fill in. Many travel insurance policies will then allow reasonable expenses on clothes and other essentials.

Left luggages: For a small charge, luggage may be left at railway stations or offices of the Compagnie Transport Marocain (CTM): it should be safe enough.

MEDICAL SERVICES

There are private clinics in all main towns, and government hospitals in many. Consulates may be able to give advice about English-speaking doctors; or tour companies' representatives (and noticeboards) at hotels. All services will be charged for immediately, except in cases of need or emergency: if your travel insurance is not explicit on the point of medical treatment, and you have to pay, ask for and keep receipts.

Pharmacies in towns sell many kinds of medicines, drugs and contraceptives (but not tampons or sanitary towels—these may be available from general stores in town). Medicines are expensive: aspirin, insect bite cream and stomach settlers are best bought at home. There is a late night pharmacy in each major town: it's often the town hall (*Municipalité*) which houses an all night dispensary.

GETTING AROUND

ORIENTATION

Reaching a Moroccan town or city is often a bewildering experience. The largest are divided into the old and new towns. The old town—or *medina*—is the Moroccan quarter. Often surrounded by ramparts and entered through grand gateways, it will contain a disorientating maze of narrow streets and *souks* running between squares. It may also contain the fortified *kasbah*—ramparts within ramparts. At the other extreme is the *nouvelle ville*—usually planned and laid out by the French, with grand, straight avenues connecting roundabouts. The grandest avenue is often named after Mohammed V, and it's usually here or in the main square of the new town that you'll find the tourist office (addresses below). This is the place to find an *official guide* (see below): the quickest and simplest method of orientation. On the roads, there are few problems with navigation: signposts are clear, and the long roads have few turnings. It's worth taking local advice about the state of mountain or desert roads at any time of year, but particularly in the mountains during the winter season.

Guides—official and otherwise: the experience of arriving in an unfamiliar town or city is, in Morocco, inevitably accompanied by the offer of a guide's services. The guide may be a small grubby boy, a schoolboy, a student; he may claim to be any of these things; and he will be persistent, rarely taking your first no for an answer. If you've decided you need a guide, such meetings can be fruitful, as long as you explicitly agree on a fee in advance (10 dirhams an hour is fairly standard, and perhaps round it up a little when you've finished).

The rate for *official guides* in Marrakesh

in the winter of 1988 was 50 dirhams a half day, 90 for a full day. The half-day rate is a minimum charge, so it's worth starting out when the tourist offices open, or even booking a guide in advance. Remember that monuments often close in the middle of the day: half-day guides often like to finish at noon.

MAPS

The most accessible and reliable maps produced by European companies are: Hallwag (1:1,000,000: £3.95); Lascelles (1:800,000: £3.95); Michelin no. 969, *Maroc Nord et Centre* (1:0,000,000: £3.40). Tyre companies in Morocco sometimes sell road maps (in the style of Michelin maps), or try for a *librairie* in major towns. Serviceable town and city plans are available free of charge from the National Tourist Office (available in advance from the Moroccan National Tourist Offices abroad). Large scale topographical maps of the Atlas are difficult to obtain. Main agent in the UK is West Col Productions, Goring, Reading Berks. RG89AA.

In the USA: Michael Chessler Books, PO Box 2436, Evergreen, CO80 439-2436. IGN maps of Toukal National Park are available at Imlil and Asni.

AIRPORT/CITY LINKS

There are taxi services links between international airports and their respective towns. With the exception of Casablanca, distances are small, so that taxi fares should remain low. There are official fare tables published, but you're unlikely to see them around the airport: most of the *grands taxis* on the airport run will be unmetered, and drivers may want to haggle over fares. Use the guide prices below as a rough estimate. **Casablanca** airport is nine miles (30 km) south of the city: the taxi fare will be up to 100 dirhams. **Agadir** airport is five miles (eight km) south of town, and the taxi fare around 40 dirhams; **Fez** airport is six miles

(10 km) south of the town (taxi around 40 dirhams); **Marrakesh** airport is 5 km south-west of the city (taxi around 45 dirhams); **Tangier** airport is seven miles (12 km) south-west of the city (taxi at least 45 dirhams). During the day there are also bus services from the airports at Casablanca, Agadir, Marrakesh and Tangier.

CITY TRANSPORT

Much cheaper for cities are *petits taxis*: small saloon cars, theoretically metered, and with a different livery (and often different rates) in each town. They'll take up to three people. It's wise to ask the fare before you get in to a cab: and there's no harm in politely but firmly disputing an exorbitant fare at the end of a journey. In the end, as with so much in Morocco, the price depends on the agreement of the driver and the driven.

In **Marrakesh** (and also in Taroudant), an alternative means of urban transport are the glossy horse-drawn *calèches*, with large wheels, loud horns and folding leather canopies. These can be as cheap as taxis for three or four people, though increasingly exorbitant prices prevail when tourists are many. The same rules of haggling apply. City buses are occasionally useful and always cheap (but usually crowded).

LOCAL TRANSPORT

The choice in local transport is between trains, buses and taxis. **Railway lines** are confined to the major cities; the network extends south to Marrakesh, and links up with Safi, Casablanca, Rabat, Tangier, Fez, Méknès and Oujda. There are three classes on Moroccan trains: first class has air-conditioning and is still cheap (around 25 dirhams per 62 miles/100 km). Groups of ten or more receive a discount of 20 to 30 percent: travellers under the age of 26 can use Eurotrain or Inter-Rail passes on Moroccan trains. Train stations are usually found near the centre of the *ville nouvelle*. Tourist offices outside Morocco can provide timetables.

Bus travel is the cheapest way to get around, and there's no better way to get to know Morocco in detail. There is a national network, CTM; a network between Casablanca, Agadir and the south, SATAS; and a lot of small local companies who may or may not run according to a timetable. Allow plenty of time to travel by bus: all of them stop frequently. Fares are usually some 20 percent cheaper than trains (as a *very* rough guide, say 20 dirhams per 62 miles/100 km). Comfortable express coaches run by **ONCF** (the railway company) along the southwest and northern coasts (where the railway doesn't run): these cost 50 percent more than standard bus fares.

Grands taxis are large cars, usually Mercedes, which rattle along with up to six passengers on routes from town to town, charging a fixed price. They will leave when they are full: it's possible to charter an entire taxi, but make sure you know the going rate. The fare is liable to be a third as much again as a bus, but the journey is likely to take half the time, or less. In remote or desert areas, Land Rovers may replace taxis, and open trucks act as local buses.

PRIVATE TRANSPORT

Car: Drivers must be over 21, and be fully insured against claims by third parties. The insurance is automatic on renting a car. If taking your own car, the European insurance green card is valid (motoring organisations and insurance companies will give details); you will also need the registration document. Your own national licence is valid, but it does no harm to carry an International Driving Permit as well (it has French and Arabic translations; available from motoring organisations). An international customs carnet is required for caravans.

The rules of the road are to drive on the right, and give priority to the right (the same system as the French *priorité á droite*). Major roads are well surfaced, minor ones good with lapses (some treacherous potholes) and mountain roads often not as bad as you'll have been led to expect. Although there is only one motorway (between Rabat and Casablanca), outside cities driving is fast. Beware, though, of other drivers. The driving test in Morocco is notoriously open to corruption. Fuel (*essence* or, more likely, *super* for petrol/gas; *gas-oil* for diesel) is available in towns of even modest size, but fill up before striking out on a long journey away from main roads. It gets cheaper to the south, but costs around six dirhams a litre on average (about £2 per gallon: Agadir, 1989). Parking in all towns of any size is likely to cost a few dirhams, collected by an official attendant, who may offer car cleaning services at a price.

Hiring a car: The major international hire companies are all represented in Morocco. It is possible to arrange for a car to be picked up at any of the international airports. In the cities, too, there are always several local companies, who will undercut the rates of the major companies considerably, possibly by as much as half. This will be useful for short rentals (which are proportionately more expensive): but for a rental lasting the whole trip, it may be cheaper to organise a car in advance on a special **holiday tariff**— either through a travel agent or direct with one of the major rental companies.

Car hire prices are usually quoted exclusive of a 19 percent government tax: be sure this has been added to the price which is agreed. A week's inclusive hire of a basic car (Renault 4) for a week will be about 2,000 dirhams (around £150) from small local companies. Booked from London, prices from specialist brokers start at roughly the same level, but prices from the majors start at around £210. Remember that the large international companies are likely to have a better network of offices if anything goes wrong with the car. For gruelling itineraries with a lot of mountain driving, consider hiring cars from group B (Fiat Uno) or C (Renault 5): they feel a bit more secure on tight corners. Land Rovers for more adventurous routes can be hired locally, often supplied with a chauffeur.

The Casablanca offices (agencies) and telephone numbers of the major companies, who can advise on hire throughout Morocco, are listed below.

Avis: 19 Avenue des Forces Armées Royales. Telephone: 314451. Telex: 23080.
Budget: Tour des Habous, Avenue des Forces Armées Royales. Telephone: 313943. Telex: 24911.
Europcar: 144 Avenue des Forces Armées Royales. Telephone: 367973. Telex: 21813.
Hertz: 25 Rue de Foucauld. Telephone: 312223. Telex: 21884.
InterRent: 44 Avenue des Forces Armées Royales. Telephone: 313737. Telex: 22990.

INTERNAL FLIGHTS

There are internal flights between most cities, even as far south as Layounne and Dakhla. The advantages of flying are clear cut: speed and reliability. The chief drawback is equally obvious: cost. The best reason to use an internal flight would be to complete the lion's share of a long circuit. For example, the journey from Tangier to Marrakesh costs around 520 dirhams, or nearly 90 dirhams per 60 miles/100 km)—three or four times bus or train fares. But the journey time is two instead of 10 hours.

ON FOOT & BY THUMB

With public transport so cheap, and distances so vast, walking and hitchhiking by visitors aren't that common. Arranging lifts with other tourists is sometimes easier at campsites. Tourists are more likely to be a source of rides—for other visitors or for Moroccans. If you accept a ride from a Moroccan driver, or ride on a truck, you may be asked for money: if you're using the only means of transport around, this is fair enough. But watch out for exorbitant "fares", and don't pay until you arrive at your destination (or you may be left stranded).

In cities, contact the tourist office, the *Sûreté* or *Gendarmerie*; even the hotel may be able to help resolve problems. On the road, if you're following a major route, the chances of a *Gendarmerie* road block are high; this can be a good place to air problems (as long as everybody remains reasonably calm). In remote areas, travelling off roads or in the desert, the intrepid traveller will be literally beyond help: remember this before setting out.

WHERE TO STAY

HOTELS

Most Moroccan hotels are classified, and their rates set, by the government. The exceptions are five star hotels, who are free to set their own prices, and unclassified hotels, usually simple central establishments without baths or showers, probably in the medina (the local *hammam*, or steam bath, takes the place of hotel baths). The tariffs for 1988, shown below, are a guide: but it's worth noting that some hotels, while charging the official rate for their standard rooms, will quietly slip you into a superior room—away from the road, or with an extra sitting-room—which is undeniably more pleasant, but can end up much more expensive. Check the rate when you check in. Local tourist offices are prepared to investigate inflated prices.

You will usually find it easier to contact hotels in the country by post than by telephone, even when in Morocco. There are several specialist companies in London who will tailor make an itinerary and take care of all the bookings: see section on *Things to do*. There are **campsites** all over the country, especially along the coast: they act as meeting places for budget travellers, both Moroccan and visiting. Prices start at around 8DH per night for one person and a tent. You may be able to hire a tent if you don't possess one. Security can be a problem: don't leave valuables unattended. There are half a dozen **youth hostels**, all but one in cities: Casablanca, Fez, Marrakesh, Méknès and Rabat. The sixth is at Asni in the High Atlas, a popular hiking base. Here is a list of some of the best hotels:

• Casablanca
Hotel Riad Salam Meridien: 5 star: beachside; 100 rooms, 12 suites, 50 bungalows, sea water therapy institute. Telephone: 363535/367922. Telex 24692.

• El Jadida
Club Salam des Doukkala: 4 star B: Avenue El Jamaiaa Al Arabia; sporty beach club hotel; 82 rooms. Telephone: (34) 3622/3575. Telex 78014.

• Essaouira
Hotel des Iles: 4 star A: well-run, popular with British; 77 rooms. Telephone: (47) 2329. Telex: 31907.

• Fez
Hotel Palais Jamai: 5 star: Bab Guissa; 18th century palace with beautiful gardens and views of Fez; superb cuisine; 115 rooms, 25 suites. Telephone: (6) 34331/24746.

• Immouzer Des Ida Outanane (Agadir region)
Hotel des Cascades: 3 star B; small hotel in superb site by pretty waterfalls; 14 rooms. Telephone: Immouzer Des Ida Outanane 14.

• Layounne
Hotel Parador: 4 star A; central, with bedrooms giving on to lush courtyards, good food; 31 rooms. Telephone: Layounne 2245/2200. Telex 28800.

• Marrakesh
Hotel La Mamounia: 5 star luxe; Avenue Bab Jdid; former palace at the city's edge: expensive but truly luxurious, after complete refurbishment in the mid 1980s; superb gardens; 180 rooms, 48 suites. Telephone: (04) 48981. Telex: 72018.
Hotel Tichka: 4 star A; Route de Casablanca; in the modern hotel quarter, a designer's treat, with a fine pool; 140 rooms. Telephone: (04) 48710. Telex: 74855.
Hotel Tafilalet: 4 star; Route de Casablanca; polished, personal service, a little way out of town; 84 rooms. Telephone: (04) 34518. Telex: 72955.
Hotel Imilchil: 3 star; Avenue Echouhada; Moroccan decor, pool but no bar at this good value hotel; 82 rooms. Telephone: (04) 47653. Telex: 72955.

• Val d' Ouirgane (High Atlas)
Residence de la Roseraie: 4 star A; BP 769 Marrakesh; folded into the mountains, with rose garden, pool, stunning views, bungalows and apartments; 9 rooms, 16 suites. Telephone: Ouirgane 4/5.

• Ouarzarzate
Hotel Tichka: 4 star. Avenue Mohammed V; 113 rooms; tennis, pool, nightclub, in southern style. Telephone Ouarzarzate 2206.

• Rabat
La Tour Hassan: 5 star; Avenue de Chellah; central, traditional style hotel with facilities kept up to modern standards; 150 rooms. Telephone: (07) 21401/33814. Telex: 31914.

• Tafraoute
Hotel aux Armandiers: 4 star B; ochre-coloured, kasbah style, above the town square: atmosphere and setting striking, decor a little worn; 60 rooms. Telephone: (Tafraoute) 8.

• Tangier
Hotel el Minzah: 5 star; Rue de la Liberté; smart but relaxed hotel with Moorish decor (it was formerly a private home) overlooks the Straits of Gibraltar; 100 rooms. Telephone: (09) 35886/7/8. Telex: 33775.

• Taroudant
Gazelle d'Or: 5 star; three kilometres from town, a sybarite's escapist dream; pool, tented restaurant and bungalows under the High Atlas; 30 rooms. Telephone: (85) 2039/2048. Telex: 81902 Gazelor.
Hotel Palais Salam: 4 star A: a palace built in to the city walls, with luxuriant banana palms. Thoughtful service, mediocre food; 75 rooms, 38 suites. Telephone: (85) 2130. Telex: 81679.

• Zagora
Hotel Tinsouline: 3 star A; desert's edge hotel, unpretentious and French-feeling, with good food; 90 rooms. Telephone: Zagora 22.

FOOD DIGEST

The following are the staples of Moroccan menus. The first three are available almost everywhere, from roadside cafés to top class hotels.

Brochettes: cubes of meat on kebabs, most often made from lamb or mutton; *kefta* are kebabs made from balls of mince.

Harira: thick, spicy, sometimes creamy soup, based on beans and pulses. It's often offered as a starter, but beware: it is enough to be a meal in itself.

Tajine: stew—meat or fish slowly cooked over charcoal in an earthenware pot on a bed of oil, vegetables, fruits and spices. One of Morocco's most visible dishes (because of the distinctive conical topped dish in which it is served).

M'choui: whole lamb, spit or oven roasted. Although traditional, *m'choui* is usually found only on special occasions—at festivals, say—or in the more "traditional" restaurants.

Poulet: chicken—whether cooked with lemon and saffron or olives, or with dates and nuts, or just plain roasted—is common to many more sophisticated (or expensive) menus.

Pastilla: spiced pigeon meat encased in flaky, *warkha* pastry, often dusted with sugar or cinnamon—a traditional delicacy.

Fish: Sea bream, whiting and sardines are the most common fish. In stews, baked or grilled, they are most usual (not unnaturally) on the coast.

Bread: for mopping up harira or tajines, the traditional flat round loaves are ideal. Fairly dry, with a grainy texture.

Cous-cous: a huge bowl of steamed semolina grains with vegetables and meat—usually mutton or chicken. It's supposed to be eaten by hand, but spoons are usually provided for Westerners, which is just as well. More of a domestic meal than a meal eaten out—at least as far as the Moroccans are concerned.

Fruit: good quality fresh fruit is everywhere: dates, grapes, melons, peaches, oranges, cherries or bananas. Fruits that you can peel are the least likely to damage your health. One more fruit, rarely on menus but often sold in the streets, is the sweet and juicy cactus fruit, prickly pear or Barbary fig.

Moroccan-style meals are available in most four and five-star hotels, in traditionally furnished restaurants. In cities such as Fez and Marrakesh, there are several restaurants in the medina which specialise in Moroccan meals combined with a floor show. These are mainly the preserve of the tourist trade, since Moroccans tend not to eat out.

The design of a Moroccan dining-room is similar everywhere. Low banquette seats against the wall, and even lower tables, are the norm in both restaurants and private homes. The classic Moroccan meal is eaten with two fingers and thumb of the right hand—but hotels and restaurants may not insist! When tea or coffee is served, it is a sign that the meal is at an end: you should prepare to leave after three cups or so.

You will probably need to book such meals in advance (even in your hotel): occasionally you may need to be part of a group to order a certain dish. If you're looking for a good restaurant, rely on word of mouth from other visitors rather than the recommendations of guides: the restaurants themselves pay a hefty commission to the guides.

European style meals are served in three, four and five-star hotels, and in several city restaurants; Fez also boasts a typically Chinese restaurant (Young Tse on Avenue Salaoui). Especially in Agadir, but also elsewhere, the number of pizza and spaghetti restaurants is rising. But there will always be cheap roadside or medina cafés—pick the cleanest and busiest.

•Agadir

Agadir likes to think of itself as a cosmopolitan resort, and this is reflected in the restaurants—sadly rather too many pizza, burger and pasta establishments, most of which are on Boulevard du 20 Août. However, there are also some good fish places. Try, **Restaurant du Port**—unsurprisingly, at the port entrance.

•Asilah

Of all the small fish restaurants just outside the medina, **Pepe's** is perhaps the best. Simply cooked sardines, squid, swordfish, prawns, sole, sea wolf is served with bread and salads. Pavement tables provide a good view of the evening promenade.

•Casablanca

The city may not have much to recommend it from the point of sight-seeing but it has good restaurants. These include the outstanding **A Ma Bretagne**, Sidi Abderahmen (tel: 36 62 26), the expensive **Al Mounia** (Rue du Prince Moulay Abdallah, off the Boulevard de Paris) and **Sijilmassa** (Rue de Biarritz). The Moroccan character of both extends to providing floor shows.

Less expensive are **Ouarzazate** (Rue Mohammed el Qorri, off Boulevard Mohammed V) and **Bahja** (Rue Colbert, off Boulevard Mohammed V).

Restaurant du Port de Pèche (through the port entrance) is the best fish restaurant, with only moderately expensive prices.

•Essaouira

Expect to find both these restaurants busy with French surfing crowds:

Chez Sam's, inside harbour perimeter, i.e. through the gate. Excellent seafood and large portions, and lively atmosphere.

Châlet de la Plage: large portions of good French food at reasonable prices. It is possible just to drink at the bar and eat *tappas*—particularly useful when the few other bars existing in the town have closed.

•Fez

The restaurant with an international reputation is **L'Anmbra** (47 Route d'Immouzer, Tel: Fez 25177). It is famous for its Moroc-

can specialities, particularly *pastilla*. It is essential to book.

Hotel Palais Jamai, Fez's most stunning hotel, contained in a former palace, has a very good Moroccan restaurant. Book on Fez 34331.

Dar Saada (tel: Fez 33343), 21 Rue Attarine, near the Attarine Medrassa and **Palais de Fez**, opposite the Kairouyine Mosque (16 Boutouil, tel: Fez 347 07) are decent alternatives, but their locations are reflected in their overwhelmingly tourist clientele and high prices.

As a change from Moroccan cuisine, **Young Tse** (Avenue Salaoui) is a popular Chinese restaurant. (Tel: Fez 23681).

•Marrakesh

In contrast to the more expensive restaurants listed is a humble and anonymous café on Djemma el Fna close to the Café de France. It can be identified by two vast cauldrons, containing *harira* and vegetable soups, on its raised terrace. Prices are the lowest you'll find in Morocco (literally a few dirhams) and the food is fresh and delicious. Inside, standards of hygiene may make the nervous diner blanch, but trade is reassuringly brisk.

Yacout, 79 Sidi Ahmed Soussi, is at the other end of the price spectrum (approximately $50 per head). The newest (it opened in 1988) and most fashionable restaurant in town (it attracts international names). Classic Moroccan dishes, superbly cooked and presented; a terrific ambience; and exquisite decor. Necessary to book on Marrakesh 41903.

La Maison Arabe (5 Derb Ferrane; Tel: Marrakesh 22604); open from November to March. Its reputation rivals, if not surpasses L'Anmbra in Fez. This restaurant must be booked well in advance and it may be necessary to discuss the menu with the French patron beforehand. Recently it has been criticised for resting on its laurels. These days gourmets with the money to spend may prefer Yacout.

Restaurant de France on Place Djemma el Fna. Fairly good Moroccan food and traditional decor beyond the very popular bar. Relatively inexpensive, popular with tourists, and not necessary to book.

Restaurant Foucald, Rue el Mouahidine, is a Moroccan restaurant again popular with tourists—possibly because it serves large portions!

The Moroccan restaurants in **La Mamounia** and **Tichka** hotels are excellent—and expensive.

Petit Poucet (56 Avenue Mohammed V, Gueliz) is still the restaurant most frequented by European residents (Tel: 32614). French cuisine.

●Méknès

Hotel Transatlantique, Rue El Merinyine (Tel: Méknès 200 02). This is a long established luxury-class hotel; it serves old-fashioned Moroccan food at its best. It is expensive.

Hacienda, about 2 miles (3 km) outside Méknès on the Fez road, is a good French restaurant, with bar, dancing and al *fresco* dining. (Tel: Méknès 210 91).

●Ouarzazate

Chez Dimitri, on Boulevard Mohammed V, looks from the outside like an upmarket café. Serves throughout the day and evening. It has a French Legion feel: large old-fashioned bar, wooden tables and chairs, old military memorabilia on the walls. Its owner, Dimitri, is reputed to have once had a monopoly on alcohol in the south. The price of beer here is in fact very low. At dinner there is usually a *table d' hôte* menu as well as *à la carte*. Choices include hearty casseroles, such as rabbit and lamb. Extremely reasonable prices and obliging staff.

● Rabat

L'Oasis, off the Place Pietry (site of the flower market) and **Le Mont Doré** in l'Ocean (next to the medina) are inexpensive traditional restaurants.

Alternatively **La Pagode**, behind the railway station, and **Le Dragon d'Or**, out of town, next to the Supermarche Souissi on Lotissement ben Abdallah, are good Chinese restaurants.

For pizza: **Sorrento** in the Place de Bourgogne and **La Mamma** behind Hotel Balima opposite La Gare de Ville.

● Tangier

Tangier, perhaps as a legacy from its international days, is well served by restaurants. It also has numerous good *tappas* and sandwich bars.

Restaurant Hammadi (end of Rue Italie) provides authentic Moroccan cooking, well-presented, but it is not one favoured by locals; customers are generally tourists.

Le Marquis, Rue Tolstoy; **Nautilus**, Rue Velasquez; **Guitta's** (famous in the international era), Place Kuwait: all recommended, but expensive. French Restaurants.

La Grenouille (Rue Rembrandt), **Couer de Tanger** (Boulevard Pasteur) are other good French options; La Grenouille, popular with the English, is probably the best value restaurant in town.

For a change from Moroccan or French food, there are **Pagode**, a very expensive Chinese restaurant, and **San Remo-Chez Toni** in Rue Murillo (excellent Italian).

●Taroudant

La Gazelle D'Or contains another of Morocco's very best traditional restaurants. The hotel is situated in extensive grounds outside town. Tel: Taroudant 2039 (closed during summer months).

DRINKING NOTES

Mint tea (*thé à la menthe*) and mineral water are the most common beverages in Morocco. There is more or less ceremony attached to the making and pouring of it, depending on whether you are drinking in a home a shop or a hotel. But the basic brew is consistent—green or black tea, sugar and mint, poured from a height into small glasses. Light, thin and refreshing on the first cup, it can quickly become slightly astringent, and is often gulped down quickly.

Coffee: Turkish coffee is the traditional type of coffee—drunk at any time during the day. *Café au lait* (with milk), *coffee cussé* (with a dash of milk), and *lait cussé* (mainly milk) can all be ordered in the cafés.

Islam and alcohol are strictly speaking incompatible: hence the popularity of Moroccan mineral water, still or sparkling (gazeuse, or use the brand names *Oulmés*, or *Sidi Harazem*, which come from sources close to Fez). It may be difficult to find anywhere serving alcohol in remote areas, especially during Ramadan, or on religious holidays.

However, you can usually buy Moroccan **wine** and **beer** in restaurants used to tourists. Robust red wines such as Cabernet, make a good accompaniment to a spicy meal (30 to 50 dirhams). Local beer is good—Flag Pils and Flag Spéciale (10 to 12 dirhams, though can be as low as six). The price of spirits is outrageous—easily 25 dirhams for a single measure (but it is larger than a British single), more for a simple cocktail. Visit the duty free shop on your way, and bring your own.

THINGS TO DO

Mosques, medersas and monuments: the great imperial cities all glory in vestiges of their splendid past. But all mosques and many *zaouias* (the centres of a saint's cult) are closed to non-Muslims, so that the number of monuments you can actually visit is reduced. But the ornate gateways (*babs*) into the walled medinas, and the decorated towers (*minarets*) of the mosques are impossible to miss.

The *kasbah* is often worth a visit, and the cool of luxuriant *gardens* usually a relief after a few hours' heavy sightseeing. Palaces and mansions in many cities have been converted to luxurious hotels, or to galleries and museums (see below); and it's usually possible to visit a mausoleum or *medersa* (once lodging-houses for students at the mosque-universities, and often elaborately decorated). Officially-run monuments charge three dirhams per person; smaller sights and *medersa* are supervised by a *gardien,* who will expect a tip of a couple of dirhams.

The imperial cities—essential sights: The really unmissable city monuments.

Fez: *Kairouyine* Mosque; its university is older than those of Oxford and Bologna; Medrassa Atarine, Medrassa Bou Inania, Medrassa Seffarine; Zaouia Moulay Idriss, one of the holiest shrines in Morocco; Place Nejjarine, with its ornately portalled *fondouk* (an ancient inn-cum-warehouse) and tiled fountain.

Marrakesh: Koutoubia minaret; the Saadian tombs, and Medrassa ben Youssef, both fabulously rich in decoration, outshine all the other ruined monuments.

Méknès: Bab Mansour, one of North Africa's finest gateways; the mausoleum-mosque of Moulay Ismail, open to non-Muslims; the Medrassa Bou Inania.

Rabat: Tour Hassan; Mohammed V mausoleum; Kasbah des Oudayas; the Roman remains and Islamic necropolis of Chella.

Arts, crafts and museums: art, craft or folklore museums usually occupy converted palaces or mansions (smaller towns also sometimes have local museums containing craft displays).

Despite their superb settings, they rarely have much to offer in the way of relevant literature.

Fez: Museum of Moroccan arts, Dar Batha Palace; Weapons Museum, in the fort overlooking the city, Borg Nord.

Marrakesh: Moroccan Arts Museum, in the Dar Si Said palace.

Méknès: Museum of Moroccan Arts, in the Dar Jamai palace

Rabat: National Archaeological Museum, near the Royal Palace; Museum of Moroccan Arts, in the palace of the kasbah; Museum of Handicrafts, rue des Consuls.

Tangier: Museum of Antiquities in the palace of the kasbah.

Souks: a major part of city sightseeing is bound to be wandering through a city's souks. Keep a hand on your bag, and see the section on shopping for buying advice. A visit to the *Maison* or *Centre de l'Artisanat* is somewhere between museum-going and shopping. In each regional centre is a handicrafts co-operative, where as well as craftsmen in small workshops, there will be a crafts shop with fixed prices (it's also possible to buy from the *artisans* themselves; they may or may not be prepared to haggle). Occasionally there is a craft college attached to the centre.

Unexpected pleasures: If there comes a time when you are hot and bothered and there is no bath in which to relax, then a visit to the *hammam* could be the answer. Most towns (of any size larger than village) have one: a public steam bath, part of Islam's requirement of cleanliness, and Morocco's answer to the sauna (without the birch twigs).

A *hammam* is usually open to women during the day, to men from six or seven in the evening, though arrangements differ from place to place. In a fairly shy atmosphere (nobody strips completely) bathers line the edge of a steam room; after as much steam as they can take, it's time for a cold water dousing, usually from buckets (more modern *hammams*, e.g. in hotels, use cold showers). An attendant will physically "scrub" you with pumice and a black, tar-like soap. In the men's *hammams* massage is often also provided. In the traditional *hammams* the cost is between two and five dirhams. Unfortunately, some male *hammams* prohibit non-Muslims.

A good sweat sounds like the last thing one wants after a sticky day, but it clears the pores and relaxes the body—and nobody is likely to hassle you. The same is true (at least for men) while sitting in the barber's chair for a *wet shave*. There are an extraordinary number of barbers in the larger towns, packed with fathers and sons waiting for a cut in the early evening and other customers are swathed in pints of foam.

For other leisure pursuits, see section on *Sports*.

COUNTRY

There is, of course, an infinite number of touring routes and excursions throughout Morocco that could be contrived: and the main text of this book should help in the contrivance of a suitable itinerary. Below, however, are lists of the must-see excursions and routes radiating from the most popular holiday centres.

From **Agadir**: the mountain villages and scenery around **Tafraoute**, 95 miles (150 km) south-east; the old Portuguese fishing port of **Essaouira**, 112 miles (180 km) north.

From **Marrakesh**: the pass roads through the High Atlas of **Tizi n-Test** (to the south) and **Tizi n-Tichka** (to the southeast); the highest peak of Morocco, **Jebel Toubkal**, due south, visible for miles around, and climbable from Asni or Imlil; the **southern valleys** of oases and kasbahs, east and south of Marrakesh and reached via Ouarzazate 130 miles (210 km)—specifically the **Draa** valley, the **Dadès** valley and gorges, and the **Todra** gorge; the really dedicated will press further east into the Sahara to the **Tafilalt** to watch sunrise over the dunes; via Beni-Mellal 125 miles (200 km northeast), you can reach the reservoir at **Bin el Ouidane** and the waterfalls (*cascades*) at **Ouzoud**.

From **Méknès or Fez**: the cedar forests around **Azrou** and **Ifrane** (50 miles/80 km and 37 miles/60 km south of Fez); the **Kandar massif** (19 miles/30 km south of Fez); the holy city of **Moulay Idriss** and the nearby Roman ruins of **Volubilis** (19 miles/ 30 km north of Méknès); the end of the Middle Atlas mountains to **Taza**, and further east, the end of the Rif at the **Beni-Snassen** mountains.

From **Rabat**: head inland! There are only coastal towns to visit closer than Méknès: **Salé**, Rabat's other half; south via **Casablanca** (56 miles/90 km) to **El Jadida** (117 miles/187 km).

From **Tangier**: the large market town of **Tetouan** and the pretty white houses at **Chaouen** and **Ouezzane** are in the foothills of the Rif. Asihah and Larache on the west coast.

Further afield: Hiking into the mountains and riding into the desert can both be arranged with relative ease. English speaking travel agencies arrange Land Rover "safaris" deep into the desert, along prearranged routes, and this obviously has considerable attractions over random forays, especially since reliable maps are hard to come by. Hiking in the High Atlas is well catered for, with mules, guides and mountain huts—the latter maintained by the French Alpine Club (CAM). First base is at Asni, two hours by bus from Marrakesh. Again, there's safety in numbers, and specialised tour operators can provide guaranteed expertise, as well as a bit of security for your adventure. But there's no reason to ignore independent possibilities, at least if it's summer and you're reasonably fit. The Toubkal National Park is well charted (IGN maps available from either Imlil or Rabat), the terrain not difficult (except for coping with the loose scree underfoot). All in all, very little specialist equipment is necessary.

Travel packages and tour operators: package travel to Morocco divides into the mass market—chiefly winter-sunshine packages to the coastal resorts, Fez or Marrakesh—and the specialist, either up-market (tailor-made itineraries and specialist hobby holidays) or budget (adventure holidays, treks or expeditions). Tour operators operating from the UK are listed below.

Tour operators—general: based on information and telephone numbers supplied by the Moroccan National Tourist Office based in London.

Abercrombie & Kent: up market hotels in Tangier, Mohammedia, Marrakesh, Fez and Taroudant. Telephone: 01-730 9600.

Cadogan Travel: good hotels in Agadir, Tangier, Marrakesh; Imperial Cities tour. Telephone: (0703) 332551.

Cosmos Holidays: Tangier, and Moroccan Adventure tour. Telephone: 01-464 3400.

Club Méditerranée: Club holidays in Agadir, Marrakesh and Ouarzazate. Telephone: 01-581 1161.

Enterprise Holidays: Tangier, Agadir and Marrakesh. Telephone: (0293) 560777.

Hayes & Jarvis: Imperial Cities Tour; Agadir and Marrakesh. Telephone: 01-245 1051.

Horizon Holidays: Agadir and Marrakesh. Telephone: 021-632 6282.

Kuoni: Imperial Cities and Discovery Tours; Marrakesh and Agadir. Telephone: (0306) 740500.

Martin Rooks: Agadir and Marrakesh. Telephone: 01-730 0808.

Sovereign Holidays: Agadir, Marrakesh and Tangier. Telephone: (0293) 517866.

Stallard Holidays: Agadir, and two or three night breaks to Tangier, Casablanca and Marrakesh. Telephone: 01-254 6444.

Thomson Holidays: Agadir, Tangier and Marrakesh; Valley of 1,000 kasbahs tour. Telephone: 01-387 8484.

Travelscene: telephone: 01-486 6411.

Wings: Agadir. Telephone: 021-632 6282.

Specialist companies: you can expect these companies to offer a wider choice of packages, to have rather more local knowledge, to tailor itineraries (and to charge more than the above).

Creative Leisure: Agadir, Tangier, Marrakesh, Ouarzazate, Fez, Rabat, Mohammedia, Casablanca, El Jadida, Essaouira, Taroudant; golf, shooting, trekking and birdwatching holidays. Telephone: 01-235 0123.

Just Morocco: Imperial Cities tour; South & Kasbahs tour; Agadir, Casablanca, Tangier, Marrakesh. Telephone: 01-372 6161.

Longshot Golf Holidays: golfing in Rabat, Mohammedia and Marrakesh. Telephone: (0730) 66561.

Moroccan Sun: Imperial Cities tour; Discovery of Morocco tour; Agadir, Casablanca, Fez, Mohammedia, Marrakesh, Rabat, Tangier, Taroudant; fly-drive package. Telephone: 01-437 3968.

Moroccan Travel Bureau (not listed by the tourist office: phone for brochures). Telephone: 01-373 4411.

Morocco Bound: Imperial Cities tour; Great South tour; Grand Tour; Agadir, Marrakesh, Casablanca, El Jadida, Essaouira, Layounne, Mohammedia, Ouirgane, Taroudant, Rabat, Tangier, Fes, Méknès, Smir-Restinga, Al Hoceima, Ouarzazate, Zagora; fly-drive tour. Telephone: 01-734 5307.

The Best of Morocco: Imperial Cities tour; Great South and Kasbahs tour; Discovery of Morocco tour; Agadir, Casablanca, Essaouira, Fez, Marrakesh, Mohammedia, Ouarzazate, Taroudant, Tangier. Telephone: (0622) 46678.

Adventure and expeditions:
Guerba Expeditions, telephone: (0800) 373334.
Encounter Overland, telephone: 01-370 6845.
Exodus Expeditions, telephone: 01-870 0151.
Explore Worldwide, telephone: (0252) 319448.
Sherpa Expeditions, telephone: 01-577 2717.

NIGHTLIFE

Resort nightlife is restricted to Tangier, Casablanca and its outskirts (Ain Diab and Mohammedia) and Agadir (where it is, in fact, fairly subdued). The most exciting city at night, and with the most Moroccan feel, must be Marrakesh, but Tangier still has claim to being the late-night town.

Bars: are a late 20th century addition to Moroccan nightlife, and not always a happy one. It's as though they are symbols of the clash between Moroccan Islam, with its traditional rule of total abstinence from alcohol, and Moroccan modernity, with its liberal, urban, Westernised way of thinking. They can be loud and intimidating or furtive and uneasy. **Hotel bars** are a different matter, and can be insular.

Nightclubs (often with belly dancing) and **discos** in tourist centres and cities are aimed at the tourists and the Westernised urban population. Sometimes they take place within hotels (particularly in Agadir).

Casinos: There are casinos in Marrakesh (in the Hivernage district of the new town) and in the resort area of Mohammedia, just north of Casablanca.

FOLKLORE/FANTASIAS

In *medina* restaurants or on main roads out of town, the most common evening entertainment is a combination of a typically Moroccan meal with a display of folklore: folk music and dancing, or (in the open countryside) an equestrian fantasia. Although these evenings often have a rather "packaged" feel, they can be genuinely spectacular—especially the fantasias. There may, of course, be the chance of coming across real festivals (while touring, for example), where the excitement is more spontaneous. The early evening in any town or city is vibrant and feels animated, as everyone comes out after an afternoon siesta. Evening street life is notably exciting in Marrakesh, where the celebrated *Djemma el Fna* whirls with people; dancers, snake charmers, traders, beggars and musicians and tourists. Have plenty of change in your pocket while you watch the performers: a contribution is expected from everyone, visitors above all—and especially from all photographers.

SHOPPING

In Morocco touting is an everyday occupation; selling is a polished and sinuous art form, the rigmaroles of buying can be prolonged, even wearisome. One thing is worse: attempting *not* to buy articles is completely exhausting.

Dealing with it: The only rule about bargaining for something you really want is to know the price you are prepared to pay, and start well under it (at, say, half or a third). Tactics and strategies on both sides (incredulous laughter, walking towards the door), and bids, which come gradually closer, will probably end with the buyer paying a little more than his original maximum; part of the seller's art is to determine how much more!

Fixed prices: The first priority, then, is to ascertain a fair market price for goods on offer. This is often possible in the state-run Handicraft Centres (*Centre* or *Maison de l'Artisanat*) in major towns. The quality of goods here is underwritten by the government, and there is always a shop with fixed prices on display. These will be higher than the prices that should be possible through bargaining, but the lack of hustle and pressure mean that some people are bound to prefer shopping here.

The Moroccan authorities, as well as the traders themselves, recognise that bargaining makes many visitors nervous; and many of the souks, as well as city shops, are beginning to display *prix fixes*, for everything from room-sized carpets to small brass trinkets. Although haggling is not about to die, these are depressing sights, alongside the credit card signs.

The traditional crafts of Morocco still make the best bargains. First and most prominent of the handicraft traditions are **carpets**, hand knotted and in some cases, still coloured with vegetable dyes. Designs (apart from the Turkish inspired patterns of Rabat carpets) are predominantly traditional to Berber tribes. Their use of colours and schemes of stylised illustration are supposed to enable experts to pin down not only the area but sometimes the individual tribe or even family that made them. Top quality carpets sell for thousands of dirhams (compare shop prices in Europe and the USA); more affordable and more easily portable are Berber rugs, kilims or blankets. A reasonable rug might cost 300 dirhams: but check prevailing price levels wherever possible: a lot depends on the quality (density of the fibres and knotting, etc). For Berber patterns, try the small country souks around Marrakesh.

Leather goods are widespread: from unpolished leather bags and belts, through the distinctive pointed slippers known as *babouches*, to ornate *pouffes*, studded and dyed. Some leather goods are finished in a style closer to Italian designer luggage—in all cases, price should go hand in hand with quality, so check the hide and workmanship before buying. Printed boxes and bookbindings are often on show, but, with their shiny tooling, have become the victims of their imitators and too often look merely tacky.

Jewellery is available everywhere, although the most exciting place to buy it is Tiznit, with its famous silversmiths' souk. Dull silver is the basic material: heavy but beautifully decorated bracelets, delicate filigree rings, chunky necklaces of semi-precious stones (or occasionally of plastic, for the unwary), are the commonest pieces. Slightly more unusual, and sometimes antique, are decorated daggers, scabbards, or Koran boxes, covered with silver-wire decoration. Whatever the piece, the fastenings are often a weak point. Beware, too, of silver-plating masking what the Moroccans call *b' shi-b' shi*—meaning rubbish.

Marquetry is another traditional craft: wooden furniture, ornaments, chess-sets, and small wooden boxes made in cedar, thuya, and oak. Many wooden goods are inlaid with contrasting veneers or mother of pearl. Often the quality of finish is less than ideal: hinges or joints are points to watch. The woodworkers' *ateliers* at Essaouira are an ideal place to buy (and to watch the manufacture).

Pottery ranges from the rough earthenware of household pots and crocks to gaudy (and predominantly tourist-orientated) designs in the main towns and markets.

Whether you're looking for egg-cups or Berber carpets, it's worth visiting craft museums to determine what is traditional, and what is tat. In the end, however, visitors will end up by buying what they like and paying what they think it's worth.

EXPORT PROCEDURES

Beware of buying anything that can't be carried away. Many traders will offer export facilities (e.g. for large carpets) and, although there are no customs formalities to be met, the shipping of goods could take months. There is little comeback against a souk trader who has been paid in cash and fails to deliver. However, paying by credit card is getting easier, and the networks of the card companies may well provide a back-up.

COMPLAINTS

Complaints can be taken to the local police. A complaints book is supposed to be kept by every classified hotel, specifically for tourists' complaints (albeit usually complaints about accommodation, as might be expected). Copies of complaints are then forwarded to the headquarters of the tourist office in Rabat. The *Syndicat d' initiatif* or ONMT offices should also be able to help in passing on complaints, or advising on any appropriate action.

SPORTS

PARTICIPANT

Golf: It is said to be King Hassan II's enthusiasm for golf which has led to courses sprouting near major cities and resort areas through the country. The following list includes daily green fees and telephone numbers. Lessons (20 to 90DH per half hour) and caddies (25 to 90DH per 18 holes) are available at all courses.
Rabat: 45 holes; 200DH; (7) 55864.
Casablanca: 9 holes; 200DH; 361026.
Mohammedia: 18 holes; 200DH; (32) 2052.
Marrakesh: 18 holes; 120DH weekdays, 150DH Saturday and Sunday; (4) 44341.
Agadir: 9 holes (but due to be extended to 45 holes, according to the tourist office); 80DH; (8) 31278.
Tangier: 18 holes; 80DH; (9) 38925.
Méknès: 9 holes; 30 DH; (5) 30753.

Hunting: From the first Sunday in October, on Sundays and public holidays until January or early spring, it's open season on game birds and wild boars. In the Arbaoua Game Reserve, most notably, but elsewhere too, abundance of wildlife has led to the government licensing shooting. Victims include quail (season closes late January); snipe woodcocks, pigeons and turtle doves (there is a separate season in May and June for the doves); and partridges, ducks, rabbits and hares (season closes early January). The season for wild boar runs until mid-February, on Thursdays as well as Sundays and holidays; but hunting is only allowed with beaters. **Licensing** is strictly controlled, and hunting without a licence is an offence. It is theoretically possible to organise the temporary import of one's own guns, but it is more convenient to leave to an expert the formalities and the procurement of a local shooting licence (which, in 1989, cost visitors 300DH and nationals 100DH, or 500DH and 100DH for boar). The specialist company in Morocco is Sochatour, who co-operate with the Ministry of Agriculture and the *Administration des Eaux et Forêts*. Sochatour, 72 Boulevard Zerktouni, Casablanca. Telephone: 277513.

Fishing: Trout fishing is hugely popular in Morocco: to the extent that the rivers and lakes that are easily reached have been over-fished. The fly fisher's choice is extreme: fishing in isolated streams and pools of the Middle and High Atlas, or casting into custom-stocked lakes (most of them in the Middle Atlas) where the permits are expensive and the catch weighed before leaving.

Coarse fishing: Lakes and reservoirs of the Middle Atlas are the most popular setting for coarse fishing; around Azrou, Ifrane and Immouzer du Khanda in particular, and in the reservoir of Bin el Ouidane. Species include some of the world's largest pike, as well as black bass and perch.
Permits are required for trout and coarse fishing; these are usually available locally (through hotels or tourist offices) or from the *Administration des Eaux et Forêts*, 11 Rue Revoil, Rabat (Telephone: 07 25335). The *Administration* also sets the fishing seasons year by year.

Sea fishing is rich, too, and does not require a permit. From massive sea bass off Dakhla and Layounne in the south, to the summer visits of tuna north of Casablanca, and swordfish off Tangier or lobster and langouste in Rabat and Agadir, fish are populous and varied. Bream, mackerel and sardines are common also. The Mediterranean and the South Atlantic coasts are the most fruitful: deep sea fishing from boats is relatively easy to arrange, and spearfishing with aqualung is possible with a permit.

Skiing: The peculiarity of the High Atlas climate enables the tourist board to boast of Marrakesh being a base from which you can go skiing in the morning and sunbathing in the afternoon. The ski resort of Oukaimeden (altitude 8,700 ft; 2,650 metres), around an hour's drive south of Marrakesh, expects snow from December to April—but the snow is not to be relied on. The skiing is stiff; skis and boots can be hired. The other resort, Mischliffen, is on a volcanic crater, reached through cedar forests from Azrou or Ifrane: the setting rather than the skiing is the attraction. There are plans afoot to develop Ketama further as "the Moroccan Switzerland". In the meantime, or at least until it loses its reputation as the Moroccan drug capital, the casual visitor might care to think twice about sampling the (undeniably attractive) slopes of Mount Tidighine in the Rif mountains.

Bird-watching: Some of the migratory birds lucky enough to have avoided death by shotguns are rare and beautiful: Morocco lies under one of the two major migratory routes for European birds wintering in Africa. Storks, ibis, and flamingoes are seen in the wetlands of river estuaries and coastal lagoons. Eagles and falcons sometimes wheel high in a semi-desert sky. Several tour companies offer specialised bird-watching holidays; their expertise will help determine the place and time to go.

Other sports: Tennis, and (along the coast) watersports are easy to find in most tourist areas, conveniently through hotels. One of the most popular activities, though, is riding—whether it is mule-trekking in the rugged terrain of the mountains, or galloping on horseback along the sandy beaches of the coast.

For most sports, it is easy (with the help of the Moroccan Tourist Office) to find a specialist who will sell (or arrange for you) an inclusive holiday. It is, of course, also possible—and certainly cheaper—to arrive and to arrange for a few days' sport *in situ*.

SPECIAL INFORMATION

DOING BUSINESS

Business customs are a mixture of Arab and European; the French influence remains in many of the country's industrial concerns. Personal contacts and hospitality are important: urgency and on the spot decision-making are not. Intermediaries who have set up business deals or contacts may expect commissions as a matter of course; businessmen should be careful in such cases, since to suggest that such conduct is less than honest could give offence. Signs of impatience are also considered rude: the best signs of a successful deal are meetings with a series of executives from the same company. Promotional literature, if any, should be supplied in French. Useful addresses for businessmen include:

Chambre de Commerce et d'Industrie de Casablanca, 98 Boulevard Mohammed V, Casablanca. Telephone: 221524.

Office for Industrial Development (ODI), 10 Zankat Ghandi, PO Box 211, Rabat. Telephone: (07) 68460. Telex: 31053.

British businesses should contact the Department of Trade and Industry for useful information in the leaflet *Hints to Exporters: Morocco*, available from DTI, Overseas Trade Division 4/1c, 1 Victoria Street, London SW1H 0ET. Telephone: 01-215 4947.

GAYS

Morocco no longer offers visitors the free and easy attitude it once did towards male homosexuality. Tangier in particular has been officially cleaned up. What the Moroccan law describes as an "unnatural act" between two persons of the same sex is now punishable by imprisonment (six months to three years) and by fines. The British embassy in Rabat stresses this. Despite all this, and regional taboos, male gay sex is still available, and in some cities (Marrakesh, for example) young male hustler-prostitutes are becoming more evident. In common with the whole of Africa, the risks of sexually-transmitted diseases (including AIDS) must be considered (although there are few figures available). In general, Marrakesh is associated with French homosexuals, and Tangier attracts an English gay community.

DISABLED

No official register exists of facilities within Morocco for people with disabilities. Relatively few hotels are overtly suitable for wheelchair access, particularly those converted from older buildings such as palaces. That said, the Moroccans' attitude to disability is extremely solicitous. UK tour operators able to cater for disabled travellers are Cadogan Travel, Horizon Holidays, Intasun Holidays, and Kuoni Travel.

STUDENTS

There are few official discounts available to students in Morocco. Chief benefits of student status are the use of an Inter Rail pass on the railways. There are also discount fares for students from Royal Air Maroc. Domestic discount fares can be booked in advance from RAM offices (but not on spec at the airport) on proof of student status. Some international discounts are also available: check your local office for details.

LANGUAGE

agadir	fortified granary
agdal	garden
Aid el Kebir	feast day celebrating Abraham's Sacrifice of the Lamb
Aid es Seghir	feast day held after the first sighting of the moon after Ramadan
El Andalus	Muslim Spain
aït	community
bab	gate
baraka	blessing, often thought magical
bled el makhzen	land of government
bled es siba	land of dissidence
caid	district judge
djemma	assembly, but also mosque
djinn	spirit
Fasi	person from Fez
foundouk	lodging house with stables
Gnouai	a black African tribe in the south
Hadith	the written traditions of Islam
Hadj	the pilgrimage to Mecca
hammam	steam bath
horm	sanctuary
imam	prayer leader
jebel	mountain
koubba	white, domed building containing the tomb of a saint
ksar (ksour)	fortified *pisé* building or community (plural)
l'tam	veil
Maghreb	collective name for Morocco, Algeria and Tunisia
makhzen	government
marabout	saint
Marrakshi	person from Marrakesh
mechouar	square, assembly area
medrassa (medersa)	Islamic college and living quarters for students (plural)
medina	old town
mellah	Jewish quarter
mihrab	niche indicating direction of

	Mecca in mosque
minaret	tower of mosque
Moriscos	Muslim refugees from Spain in 15th century
moujehaddin	Islamic soldiers engaged in Holy war
Moulay	indicates descendancy from the Prophet
Mouloud	Prophet's Birthday
moussem	religious festival
msalla	prayer area
muezzin	caller to prayer
oued	river
pisé	mud and rubble
quibla	direction of Mecca in a mosque
Shia	branch of Islam which recognises Ali as the successor to Mohammed
shouaf	fortune teller
shereef	ruler who is descendant of Prophet
stucco	elaborate plaster work
Sufi	religious mystic
Sunni	orthodox Muslim
tizi	mountain pass
tabia	mud used in *pisé* architecture
zaouia	religious fraternity
zellige	elaborate tile mosaics

FURTHER READING

Barbour, Neville. *Morocco.* London: Thames & Hudson, 1965. The standard historical work from the Phoenicians to the 1960s.

Bowles, Paul. *The Spider's House.* London: Arena Publishing. Good introduction to the work of a writer working in and out of Moroccan traditions, translating and fictionalising. This is a novel set against daily life in Fez.

Canetti, E. *The Voices of Marrakesh.* London: Marion Boyars. Impressions by Nobel Prize winner.

Carrier Robert. *Taste of Morocco.* Century, 1988. Excellent introduction to food and recipes, plus social customs.

Choukri Mohamed. *For Bread Alone.* Grafton 1987. Autobiography of a man who grew up poor and illiterate. Translated into English from classical Arabic by Paul Bowles.

Harris, Walter. *Morocco That Was.* London: Eland Books, 1983 (first published 1921). Accounts of the end of feudal Morocco and the beginning of French rule from London *Times* correspondent who died in 1933.

Landau, Rom and Swaan, Wim. *Morocco.* London: Elek Books, 1967. Worth tracking down for photographs, which include mosque interiors.

Mayne, Peter. *A Year in Marrakesh.* London (Eland Books). Engrossing, personal account superbly written.

Maxwell, Gavin. *Lords of the Atlas.* London: Century, 1983. The story of the Glaoui dynasty in the last two centuries: compellingly written.

Meakin, Budgett. *The Moors: a comprehensive description.* London: Sonnenschein, 1902. Comprehensive indeed, long certainly, with a good claim to be the first guide book to Morocco.

Mernissi, Fatima. *Beyond the Veil*. London: Al Saqi Books. Classic polemic on women's position in Islam by Moroccan feminist educated in Morocco and America.

Mrabet Mohammed. *The Lemon*. Al Saqi Books; and *Love with a few Hairs*. Al Saqi Books. Fiction by one of the leading Moroccan novelists.

Porch, Douglas. *The Conquest of Morocco*. London: Jonathan Cape, 1986. French colonial adventurism and Moroccan history at the turn of the century.

FILMS

There is little state support or interest in Moroccan film-making, most energy being employed in promoting Morocco's advantages as a film-location. The following films are worth catching.

Hamid Benani's *Traces* (1970). About an orphaned boy adopted by a strict Muslim father.

Souhel Ben Barka's *A Thousand and One Hands* (1972) about the problems of dyeworkers; *The Petrol War Won't Happen* (1975); and *Amok* (1982).

Moumen Smihi's *El Chergui* (1975) is about a young wife's problems.

Ahmed el Maanouni's *Oh, the Days* (1978) is concerned with harsh peasant life and the lure of France.

Mohammed Reggab's *The Hairdresser from a Poor District* (1982); Abderrahmane Tazi's *The Great Voyage* (1981).

Moustafa Derkaoui's *The Beautiful Days of Scheherazade* (1982).

Jilali Ferhti's *Reed Dolls* (1981) about the plight of a widowed woman.

USEFUL ADDRESSES

TOURIST OFFICES

Outside Morocco
London: 174 Regent Street, London W1R 6HB. Telephone: 01-437 0073.

New York: 20 East 46th Street, Suite #503, New York NY 10017. Telephone: (212) 557 2520. Telex: 236040.

Orlando: EPCOT Centre, Walt Disney World, Orlando, Florida 32830. Telephone: (305) 827 5337. Telex: 856487.

Toronto: 2 Carlton Street, Suite 1803, Toronto, Ontario M5B 1K2, Canada. Telephone: (416) 598 2208. Telex: 6219760.

In Morocco
National Tourist Offices (Office Nationale Marocain du Tourisme, ONMT: headquarters in Rabat) are often complemented by a municipal *Syndicat d'Initiatif*. Both can give plans, maps, advice and provide guides, but the ONMT are usually better staffed, with more guides on hand. Most are open Monday to Saturday mornings from 8 a.m.

Agadir: Avenue du Prince Heritier Sidi Mohammed (off street: on first floor level of paved square opposite post office).

Casablanca: 55 Rue Omar Slaoui.

Fez: Place de la Resistance, Boulevard Moulay Youssef.

Marrakesh: Place Abd el Moumen Ben Ali, Boulevard Mohammed V.

Oujda: Place du 16 Août.

Rabat: 22 Avenue al Jazair (Ave d'Algier).

Tangier: 29 Boulevard Pasteur.

Tetouan: 30 Avenue Mohammed V.

CASABLANCA

Great Britain: 60 Boulevard d'Anfa. Telephone: 221653.
United States of America: 8 Boulevard Moulay Youssef. Telephone: 224149.

RABAT

Canada: 13b Rue Jaáfar Assadik (Agdal). Telephone: 71375/6. Also represents **Australia**.
Great Britain: 17 Boulevard de la Tour Hassan. Telephone: 20905.
USA: 2 Avenue de Marrakesh. Telephone: 62265.

TANGIER

Great Britain: Trafalgar House, 9 Rue Amerique du Sud. Telephone: 35897.
USA: 29 Rue el Achouak. Telephone: 35904.

American Express agencies

American Express is represented by Voyages Schwartz in Morocco. These English speaking travel agencies can be useful for anyone, but particularly those carrying an Amex card or travellers' cheques. Cardmembers can also use the offices for drawing cash in emergencies, mail forwarding and poste restante.

Agadir: 87 Place du Marché Municipale. Telephone: 20252.
Casablanca: 112 Rue du Prince Moulay Abdallah. Telephone: 273133.
Marrakesh: Rue Mauritania, Immeuble Moutaoukil. Telephone: 33022.
Tangier: 54 Boulevard Pasteur. Telephone: 33459.

ART/PHOTO CREDITS

INDEX

A

Abd el Krim, 50
Abd el Moumin, 42
Abdallah ben Hassan, Sidi, 161
Abids, the, 47
Abou el Hassan, 43
Achabou, 254
Acmed el Raisuni, Shereef, 145
Agadir, 275-8
Agdal Gardens, 232
Agoudal, 251
Aguedal Basin, 204
Ahmed el Mansour el Dehbi, 45, 46
Aït Benhaddou, 248
Al Hoceima, 139
Alaouites, 46, 47, 95
Ali ben Youssef Medrassa, 226
Ali ben Youssef Mosque, 225
Allal ben Abdallah, 53
Almohads, 42, 95
Almoravids, 41, 42, 95
American Legation, Tangier, 122
Andalous quarter, Fez, 196
Arabic, 62
Asilah, 145, 146
Atlas Mountains, 243-56
Averroes, 42, 95
Azemmour, 173
Azurki, 105

B, C

Bab Boujeloud, 189
Bab Mansour, 202-3
beer, 87
ben Aissa, Sidi, 205
Beni-Mellal, 255
Borj Nord, 186
Bou Guemez Valley, 104, 249
Bou Iblane, 103
Bou Inania Medrassa, Fez, 189-90
Boulevard Pasteur, Tangier, 119
Bowles, Paul, 75, 76, 77, 78
Burroughs, William S, 78
Casablanca

Hassan II Mosque, 168-9
Quartier Habbous, 168
Caves of Hercules, 126
Ceuta, 66-7
CFAMM, 249
Chaouen, 135-6
Chella Necropolis, 158-60
Churchill, Winston, 232
Cotta, 126
couscous, 85

D, E

Dar Batha Palace, 197
Dar el Bahr, 174
Dar el Glaoui, 232
Dar el Makhzen, Fez, 94
Dar el Makhzen, Rabat, 158
Dar Si' Palace, 232
Demnate, 250
Djemma el Fna, 223
dyers' quarter, Fez, 194
El Badi Palace, 94, 229, 231
El Jadida, 174
El Kelâa des M'gouna, 267
El Mansour (Youssef Yacoub), 42
El Minzah Hotel, 120
English Church, Tangier, 121
Er Rachidia, 264
Erfoud, 265
Essaouira, 237-9

F, G

Fez
   Andalous quarter, 196
   Bab Boujeloud, 189
   Borj Nord, 186
   Bou Inania, 189-90
   Fez el Bali, 184
   Fez Jdid, 196-7
   Fondouk Tsetaouyine, 192
   Kairouyine Mosque, 185, 193-4
   Kissaria, 192
   medina, 186-9
   mellah, 196-7
   Moulay Idriss II, shrine, 192
   Museum of Moroccan Arts, 197
   Palais Jamai, hotel, 196
   Talaa Kebira, 190
Figuig, 264
Fondouk Tsetaouyine, 192
Forbes, Malcolm, 124
Forbes Museum of Military Miniatures, 124
France, 49, 50-51
gnaoua, 100
Goulimine, 283, 287
Grand Mosque, Tangier, 122

Grand Socco, 121-2
Green March, 61
Gueliz, 232
Guelmim, 283
guides, 187, 230
Guillaume, General Augustin, 52, 53

H, I, J

Harris, Walter, 121
Harun el Rashid, 41
Hasan II, King, 58
hashish, 134
Hassan Mosque, Rabat, 152
Hassan II Mosque, Casablanca, 168
Hassan Tower, 151
Heri as Souani, 204
Hotel La Mamounia, 232
Hutton, Barbara, 79
ibn Toumert (The Torch), 42
Idriss I (Idriss ibn Abdullah), 36, 41
Idriss II, 41
Ifrane, 257
Imilchil, 255, 256
Imlil, 245
Imouzzer des Ida Outanane, 239
Islam, 24, 71
Isles Purpuraires, 238
Istiqal Party, 52, 57, 58, 63
Jaffar Cirque, 256
Jews, 24, 32, 122, 195-6, 229, 237
Juba II, King, 32

K, L

Kairouyine Library, 194
Kairouyine Mosque, 185, 193-4
Kairouyine University, 41
Kasbah de Mehdiya, 147
Kasbah Mosque, Marrakesh, 228
Kasbah of the Oudayas, 153
Kechla, 174
Ketama, 134, 138
kif, 134
Kissaria, 192
Koubba el Baroudiyin, 225
Koubbet el Khiyatine, 203
Kousser, 254
Koutoubia Mosque, 226-7
Ksar el Kebir, 147
ksour, 93, 262
La Bahia, 231
Larache, 145, 146
Lawrence of Arabia, 269
Layounne, 286
Le Détroit, café, 124
Lixus, 146
Lyautey, Marshal Hubert Gonzalve, 50-51

M

magic, 24
Marrakesh
    Ali Ben Youssef Mosque, 225-6
    Dar el Glaoui, 231
    Dar Si' Palace, 231
    Djemma el Fna, 223
    El Badi Palace, 229, 231
    Hotel La Mamounia, 232
    Kasbah Mosque, 228
    Koubba el Baroudiyin, 225
    Koutoubia Mosque, 226-7
    La Bahia, 231
    mellah, 229
    Museum of Moroccan Arts, 231
    souks, 224
    Tombs of the Saadis, 228
    Zaouia of Sidi bela Abbes, 229
    Zaouia of Sidi ben Slimann, 229
"Mauresque" architecture, 51, 95, 167
medersa, 43, 92
Mehdi ben Barka, 58, 59
Melilla, 67
mellah, Fez, 196-7
Menara Gardens, 232
Merinids, 43, 95
Merzouga, 265, 266
Meski, 264
Méknès
    Aguedal Basin, 204
    Bab Mansour, 202-3
    Heri as Souani, 204
    history, 46-7
    Koubbet el Khiyatine, 203
    Museum of Moroccan Arts, 205
    New Town, 202
    Old Town, 202
    walls, 201-2
Mgoun, 254
M'Hamid, 270
Midelt, 262
Mischliffen-Jbel Hebri, 103, 257
Mogador, 237
Mohammed V (Mohammed ben Youssef), 51, 52, 53, 55, 57, 153
Mohammed ibn Abdullah, 47
Mohammedia, 163
mosques, 92
Moulay Ali Shereef, tomb of, 265
Moulay Bousselham, 147
Moulay Hassan, Crown Prince, 58
Moulay Idriss II, Shrine, 192
Moulay Idriss, 41, 207-9
Moulay Idriss, I, 41, 203, 207-9
Moulay Ismail, 46, 47, 95, 201, 202, 204, 211
Moulouya, river, 140
Msemrir, 252
Musa ibn Noseir, 35
music, 99-100, 140

N, O, P

Nador, 139, 140
nationalist movement, 51-2
Okba ibn Nafi, Sidi, 35
Oualidia, 174
Ouarzazate, 267, 269
Oudaya Gate, 155
Ouezzane, 137-8
Oujda, 140, 141
Oukaimeden, 103, 247
Ourika Valley, 244
Palace Museum, Tangier, 124
Palais Jamai, hotel, 196
Petit Socco, 123
Pillars of Hercules, 66
Place Seffarine, 194
Plateau des Lacs, 255
Plaza Uta el Hamman Chauen, 136
Polisario Front, 62
pottery, 162, 174, 196
Protectorate Treaty, 50

Q, R, S

Quartier Habbous, Casablanca, 168
Rabat
    Chella Necropolis, 158-60
    Dar el Makhzen, 158
    Hassan Mosque, 151
    Kasbah of the Oudayas, 153
    medina, 155-6
    Mohammed V's Mausoleum, 153
    Museum of Moroccan Arts, 155
    Oudaya Gate, 155
Ramadan, 86
Rif, the, 131-41
Rissani, 265
Route de l'Unité, the Rif, 141
Saadians, 44, 46, 95, 228
Safi, 174
Saharan Arab Democratic Republic (SADR), 62
Sala Colonia, 158-60
Salé, 161-2
Setti Fatma, 244
Shrine of Moulay Idriss II, 192
Sidi ben Slimann, 229
Sidi bela Abbes, 229
Sidi Chamharouch, 245
Sidi Okba ibn Nafi, 35
Sidi Yahya, 141
Sigilmassa, 265
skiing, 103-5, 247, 257
Skoura, 267
Spain 49, 51, 52, 66-7

T

Tabant, 249
Tafilalt, 261
Tafraoute, 281
tajine, 85-6, 245
Talaa Kebira, 190
Tamgrout, 270
Tamtetoucht, 252
Tan Tan, 283-4
Tangier
    American Legation, 122
    Boulevard Pasteur, 119
    El Minzah Hotel, 120
    English Church, St Andrews, 121
    Forbes Museum, 124
    Grand Mosque, 122
    Grand Socco, 121-2
    Le Détroit, café 124
    Palace Museum, 124
    Petit Socco, 123
tanneries, Fez, 194
Targuist, 139
Tarik ibn Ziad, 35
Taroudant, 271
Tazzeka, 257
tea, 87
Tetouan, 131, 133, 135
Thami el Glaoui, 231
The Rif, 131-41
Tindouf, 263
Tinerhir, 252-3
Tiznit, 282
Tombs of the Saadis, 228
Toubkal, 245
Toubkal Massif, 104
Tuareg, 287

V, W, Y, Z

Volubilis, 211-14
water-clock, Bou Inania, 190
Wattasid dynasty, 44
wine, 87
Youssef ibn Tashfin, 41
Youssef Yacoub (El Mansour), 42
Zagora, 268
Zaouia of Sidi bela Abbes, 229
Zaouia of Sidi ben Slimann, 229